JACQUELINE
KENNEDY

Jacqueline Kennedy

JACQUELINE KENNEDY

Historic Conversations

ON LIFE WITH

JOHN F. KENNEDY

INTERVIEWS WITH

ARTHUR M. SCHLESINGER, JR.

1964

FOREWORD BY

CAROLINE KENNEDY

INTRODUCTION AND ANNOTATIONS BY

MICHAEL BESCHLOSS

HYPERION

NEW YORK

Transcription of taped conversations is almost always an art, rather than a science, and the most reliable source for exactly what Jacqueline Kennedy and Arthur Schlesinger, Jr., said to each other in the spring of 1964 is the accompanying audio version, which has been digitally re-mastered, but not altered. In order to make this book as comprehensible for the reader as possible, and in the style of other published oral histories, we have deleted some interjections and broken phrases where they interrupted the flow of the conversation, but only where such changes would not alter the meaning.

The photograph credits on page 357 constitute an extension of this copyright page.

Library of Congress Cataloging-in-Publication Data has been applied for.

ISBN: 978-1-4013-2425-4

Hyperion books are available for special promotions and premiums. For details contact the HarperCollins Special Markets Department in the New York office at 212-207-7528, fax 212-207-7222, or email spsales@harpercollins.com.

BOOK DESIGN BY SHUBHANI SARKAR

First Edition

10   9   8   7   6   5   4   3   2   1

SUSTAINABLE FORESTRY INITIATIVE
Certified Fiber Sourcing
www.sfiprogram.org

THIS LABEL APPLIES TO TEXT STOCK

We try to produce the most beautiful books possible, and we are also extremely concerned about the impact of our manufacturing process on the forests of the world and the environment as a whole. Accordingly, we've made sure that all of the paper we use has been certified as coming from forests that are managed, to ensure the protection of the people and wildlife dependent upon them.

CONTENTS

THE FIRST CONVERSATION

John F. Kennedy's presidential aspirations • 1956 vice-presidential nomination • Fight for control of Massachusetts delegation • 1953–54 Boston politics • Early married life • 1954 surgery • JFK's temperament • Georgetown social life • White House parties • JFK's impact on others • Adlai Stevenson • 1958 Massachusetts Senate campaign

THE SECOND CONVERSATION

JFK's reading habits • JFK's childhood interests and heroes • JFK's opinions of Thomas Jefferson, Theodore Roosevelt, Franklin D. Roosevelt • Joseph P. Kennedy • JFK's temperament • Charles de Gaulle • 1960 rivals • 1960 campaign • *Profiles in Courage* authorship • JFK–Robert F. Kennedy relationship • JFK's political courage • 1960 campaign • Wisconsin and West Virginia primaries

THE SIXTH CONVERSATION

U.S.-German relations • Berlin Crisis • JFK's temperament • Jawaharlal Nehru and Indira Gandhi • Nuclear disarmament • Harold Macmillan • Hickory Hill Seminars–JFK on Lincoln • Steel Crisis • J. Edgar Hoover • Civil Rights • 1963 March on Washington • Martin Luther King, Jr. • The Cuban Missile Crisis • Lyndon Johnson • Mike Mansfield • Other staff and friends

THE SEVENTH CONVERSATION

Harold Macmillan and Skybolt • Charles de Gaulle and the Common Market • JBK's trip to India • JFK and State Department • Vietnam • Henry and Clare Boothe Luce • Latin America • JFK and Dean Rusk, Chester Bowles, Averell Harriman, Douglas Dillon • Supreme Court appointments • *New York Times v. Sullivan* • JBK on her "image" • JFK's relations with staff • JFK and children • JFK's plans for second term • 1964 campaign

FOREWORD

by Caroline Kennedy

IN 1964, AS PART OF AN ORAL HISTORY PROJECT on the life and career of John F. Kennedy, my mother sat down with Arthur M. Schlesinger, Jr., to share her memories and insights. Recorded less than four months after the death of her husband, they represent a gift to history and a labor of love on her part. In order to treat them with the appropriate respect, my children and I took very seriously the decision to publish them now, in connection with the fiftieth anniversary of my father's presidency. The moment seems right— enough time has passed so that they can be appreciated for their unique insight, yet the Kennedy presidency is still within living memory for many who will find her observations illuminating. I hope too that younger generations who are just learning about the 1960s will find these reminiscences a useful introduction to how history is made, and will be inspired to give back to this country that has given us all so much.

When I was growing up, my mother spent much of her time meeting behind closed doors with members of my father's administration, planning his gravesite at Arlington National Cemetery, making sure that the John F. Kennedy Center for the Performing Arts would reflect his commitment to our country's cultural heritage, executing his wishes for the John F. Kennedy Presidential Library and the Institute of Politics, and making countless decisions on the disposition of my father's official papers, personal effects, mementos, and memorabilia. She was determined that the Kennedy Library would be a living memorial, a place where students would be inspired to pursue careers in public service, where scholars would have access to the historical record, and where families could learn about the ideals that animated my father's career and his vision for America. These meetings were somewhat mysterious, but my brother and I had a sense that nothing was more important than the "oral history" that we heard about from time to time.

My parents shared a love of history. To them, the past was not an academic concern, but a gathering of the most fascinating people you could ever hope to meet. My father's interests were political—I still have his books on the Civil War and English parliamentary history, as well as his annotated copy of *The Federalist Papers*. My mother thought there weren't enough women in American history to make it as interesting as reading novels and diaries from the courts of Europe. She read *War and Peace* during the Wisconsin primary, and maintained that reading the *Memoirs of the Duc de Saint-Simon* about life at Versailles was the most valuable preparation she received for life in the White House.

After my father's death, my mother resolved to do everything she could to make sure that the record of his administration was preserved. She had confidence that his decisions would stand the test of time and wanted future generations to learn what an extraordinary man he was. She helped set in motion one of the most extensive oral history projects ever conducted up to that time, in which more than one thousand people were interviewed about their life and work with John F. Kennedy. Although it was painful for my mother to relive the life since shattered, she knew it was important that she participate. She always told us that she chose to be interviewed by Arthur M. Schlesinger, Jr., the Pulitzer Prize–winning historian, former Harvard professor, and special assistant to President Kennedy, because she was doing this for future generations, and that was why she put the tapes in a vault to be sealed for fifty years.

I first read transcripts of these conversations a few weeks after my mother's death in 1994 when the vault was opened and her lawyer gave me a copy. Everything about that time was overwhelming for me as I found myself faced with the same sorts of decisions about her possessions that she had made thirty years earlier. Knowing her wishes for the oral history made it easy—I knew I was reading something that wasn't supposed to be seen yet—and although I found it fascinating, I put it back in the vault to await its time.

A few years ago, my family began thinking about how to commemorate the fiftieth anniversary of my father's presidency. We decided to concentrate our efforts on projects that would make his legacy accessible worldwide.

Working with the staff of the John F. Kennedy Library and Foundation and generous private partners, my husband led the effort to create the largest existing digital archive of a presidency, as well as online curricula, downloadable exhibits, and a Web site—www.jfk50.org—intended to renew my father's call to service for today's generation.

The publication of these interviews is an important contribution to this commemorative effort, and one with its own story. When the director of the Kennedy Library first approached me with the idea, I asked him to search the archives to confirm my mother's wishes regarding the date of publication. Surprisingly, given the importance of the material, there was no deed of gift or transfer, nor a letter of intent regarding the date at which the interviews were to be opened. There was only a brief notation by a former government archivist that these interviews were "subject to the same restrictions as the Manchester interviews."

By way of background, there are three significant interviews that my mother gave after my father's death. The first was to Theodore H. White in Hyannis Port on November 29, 1963, only a few days after my father's funeral. In that interview, my mother famously told White that she and my father used to listen to the record of the Broadway musical *Camelot* in the evening before they went to bed, and looking back, "that one brief shining moment" reminded her of his presidency. White's article was published a week later in *Life* magazine, but the notes of his interview were sealed until one year after my mother's death. They are now open to researchers at the Kennedy Library in Boston.

The second set of conversations was with William Manchester, who was writing a book called *The Death of a President*. During the sessions my mother said more about my father's assassination than she had intended. Subsequently, she became so upset at the thought of her personal memories becoming public that she sued the author and publisher to keep them out of the book. A settlement was reached, and although much of the content made its way into the public sphere, the notes of the interviews were sealed for 100 years—that is, until 2067.

By far the most important were these oral history conversations with Arthur Schlesinger in which my mother willingly recalled the span of her married life, and shared her insights into my father's private and public political personality. The archivist's notation regarding the date of publication was not consistent with my memory, nor did it seem to reflect my mother's wishes. I checked with former members of her staff in the White House and afterward, as well as other friends and attorneys. No one had a recollection that differed from mine, and they were enthusiastic about the idea of publication.

So I was faced with a dilemma that I have confronted numerous times in connection with my mother's personal papers and correspondence. On one hand, she was a famously private person who gave no on-the-record interviews (other than these three) about life in the White House, and requested in her will that my brother and I make every effort to prevent publication of her personal papers, letters, and writings.

However, she also saved every scrap of paper that came her way—every birthday card or telegram, every letter from her parents, every date book and diary, every draft letter or memo she ever wrote. She knew that living in the White House was an enormous privilege and she was proud of the part she had played. Early on, when she discovered that one of her secretaries was throwing out notes and internal correspondence that chronicled both daily life and the official workings of the mansion, she wrote a steaming rebuke—directing everyone on her staff to save even the smallest scribbles. Her deep immersion in memoirs of the past informed her belief that she had an obligation to preserve everything that happened during her time in the White House.

In the years since her death, I have asked myself the question, When does someone no longer belong to you, but belong to history? Few people have been written about more than my mother, and I grew up feeling I needed to protect her—just as she had protected us. So at first I thought it best to leave these interviews sealed for another fifty years, rather than to expose her memory to one more round of gossip and speculation. But I also understand that the continuing interest in her life is a tribute to the immense admiration and goodwill she still commands, and I believe that open access to government is an important American value.

Over the years, I have received multiple requests to publish my mother's memos and correspondence. At times, it has been difficult to balance her wish for privacy against her public role and pay proper respect to both. Although I agonize over each request, I know that my mother trusted my judgment and felt that I understood her outlook on life. As the years pass, it has become less painful to share her with the world, and in fact, it is a privilege. As her child, it has sometimes been hard for me to reconcile that most people can identify my mother instantly, but they really don't know her at all. They may have a sense of her style and her dignified persona, but they don't always appreciate her intellectual curiosity, her sense of the ridiculous, her sense of adventure, or her unerring sense of what was right. Over time, I have tried to draw the line between her public and private life much as I think she did—I try to accommodate requests that pertain to my father's career, life in the White House, historic events and historic preservation, while denying permission for publication of her writings as a private citizen—whether as a young woman or a working editor.

These conversations are not in the same category as her personal writings, because they were recorded with the intention that they would be made accessible one day. So it was not a question of whether to publish but a question of when, and the decision was up to me. My experience with other requests informed my decision that the time was right.

In reaching this conclusion, I found it helpful to remember the context in which the interviews were conducted, and the timing of when they occurred. The goal was to create a record of my father's life and career from the memories of those who knew and worked with him. Accordingly, the questions follow a loosely chronological sequence beginning with my father's early political battles in Massachusetts, his 1956 fight for the vice-presidential nomination, the 1960 campaign, the transition to the presidency, the Inauguration, the Bay of Pigs, the Cuban Missile Crisis, official and family life in the White House, and plans for the 1964 campaign and a second term. Along the way, there are discussions that reveal much about the central characters and events of the time in both domestic politics and international affairs.

The decision was complicated by my conviction that if my mother had reviewed the transcripts, I have no doubt she would have made revisions. She was a young widow in the extreme stages of grief. The interviews were conducted only four months after she had lost her husband, her home, and her sense of purpose. She had two young children to raise alone. It isn't surprising that there are some statements she would later have considered too personal, and others too harsh. There are things I am sure she would have added, and her views certainly evolved over time. I struggled with the question of whether to delete remarks that might be taken out of context. I was aware that my intentions might be misinterpreted, even if the edited version was a more "accurate" reflection of how she really felt. After much deliberation, I decided to maintain the integrity of the audio interviews as a primary source while editing the text slightly for readability, not content, as has been done with other presidential transcripts and oral history interviews.

My reservations were mitigated by the remarkable immediacy and the informality of the conversations. Knowing my mother so well, I can hear her voice in my mind when I read her words on a page. I can tell when she is emotional, when she is enjoying herself, or is getting annoyed—though she is unfailingly polite. Even though most of her answers are about my father, by listening to the audio, people will learn a great deal about the person that she was. Much is revealed by her tone, and by her pauses as well as by her statements. I trust that readers and listeners will place her views in context to build an accurate and composite portrait of a person and a moment in time, and that her devotion to her husband will come through to others as it does to me.

In addition to their passion for history, my parents shared a conviction that American civilization had come of age. Today this seems an unremarkable proposition, but at the time the United States was just emerging as a global power, and people still looked to Europe for direction and leadership. My parents believed America should lead with her ideals, not just with economic or military power, and they wanted to share our artistic and cultural achievements with the world. My mother played a critical role in the development of what is now called "soft diplomacy." She traveled with my father and on her own, often speaking the language of the countries she visited. She was an international sensation.

She also understood that the White House itself was a powerful symbol of our democracy, and wanted to make sure it projected the best of America to students and families who visited, as well as to foreign heads of state who were entertained there. She worked hard—not to "redecorate," a word she hated—but to "restore" the White House so that the legacy of John Adams, Thomas Jefferson, James Madison, and Abraham Lincoln would be visible. She recast the White House Library to showcase classic works of American history and literature. She established the Fine Arts Committee and White House Historical Association to assemble a permanent collection of American paintings and decorative arts that would become one of the nation's finest. She made the White House the world's greatest stage and invited the world's foremost artists to perform there. She welcomed young musicians, emerging African-American opera singers, jazz musicians, and modern dancers—all to awaken and expand appreciation for American arts and culture.

She felt strongly that as our capital city, Washington, D.C., should reflect America's newly prominent place in the world. She fought to preserve Lafayette Square, and launched the effort to rehabilitate Pennsylvania Avenue—an effort that has been sustained ever since. My mother understood that the past was a source of pride for people around the world, just as it is in America, and convinced my father that the United States could build goodwill among countries like Egypt, with which we had political differences, by assisting in their historic preservation efforts. Her persistence resulted in a generous U.S. contribution to the UNESCO rescue of the temples of Abu Simbel, which were threatened by the construction of the Aswan Dam, and favorably impressed the Nasser regime. In another example of cultural diplomacy, my mother was responsible for the *Mona Lisa*'s visit to the United States, the only time the painting has ever left the Louvre.

Most important, she believed her responsibility was to help my father in every way she could. Although she became a diplomatic and even a political asset, she never thought she deserved the title "First Lady," which she disliked anyway, claiming it sounded like the name of a racehorse. But she was deeply patriotic and proud of what she accomplished, and my father was proud of her too. Their time in the White House was the happiest of her life.

Given the important role Jacqueline Kennedy played in the presidency of John F. Kennedy and its aftermath, it seemed a disservice to let her perspective remain absent from the public and scholarly debate that would accompany the fiftieth anniversary of the Kennedy administration. Fifty years seems a sufficient time for passions to have cooled, yet recent enough that the world described still has much to teach us. The sense of time passing was made more acute by the loss of my uncle Teddy and my aunt Eunice in 2009, by Ted Sorensen in 2010, and my uncle Sarge in January 2011.

But, before making the final decision, I asked my children to read the transcripts and tell me what they thought. Their reactions were not so different from my own. They found the conversations dated in many ways—but fascinating in many more. They loved the stories about their grandfather, and how insightful yet irreverent their grandmother was. They were puzzled by some of Arthur Schlesinger's questions—personal rivalries he pursued and particular issues that have not stood the test of time. They wished that he had asked more questions about *her*.

But they came away with the same conclusions that I had reached—there was no significant reason to put off publication and no one speaks better for my mother than she does herself.

—NEW YORK, 2011

INTRODUCTION

by Michael Beschloss

SO NOW, AT LONG LAST, IT IS HER TURN TO SPEAK. If you pore through the thousands of books about John Fitzgerald Kennedy, you will find the voice of one crucial witness virtually absent. As the *New York Times* obituary said the morning after her death on May 19, 1994, "Her silence about her past, especially about the Kennedy years and her marriage to the President, was always something of a mystery." She wrote no autobiography or memoir.

Jacqueline Lee Bouvier was born on July 28, 1929, in Southampton, New York, the summer family seat of both her paternal and maternal lines. Her suntanned, Yale-educated, French-American father, John V. Bouvier III, had followed his forefathers to Wall Street; his career never recovered from the stock market crash of 1929. Her mother, Janet Norton Lee, was the daughter of a self-made Irish-American tycoon in New York banking and real estate. From her Park Avenue and Long Island childhood, Jackie (she preferred Jacqueline, but friends and family rarely used her full given name) liked to ride horses, create whimsical drawings, and read books—especially art history, poetry, French history, and literature. When she was twelve, her parents were bitterly divorced, and her mother wed Hugh D. Auchincloss, Jr., a Standard Oil heir, who made Jackie and her younger sister, Lee, at home on his picturesque estates in McLean, Virginia, and Newport, Rhode Island. As a student at Miss Porter's School (Farmington) in Connecticut, where she boarded her horse Danseuse, teachers found Jackie strong-willed, irreverent, and highly intelligent.

After two years at Vassar, which did not inspire her, the young woman sprang to life during a junior year at the Sorbonne and the University of Grenoble. Returning to live at Merrywood, her stepfather's house on the

Potomac, she was graduated in 1951 from George Washington University and surpassed twelve hundred other college women to win *Vogue*'s Prix de Paris, for which she designed a sample issue of the magazine and wrote an essay on "People I Wish I Had Known" (Oscar Wilde, Charles Baudelaire, and Sergei Diaghilev). The prize offered a year as a *Vogue* junior editor in New York and Paris. She declined it—to the relief of her mother, who was inclined to take her daughter's strong interest in France as an unwelcome sign of allegiance to Jack Bouvier. Instead Jackie took a job as "Inquiring Photographer" for the *Washington Times-Herald*. In that role, she began seeing the man who would become her husband.

The first time she had met Jack Kennedy was in 1948, on a train from Washington, D.C., to New York when, as she recorded at the time, she briefly chatted with an attentive "tall thin young congressman with very long reddish hair." But the encounter came to naught. That same year, her family friend Charles Bartlett took her "across this great crowd" at his brother's Long Island wedding to meet Jack Kennedy, but "by the time I got her across, why, he'd left." Finally in the spring of 1951, in Bartlett and his wife Martha's Georgetown dining room, Jack and Jackie had their official introduction. After what she called "a spasmodic courtship," the Francophile aesthete and the fast-ascending senator from Massachusetts married in Newport on September 12, 1953, launching the decade of their life that you will read about in this book.

During the months after John Kennedy's murder, his thirty-four-year-old widow found memories of their White House life, which she calls in this volume "our happiest years," so traumatic that she asked her Secret Service drivers to please arrange her trips so that she would never accidentally glimpse the old mansion. She intended to stay away from the White House for the rest of her life—and she did, with only one exception. (In 1971, when Aaron Shikler finished his official portraits of the thirty-fifth president and his wife, she agreed to make a very private visit with her children to the White House, where they viewed the portraits and dined with President Richard Nixon and his family.) At the end of 1963, Mrs. Kennedy feared that reminiscing at length about life with her husband would make her "start to cry again," but she was determined to win Jack a fair hearing from historians. Since JFK had been deprived of the chance afforded other presidents of defending their historical record in books, articles, and public comments, she felt an overwhelming obligation to do whatever she could. To ensure that he was not forgotten, within days of Dallas, Jackie was already trying to imagine the architecture of a future Kennedy Library—planned for Harvard, on a Charles River site selected by the President just a month before he died.

At the start of December 1963, when the widow and her children had not yet departed their White House quarters, her husband's aide Arthur Schlesinger, Jr., amassed some of the most moving letters he had received about his late boss and sent them upstairs to the widow. The bow-tied Schlesinger, known for "his acid wit and a magnificent bounce to his step," was an ex–Harvard history professor, one of the nation's most respected scholars, author of award-winning books on the "ages" of Andrew Jackson and Franklin Roosevelt, and speechwriter during Adlai Stevenson's two campaigns for president. He had known JFK since they were Harvard students together, but his friendship with Jackie had really begun during the 1960 presidential campaign, when her husband, wishing not to be seen encircled by liberal academics, had asked Schlesinger to send him tactical advice through her. Now, in the wake of the assassination, the historian was already planning research for the book on the thirty-fifth presidency that JFK and his other aides had always presumed that Schlesinger would one day write.

From her White House rooms, Jacqueline replied in longhand to Schlesinger's note: "I return your letters—I am so happy to have seen them—I have not had time to read any yet." She wrote that someone had urged that the Kennedy Library try to sustain her husband's influence on the young: "Well I don't see how it can keep going without him—but you could think of a way—it would be nice to try." She told Schlesinger she had been "very impressed" by an address he had given about her husband: "It was all the things I thought about Jack—even though he didn't live to see his dreams accomplished—he so badly wanted to be a great President—I think he still can be—because he started those ideas—which is what you said. And he should be great for that." She urged Schlesinger to write about him soon, "while all is fresh—while you still remember his exact words."

As Schlesinger later recalled, an oral history project was "much on my mind after Dallas, and also on Robert Kennedy's mind." At Harvard, he had been an early champion of this new research method. Anxious that important historical evidence was getting lost because people were writing fewer letters and diaries, pioneers at Columbia University and elsewhere were interviewing historical figures, taping the conversations, and placing the transcripts in public archives. As "a matter of urgency," Schlesinger reminded Jacqueline that—in contrast to Presidents Truman and Eisenhower, who kept diaries and wrote surprisingly revealing letters—John Kennedy's leadership was often exercised on the telephone or in person, leaving no written record.[1] Without a "crash" oral history program, capturing memories from New Frontiersmen while still recent, much of the Kennedy history would disappear. In January 1964, Jacqueline and Robert Kennedy approved a plan for scholars and members of the Kennedy circle to record the recollections of "thousands" of people who knew the President—relatives, friends, cabinet secretaries, Massachusetts pols, foreign leaders, and others who had enjoyed "more than a perfunctory" relationship with him. Along with RFK's own oral history, the centerpiece of the collection would be interviews with John Kennedy's widow, which would be performed by Schlesinger himself.

Thus on Monday, March 2, 1964, Schlesinger walked to Jacqueline Kennedy's new home at 3017 N Street and climbed the long flight of wooden steps to start the first of seven interviews with the former First Lady. In her grief, Mrs. Kennedy had bought this 1794 house, which stood across the street from what was once Robert Todd Lincoln's. She was doing her best to provide a normal life for six-year-old Caroline and three-year-old John, which she saw as both her duty and her salvation. Tourist buses stopped outside throughout the day (and sometimes night), disgorging sightseers who littered her steps, pointed Instamatic cameras at her front windows, and called out her children's names, forcing her to keep the curtains in her freshly painted white living room closed.

Inside the house, passing through sliding doors, Schlesinger joined Jacqueline in the living room, whose bookshelves displayed artifacts from ancient Rome, Egypt, and Greece that President Kennedy had given her over the years. Facing away from the front windows, she liked to sit on a crushed-velvet sofa. Atop a three-tiered table beside her were two framed photographs:

---

1. In early 1963, Schlesinger had pleaded with the President to tape his own reminiscences after "major episodes." But with the exception of dictating an occasional memo for the record, Kennedy had declined. Schlesinger did not learn until 1982 that, in the summer of 1962, JFK had started discreetly taping hundreds of hours of his White House meetings and telephone calls. Even this collection covered only a small fraction of the conversations in which the President did business.

ARTHUR M. SCHLESINGER, JR.

PRESIDENT JOHN F. KENNEDY WITH CAROLINE AND JOHN IN THE OVAL OFFICE

the smiling JFK beside his desk, clapping while his children danced, another of him campaigning among a crowd. Placing his tape recorder beside a silver cigarette box on a low black Oriental table, Schlesinger would have sat to Mrs. Kennedy's right on a pale yellow chair he had seen upstairs at the White House. He urged her to speak as though addressing "an historian of the twenty-first century." As he later recalled, "From time to time, she would ask me to turn off the machine so that she could say what she wanted to say, and then ask, 'Should I say that on the recorder?' . . . In general, what I would say was, 'Why don't you say it? . . . You have control over the transcript.'" During this and the next six sittings, starting with a quavering voice that grew stronger with time, Jacqueline unburdened herself as the tape machine also picked up the sounds of her lighting cigarettes, of ice cubes in glasses, dogs barking in the distance, trucks rumbling down N Street, and jets roaring overhead.

For anyone who doubts Jacqueline Kennedy's emotional self-discipline, note that during these months of her greatest despair, she could will herself to speak in such detail about her vanished former life. And Schlesinger was not even her only interlocutor that spring. In April 1964, she sat for hours at night in that same parlor to be questioned by William Manchester, who was researching his authorized book about the assassination. In order to spare Mrs. Kennedy the agony of twice recounting those events, Schlesinger left the task to Manchester. Nevertheless, on the June day after she completed her final interview with Schlesinger, she was forced to sit in that same room to be questioned by members of the Warren Commission about her husband's final motorcade.

Read after almost a half century, the interviews in this book revise scene after scene of the history of the 1950s and early 1960s that we thought we knew. While no such work ever tells the entire story, this oral history constitutes a fresh internal narrative of John Kennedy's life as senator, candidate, and President, and his wife's experience of those years, providing new detail on what JFK and Jacqueline privately said to each other, her backstage role in his political life, diplomacy, and world crises, and her definite and consistently original views about the changing cast of characters who surrounded them both. The close student of the Kennedy years knows how Jackie expanded her husband's range with her command of French and Spanish, her knowledge about the history of Europe and its colonies, her background in the arts. But even today, many presume that she was relatively indifferent to political life. When Schlesinger met her at Hyannis Port in 1959, like others at the time, he found her "flighty on politics," asking elementary questions with "wide-eyed naivete." This behavior was not surprising, because well-bred young women of Jacqueline's generation were not encouraged to sound like intellectuals. Nor would it help her husband for her to vent her more caustic opinions around anyone but their most trusted friends. But as this oral history confirms, she knew considerably more about John Kennedy's political life than she let on to outsiders, and her influence on his official relationships was substantial.

Jacqueline Kennedy would have been the last person—during these interviews or later—to suggest that she was some kind of hidden White House policy guru. As she conveys in this volume, she considered it her role not to badger her husband about labor safety or international law, as Eleanor Roosevelt had with Franklin, but to provide JFK with a "climate of affection," with intriguing dinner guests, appealing food, and "the children in good moods," to help him escape the pressures of leading the Free World through one of the most dangerous periods of the Cold War. To the surprise of both President and First Lady—as this oral history shows, they had both worried that voters would find her too effete—she became, with her beauty and star quality, a huge political asset. Legions of American women wanted to walk, talk, dress, wear their hair, and furnish their homes like Jackie. It was not casually that in the fall of 1963, the President lobbied her to join him on campaign trips to Texas and California. On his final morning, before an audience in Fort Worth, he joked about his wife's popular appeal, mock-complaining that "nobody wonders what Lyndon and I wear!"[2]

As First Lady, Mrs. Kennedy was not a feminist, at least as the word is understood today. Betty Friedan's pathbreaking *The Feminine Mystique* was published in 1963, but the full-fledged women's movement was almost a decade away. In this book, Mrs. Kennedy suggests that women should find their sense of purpose through their husbands, and that the old-fashioned style of marriage is "the best." She describes her first White House social secretary as "sort of a feminist" and thus "so different from me." She even observes that women should stay out of politics because they are too "emotional" (views that by the 1970s she emphatically dropped). Despite such utterances, no one can argue that this First Lady did not make her own strong-minded choices about her life and work. Resisting those who counseled her to emulate her more conventional predecessors, she made it clear from the start that her supreme job was not to attend charity events or political banquets but to raise her children well amid the blast of attention around a president's family. And other public projects she undertook at no one's behest but her own. Through the run of these interviews, Mrs. Kennedy gives short shrift to those achievements. This is because Schlesinger's oral histories were intended to focus on her husband, and because, in 1964, even so knowing an historian as Schlesinger regarded a First Lady's story as a side event, which caused him to treat Jacqueline primarily as a source on her husband. This is unfortunate because among the First Ladies of the twentieth century, probably only Eleanor Roosevelt had a greater impact on the Americans of her time.

---

2. Decades later, after her death, the phenomenon persisted. Half a million people flocked to the Metropolitan Museum in New York to view the first public exhibition of Jacqueline's White House wardrobe.

One of Jacqueline Kennedy's contributions was to herald the importance of historical preservation. The 1950s and 1960s were a period when American architects and city planners were eager to raze urban monuments and neighborhoods that seemed dated in order to make room for new highways, office buildings, stadiums, and public housing. Without Mrs. Kennedy's intervention, some of Washington, D.C.'s crown jewels would have met a similar fate—for example, Lafayette Square, facing the White House, which Pierre L'Enfant, the original architect of Washington, D.C., had envisaged as "the President's park." A plan was in fast motion to destroy almost all of the nineteenth-century houses and buildings on the east and west sides of Lafayette Park, including the mansion of Dolley Madison's widowhood and the 1861 building that had been the capital's first art museum. In their place would go "modern" white marble federal office towers that would dwarf the White House.

Walking around the square, Jacqueline recalled learning while a student in Paris about how the French protected their vital buildings and places. She wished the House and Senate would "pass a law establishing something on the order of Monuments Historiques in France." (Congress did, in 1966.) As she wrote in a letter, she could not sit still while America's monuments were "ripped down and horrible things put up in their place. I simply panic at the thought of this and decided to make a last-minute appeal." In response, an eminent American architect complained that there was "practically nothing" on the square's west side worth preserving: "I hope Jacqueline Kennedy wakes up to the fact that she lives in the twentieth century." But Mrs. Kennedy prevailed. "Hold your breath," she wrote one of her co-conspirators. "All our wildest dreams come true. . . .The Dolley Madison and Tayloe houses will be saved!!!" Had someone else been First Lady, the vista seen from the Executive Mansion's north windows today might be very bleak.[3] Among other capital monuments she managed to protect was the old gray mansard-crowned Executive Office Building, built in the 1870s next to the White House, which had once housed the Departments of State, War, and Navy.

---

3. JFK sardonically quipped that the rescue of Lafayette Park "may be the only monument we'll leave." In October 1963, expanding the case into a general principle, he declared while dedicating a library to Robert Frost at Amherst College that he looked forward to an America "which will preserve great old American houses and squares and parks of our national past."

In January 1961, when the just-inaugurated President and his wife rode down Pennsylvania Avenue, they were newly reminded that L'Enfant's design for a grand ceremonial mile from Capitol to White House had given way to dilapidated tattoo parlors and souvenir stores. Sometimes at night, unbeknownst to the public, Jackie "would walk halfway" to the Capitol with Jack, as she later scrawled to her brother-in-law, Senator Edward Kennedy: "The tawdriness of the encroachments to the President's House depressed him. He wished to do something that would ensure a nobility of architecture along that Avenue which is the main artery of the Government of the United States. . . . He wished to emulate Thomas Jefferson, with whom he had such great instinctive affinity. . . . I just wanted to tell you with all my heart that this is one thing that really meant something to Jack." The President established a commission for the boulevard's redevelopment and oversaw it closely with his wife. Jacqueline recalled to Ted Kennedy that Pennsylvania Avenue was one of the last things "I remember Jack speaking about with feeling" before they left for Texas in November 1963.

She famously recast the White House as a treasure house of historic American furniture, painting, sculpture, and artifacts that would rival world-renowned museums. For the hundred and sixty years after Abigail and John Adams became its first residents, presidential families had restyled the mansion's public rooms at their whim. When Jacqueline Kennedy first scrutinized them, her heart sank. The bad wallpaper and reproductions were "early Statler," she said, almost devoid of American history. She drafted a plan to persuade wealthy collectors (employing "my predatory instincts," she privately joked) to donate important American pieces; remake the public rooms, with careful research, into proper historical venues; and establish a White House Historical Association to keep some future president's wife whose aunt "ran a curio shop" from revamping those rooms to her own ahistorical taste. Especially after Jacqueline's televised tour of the newly remade White House rooms in February 1962, which was seen by fifty-six million viewers, the project helped make Americans more aware of their traditions in the decorative arts. Enduring too are certain other ways Mrs. Kennedy changed what she described as "the setting in which the presidency is presented to the world," including the contours of state dinners and other presidential ceremonies. She transformed the austere Oval Office into "a New England sitting room" by moving in sofas and easy chairs, unsealing its fireplace, and installing the massive H.M.S. *Resolute* desk, which has since been used by five of her husband's successors. It was at Jacqueline's request that the industrial designer Raymond Loewy invented the sky-blue and white design of today's presidential air fleet.

Mrs. Kennedy also transformed the role of the First Lady. Since her restoration of the White House, a venture she conceived and assigned to herself, every president's wife has felt compelled to focus on some important public project. The thirty-one-year-old Jackie was serious when she said her preeminent job in the White House was to be wife and mother, but as Lady Bird Johnson later recalled, "She was a worker, which I don't think was always quite recognized." With that work ethic, it was natural that Jacqueline would take on the restoration project, although she knew it would prove exhausting. She had had a full-time job after graduation from college, which was unusual in her social group, and later, in 1975, when her second husband, Aristotle Onassis, had died, and both of her children were away at school, she took on a real job as a book editor at Viking and Doubleday, with a reputation for quality volumes of art and history that benefited from her taste, life experience, and expertise.

Jackie's capacity for intellectual growth manifested itself in the 1970s with her embrace of the women's movement. She told a friend she had come to realize that she could not expect to live primarily through a husband. She championed various feminist causes, including Gloria Steinem's *Ms.* magazine, and despite her aversion to giving interviews, gave one in praise of working women for a 1979 cover story in Steinem's magazine, saying, "What has been sad for many women of my generation is that they weren't supposed to work if they had families."

But in the early 1960s, all of this was in Jacqueline Kennedy's future. Retrospectively she felt that of equal importance to her White House restoration were her far less well known efforts as First Lady to save Abu Simbel. Alarmed to learn in 1962 that floods were threatening the exalted Egyptian monument, she wrote JFK, "It is the major temple of the Nile—13th century B.C. It would be like letting the Parthenon be flooded. . . . Abu Simbel is the greatest. Nothing will ever be found to equal it." Despite JFK's insistence that congressmen would dismiss Abu Simbel as some "Egyptian rocks," the First Lady's personal appeal to Capitol Hill won Egypt the necessary funds. When Egypt's president, Gamal Abdel Nasser, offered to send one of his country's treasures to America as a thank-you gift, she requested the Temple of Dendur, which she and her husband hoped to install in Washington, D.C., to "remind people that feelings of the spirit are what prevent wars."

John Kennedy would have been quick to affirm that the cultural milestones of his presidency—Pablo Casals and the American Ballet Theatre in the East Room, the *Mona Lisa* displayed in America, the dinner for Nobel laureates, the efforts to develop a national theater (now the John F. Kennedy Center for the Performing Arts), and others—would most likely have been absent had he not married Jacqueline Bouvier. Both Kennedys insisted that the arts must be included in any definition of a full American life. The affluent society of the early 1960s was a propitious moment for such a statement. Many Americans, enjoying postwar prosperity, were pondering how to spend their newfound discretionary income in leisure hours that their struggling forebears could only have dreamt of.

Jacqueline Kennedy's acute sense of how symbols and ceremony could shape American history was never more evident than during the long nightmare weekend after her husband's assassination. Remembering what she had read, while transforming the Mansion, about Abraham Lincoln's funeral, the most elaborate in the country's past before 1963, the stunned widow improvised three unforgettable days of tone-perfect ceremony—the ritual in the East Room and Capitol Rotunda, the foreign leaders walking to the strangely intimate old cathedral, JFK's beloved *Air Force One* flying in salute above the burial, the lighting of an eternal flame (like the one she had seen in Paris as a Sorbonne student). After Dallas, all of this helped Americans win back at least some portion of their self-respect. Once the melancholy pageant was over, Mrs. Kennedy's command of public gesture remained: when she and her children officially departed the White House for the last time, she saw to it that her son John was carrying an American flag.

In the summer of 1964, after finishing her interviews with Arthur Schlesinger, she told a friend that recounting her bygone life had been "excruciating." Plagued by the commotion around her Georgetown home and torturous reminders of a happier time, she moved her family to an apartment high above Fifth Avenue in New York, seeking "a new life in a new city." From her new bedroom windows, she could see, across the street, the Metropolitan Museum of Art, where, despite her preference for Washington,

D.C., the Temple of Dendur was being installed, and at night, the floodlights bothered her. That autumn, on the first anniversary of the assassination, she wrote of JFK for *Look* magazine, "So now he is a legend when he would have preferred to be a man. . . . At least he will never know whatever sadness might have lain ahead." Almost as a resolution to herself, she added, "He is free and we must live."

After writing those words in longhand, Mrs. Kennedy never again mused in public about her husband—not in 1965, when Queen Elizabeth II dedicated a memorial acre to him at the birthplace of the Magna Carta; not in 1979, when she witnessed the opening of the Kennedy Library; not ever.[4] When she and her children settled in New York, she asserted her right to be a private citizen and was content to allow the conversations in this book to be her principal contribution to the Kennedy historiography. In the spring of 1965, she read an early version of Arthur Schlesinger's forthcoming *A Thousand Days: John F. Kennedy in the White House,* and was upset to discover that the author had borrowed a number of items from their sealed conversations to describe the President's relationships with her and their children. She implored him by letter to remove "things I think are too personal. . . .The world has no right to his private life with me—I shared all those rooms with him—not with the Book of the Month readers + I don't want them snooping through those rooms now—even the bathtub—with the children." Schlesinger complied, and by the time *A Thousand Days* was published, their friendship was restored.

Despite her insistence on privacy, Jacqueline Kennedy never forgot her obligation to posterity. She knew that when this oral history was published after her death, she would have what she expected to be the almost-final word

---

4. For her family's flight to England for the Queen's ceremony in 1965, President Johnson offered a presidential aircraft. Remembering her *Air Force One* journey back from Dallas, Jacqueline wrote LBJ that she did not know "if I could steel myself to go on one of those planes again." Nevertheless, to honor her husband, she would accept: "But please do not let it be Air Force One. And please, let it be the 707 that looks least like Air Force One inside." In 1968, before boarding a presidential jet taking Robert Kennedy's casket from Los Angeles to New York, she demanded to be reassured that it was not the *Air Force One* of 1963. Though afflicted until the end of her life by such painful sensitivities, Jacqueline was blessed with loving and protective children. Once when John was reading a children's volume about his father, he called out, "Close your eyes, Mummy!" and tore out a photograph of the presidential car in Dallas before showing her the book.

on her life with her husband. It was another of her innovations. With the reminiscences in this book, Jacqueline Kennedy became the first American president's wife to submit to hours of intensive recorded questioning about her public and private life. Now, after decades in which her history has been left to others, listen to what she has to say.

The
FIRST
Conversation

MONDAY, MARCH 2

1964

*J*ackie, when do you think the President first began to think and act seriously about the presidency? When did he begin to see himself, do you suppose, as a possible president?

I think he was probably thinking about it for an awfully long time, long before I even knew, and I say this because I remember the first year we were married, I heard him at the Cape. He was in a room with his father, talking, and I came in and they were talking about something—about the vice presidency. Well, that was just the year after he had been elected a senator.

This was 1953?

Yeah. I said, "Were you talking about being vice president?" or something like that, and he sort of rather laughed. But I think it was always—he never stopped at any plateau, he was always going on to something higher. So, obviously after the vice presidential thing, well, then, he was definitely aiming for the presidency.[1] But I think it would have been—I don't know—maybe when he first ran for the Senate. It was certainly before I knew him.

---

1. ADLAI EWING STEVENSON (1900–1965) was governor of Illinois from 1949 to 1953 and Democratic presidential nominee in 1952 and 1956. At the 1956 Democratic convention in Chicago, Stevenson unexpectedly broke tradition by allowing the delegates to decide themselves who should be vice president. In the ensuing contest, JFK lost to Tennessee senator Estes Kefauver by a hairbreadth.

JOSEPH P. KENNEDY, JR., JOSEPH P. KENNEDY, SR., AND JOHN F. KENNEDY
ARRIVING IN SOUTHAMPTON, ENGLAND, JULY 1938

I am sure it was always, in some sense, in his mind. Is the story true, as has sometimes been printed, that the ambassador originally thought of—expected Joe to be the great political figure of the family?[2]

That's the sort of trite story that all these people who used to go interview Mr. Kennedy—you get so tired of people asking for anecdotes, and he'd always produce this thing that Joe would have. You know, how can I say? Because I never knew Joe. And, obviously, I suppose Joe would have run for politics, and then Jack, being so close to him, couldn't have run right on his heels in Massachusetts. Maybe he would have gone into something literary. But it's just not as simple as that story sounds. And then once Joe was dead, you know, Mr. Kennedy didn't do any strange thing of saying, "O.K., now we run you." Everything just evolved—they came back from the war—I don't know.

The story sounded, to me, too pat and mechanical. Joe was a classmate of mine at Harvard, but—

I've got a feeling, from what I think of Joe and everything, that he would have been so unimaginative, compared to Jack. He would never have—I think he probably would have gotten to be a senator, and not much higher. I don't know if that's prejudiced, but I don't think he had any of the sort of imagination that Jack did.

Well, certainly I knew him moderately well, and he did not have the imagination or the intellectual force or intellectual interest. He was a most attractive, charming fellow and would have been, I think, very successful in politics, but I don't think he would ever have carried things to the point the President did. The vice presidency then was on his mind sort of sometime before 1956?

---

2. **JOSEPH PATRICK KENNEDY** (1888–1969) was a financier, first chairman of the Securities Exchange Commission, pre–World War II ambassador to the Court of St. James's under President Franklin Roosevelt, and the father of nine children, including the thirty-fifth president of the United States. Jacqueline's comment refers to the senior Kennedy's insistence to several reporters in the late 1950s that he had originally decided that his first son, Joseph, Jr. (1915–1944), should one day be president, and that when Joe, Jr., was killed in World War II, he turned to Jack.

Well, it's funny—they were talking about that in, I guess, around October–November 1953 at the Cape. But yet I know the night that Jack ran for the vice presidency in Chicago, he didn't want to then at all. And you know, it was just a last-minute thing when Stevenson threw the convention open, and, all that taught them so much of how to do things in California in 1960 because no one was prepared. And I remember being in that office and Bobby trying to get someone to paint signs.[3] I mean, he wasn't trying for the vice presidency.

That was, when he came to Chicago in 1956, he was not coming, really, to—

No. He didn't—he didn't want it. You know, he thought Stevenson would be defeated, and it would be because—and one of the reasons would be because he would have been a Catholic on the ticket with him, so it could only have been a hindrance to him. But then when all that thing got thrown wide open, I don't know who said, "Make a race for it," or what. It just really happened that night.

There must have been some sense in his mind, because I remember Ted Sorensen coming—or perhaps, at least, in Ted's mind—coming to see me on the Cape that summer, before the convention, and discussing this—and I telling Ted that I was for it and that I knew other people in the Stevenson circle were for it. You remember then Ted had a memorandum prepared on the Catholic vote.[4]

---

3. **ROBERT FRANCIS KENNEDY** (1925–1968) was the fifth of Joseph and Rose Kennedy's nine children, a lawyer, Senate committee counsel, and manager of his brother's 1960 campaign, after which the President-elect made him attorney general. Despite his formal mandate to run the Justice Department, as his brother's presidency unfolded, RFK served as his chief adviser and enforcer on virtually all matters that faced him. In 1964, after his brother's death, RFK was elected senator from New York. Four years later, he was assassinated while running for the Democratic presidential nomination.

4. **THEODORE SORENSEN** (1928–2010) was the son of Nebraska's progressive Danish-American attorney general and his Russian Jewish wife. Ted Sorensen joined JFK's staff in 1953 and, as a speechwriter, helped give the senator his voice, with the staccato phrases, contrapuntal phrasing, soaring rhetoric, and historical references so widely praised. Later, at the White House, Sorensen served as special counsel to the President. In the spring of 1956, Kennedy had him draft and circulate a memorandum that showed how many votes a Catholic running mate might bring to a Democratic ticket in 1956. (Since the 1928 landslide defeat of Al Smith, the only Catholic candidate ever chosen for a major-party ticket, many feared that Catholicism was a liability for a nominee.) But Mrs. Kennedy is correct that

ROBERT F. KENNEDY DURING JOHN F. KENNEDY'S SENATE CAMPAIGN, MASSACHUSETTS, 1952

Ah, yes. That's right. I didn't realize it was then. The funny thing with Jack that would make it very hard in these interviews for me to sound as if I make sense, is that he never spoke of his sort of secret objectives, or of plotting things. Life with him was always so fast—of what you were doing that day. He always talked at home of what he was thinking about, or people. I mean, people say he never talked about politics at home with me, but that's all that

---

her husband did not overtly press Stevenson to put him on the ticket. When the Illinoisan made his unusual, surprise decision to throw open the nomination, and Kennedy made his hasty effort to win the prize, Joseph Kennedy, vacationing in Cap d'Antibes, was furious that his son would try something so ill planned. JFK later said he was glad that he lost, because when Stevenson was defeated by Dwight Eisenhower that fall, some Democrats might have pointed at his Catholic running mate.

SENATOR JOHN F. KENNEDY AT THE 1956 DEMOCRATIC NATIONAL CONVENTION, CHICAGO

was talked about. But he'd never sort of plot little goals and tell you when he was aiming for them then, and life with him was just so fast—that it isn't until you look back that you see what happened when.

With people, life is not like that, anyway. I don't think people have objectives which they sort of plot to reach. There are things organic in them which emerge as they continue living, and which are implanted and not sort of consciously striven for. When people do that, you get a kind of Nixon business,[5] which is unattractive,

<hr />

5. RICHARD MILHOUS NIXON (1913–1994) had served from 1947 to 1951 with JFK in the House, where they were cordial colleagues. Nixon was a senator from California when chosen by Dwight Eisenhower for the 1952 Republican ticket. On November 7, 1960, Vice President Nixon lost the presidency to Kennedy by the tiny margin of 112,827 popular votes. By "Nixon business," Schlesinger means conspicuous ambition.

and the President lived so intensely from day to day that the thing that was rather implicit in his career in both the shape of his consciousness and destiny, rather than, I imagine, explicit in his mind, or anything that he ever would talk about. You—when he decided to run for the vice presidency in 1956, what was it —just the occasion suddenly overpowered him, do you think? Or—

I was out at the convention then with him in Chicago, but I was having a baby, and so I stayed with Eunice,[6] and he lived in a hotel with Torb.[7] And I saw him—you'd see him in the day at the convention, you'd have dinner, but it was such—I can't tell you the confusion—you should talk to Torb about that. You know, he was so tired and he was working all the time. And every day was different, so I think it was when— The worst fight in his life, which you should ask me about sometime, is when he got control of the Massachusetts legislature. That was to lead the Massachusetts delegation there, wasn't it?

Yes, against Bill Burke.

Yes, against "Onions" Burke.[8] Because that was the only time in all of the fights

---

6. EUNICE MARY KENNEDY SHRIVER (1921–2009) was JFK's sister. In 1956, she was living in Chicago with her husband, Sargent Shriver, president of the city's Board of Education. Before her marriage, she had shared a townhouse with her brother in the Georgetown section of Washington. Tireless, greatly religious, Mrs. Shriver did pathbreaking work to bring the intellectually disabled into the mainstream and was always prodding Jack to do more to help the cause. (Their sister Rosemary [1918–2005] had been institutionalized in Wisconsin.) JFK indeed established the first presidential commission on mental retardation. Joseph Kennedy once said that had Eunice been a man, she might have been president.

7. TORBERT MACDONALD (1917–1976) was a Kennedy chum, captain of the Harvard football team, and one of JFK's roommates at Harvard, who was married to Phyllis Brooks, a B-movie actress of the 1930s. He served as a Democratic member of Congress, representing Malden, Massachusetts, from 1954 until his death.

8. In 1956, the chairman of the state Democratic party was a loud conservative named William "Onions" Burke (1906–1975), an onion and tobacco farmer and barkeeper from Hatfield, Massachusetts. Burke was plotting to keep the state's delegation out of Adlai Stevenson's hands at the Chicago convention by having it vote for House Majority Leader John McCormack of Boston (1891-1980) as a "favorite son." McCormack was delighted, but JFK considered the move a slap in his face. As he later explained, "I had publicly endorsed Stevenson and I wanted to make good on my commitment." Kennedy wished to avoid putting an illiberal face on the Massachusetts party, and he feared looking powerless in his home state in case Stevenson considered him for vice president. In May 1956, he launched a

he's been through in his life when I'd really seen him nervous when he couldn't talk about anything else before. So that was the big thing of all the spring, I guess was, you know, to win that fight. And it really was on his mind all the time. So, anyway, then he went out there as sort of an important person, and I guess he had rather an unsatisfactory couple of meetings with Stevenson, and suddenly there was that night. And I remember I stayed up all night at the head-quarters, and Bobby came running to me and said, "We don't know anything. What do we do about Nevada?" And I was in a little corner doing something with envelopes or getting someone to make signs, and I timidly said, "I have an uncle who lives in Nevada." And nobody ever thought I had any political relatives or anything, but this uncle was a great friend of Pat McCarran.[9] So we went in the little back room, Bobby and I, and called him up.

Who was the uncle?

Norman Biltz. And he's always been in Nevada politics. He's married to my stepfather's sister, Esther, who was, before that, married to Ogden Nash's brother. Then she married Norman Biltz, I think, and lived in Reno for the rest of her life.[10]

Norman Biltz is a Democrat?

Yeah. You know, but Pat McCarran and all these sort of types were all, I don't know, rather—I don't know if he's "shady," because I love him, but

---

major effort to depose Burke in favor of the former mayor of Somerville, Pat Lynch. This culminated in what Sorensen called "a stormy meeting—complete with booing, shoving, name-calling, contests for the gavel, and near fistfights." Since Kennedy's first election to the House in 1946, McCormack had viewed the young tiger as a threat to his dominance, and now his dread had come to pass. Burke was ousted, and JFK assumed effective control of his party in Massachusetts. The Kennedy-McCormack schism divided the state's Democrats until 1962, when Edward Kennedy defeated then Speaker Mc-Cormack's nephew Edward to win the party's nomination for JFK's old Senate seat.

9. PATRICK McCARRAN (1876–1954) was a Democratic senator from Nevada from 1933 until his death in 1954. Scourge of potential Communists in government, admirer of the Spanish dictator Francisco Franco, he commanded influence in his state far beyond that suggested by his job title.

10. NORMAN BILTZ (1902–1973) was known as the "Duke of Nevada." A Republican with many Democratic cronies, he was one of the most powerful tycoons and largest landowners in the state.

he's certainly someone to know in Nevada. And he said, "All right," because Nevada hadn't been for Jack, and the next day, all Nevada's votes were for Jack. *[Schlesinger laughs]* So all I know is that when he decided, I don't know, but I just know that I knew that he was going for vice president that day—that night. And before—I suppose Torb could tell you that, because he was closeted in the room with him.

Yes, we'll talk to Torb. That's my memory, because I can remember Stevenson's decision to throw it open, and then again Ted or someone from the President's staff getting in touch with me about things, and I think, obviously it was in the mind of some people around—before, I think, it had become dormant and then it was suddenly revived. Let's talk about the fight against Bill Burke. It was really a fight against John McCormack, wasn't it?

Yes, and again, you'd have to tell me about it, and I could tell you things that rang bells, because it's—

The great problem was the control of the Democratic state committee, and Burke had been—

And Lynch there was—

There was Lynch, who was our man—

Yeah.

And who has been state chairman through the years since. Kenny and Larry[11] were in that fight, were they?

---

11. KENNETH O'DONNELL (1924–1977), son of the Holy Cross football coach, had been a Harvard roommate and football teammate of Robert Kennedy's and World War II bombardier in England. Since JFK's 1952 Senate campaign, he had been a key member of the circle of Kennedy aides known as the "Irish Mafia," serving as appointments secretary in the Kennedy White House. Lawrence O'Brien (1917–1990) of Springfield, Massachusetts, labored on JFK's campaigns for the Senate and presidency, then as the President's liaison to Congress.

SENATOR KENNEDY WITH KENNY O'DONNELL, 1960

I think so, yes.

They were. But I think that neither of them yet had come on the senator's staff—Senate staff.

That's right. I think Kenny told me about that just now—I mean, just a couple of weeks ago. But—first, that Jack was traveling a lot then, but I can just remember every night talking. I remember at Jean's wedding—he was so busy up in Massachusetts, and she came—she had a dinner the night before she got married.[12] Well, even Jack was going all around at that dinner, talking to his father, talking to Bobby, Torb, everyone. It was sort of about this thing—it was just obsessing him. Because it was going to be known—she was married on May 6—something like that—May 19 she was married, and, I guess, the vote or whatever it is was going to come up a few days later, and I remember thinking— the only time in my life I've ever thought that Jack was a little bit thoughtless. But I didn't really think that, because you could see how worried he was, be- cause all that night, when everyone should have been making little toasts to Jean and things—which they were, and he made a touching one—he was talking to everybody at the dinner about that fight. I mean, it was just on his mind, and I've never seen him like that—in the first Cuba, the second Cuba,[13] any election—I mean, the election—the presidential election, when I think of how calm he was that night—whether it would come out well or not, but still—but that was just all that spring. And as I have—you know, you musn't think it bad that I don't have all of these political memories, because I was really living another side of life with him, but I just remember that was a terrible worry of all that spring.

I had the impression it must have been an awfully critical thing. It was the first big test of strength within the party organization. I know Kenny's told me from time to time when we've been talking about people in politics, and he would say, "So and so, he was for us in the Burke fight," which meant, we forgive him everything else. Or someone, "He was against us in the Burke fight." And this became the standard of judgment, which, years later, in the presidential years, would still be very much in everyone's mind.

And I remember all the people—it fascinated me because when I came back from my honeymoon, I was taken immediately to Boston to be registered as a Democrat by Patsy Mulkern, who was called "the China Doll," because he was a prize fighter once, and he took me all up and down that street, and

---

12. JEAN ANN KENNEDY SMITH (1928–) was JFK's youngest sister. Her husband, Stephen Edward Smith (1927–1990), shrewdly managed the Kennedy family finances and served all three Kennedy brothers as political strategist and behind-the-scenes troubleshooter.

13. Terms used by many in the Kennedy circle to refer to the failed Bay of Pigs invasion of 1961 and the Cuban Missile Crisis of 1962.

told me that "duking" people means shaking hands, and things. And then there was another man with "Onions" Burke, named "Juicy" Grenara. Well, I mean those names just fascinated me so. You know, to sort of see that world, and then we'd go have dinner at the Ritz. *[both Jacqueline and Schlesinger laugh]* Then you'd be going someplace else. It just seems it was suitcases, moving, and then you'd go to New York for a couple of days. We never had our own house until we'd been married four years. So I can't tell you—

That was in Georgetown, or out in McLean?

Oh no, that's right. We had one—for three years in Hickory Hill.[14] We didn't buy a house. You know, we'd rent January until June, then we'd go live at my mother's house, which was in Virginia, for the summer, because we didn't have a child for four years. So the summers we'd spend at her house, going up to the Cape when we could on weekends—and in the fall, we'd stay with his father—you know, living right with our in-laws. And then we'd go to his apartment in Boston or we'd go down to New York for a couple of days. It was terrifically nomadic, you know. And then we'd go away after Christmas or something for a few days to Jamaica or something. Such a pace, when I think of how little we were alone, or always moving.

I know, in the political life—you are never alone in politics. It's terrible.

And never alone. Later on, Jack said, when Teddy got married and got his house right away, "What was the matter with me? Why didn't I get our house sooner?" And I thought, why didn't I? But you were just moving and everything was so fast. And then we got Hickory Hill, but that turned out to be a mistake because it was so far out of town. That was the year after Jack's back.[15] Well, again we spent a lot of money to buy this house in Virginia, and I thought it would be a place where he could rest on weekends the year

---

14. This McLean, Virginia, estate was briefly occupied by Union Army General George McClellan during the Civil War. Jacqueline and her husband sold it to Robert and Ethel Kennedy in 1956 for $125,000, the same price they had paid for it. Especially compared to Georgetown, driving from the house to Capitol Hill took considerable time in traffic.

15. Referring to JFK's serious back surgery of 1954.

where he would be recovering from his back. And we discussed that when we bought it. Again this shows you how he didn't sort of tell me what was ahead because once we got to the house, he was away every weekend, traveling. And it was no good to him during the week—it was that much farther from his office. And then, when I lost the baby—you know, that I had made nurseries and everything for there, I didn't want to live there anymore, so that's when we moved.[16] We rented a house—no, the next year we rented a house on P Street, and then had Caroline and bought our house in 1957.[17] Yeah, we must have had Hickory Hill—no, when did we have Hickory Hill? His operation was '55. Yeah, I guess it was two years before we had a house.

You got the N Street house in '57.

'Fifty-seven. And, I guess, we got Hickory Hill the winter after his back, which was '55.

Some people have speculated, and I have written, that the operation and the sickness of the back was kind of a turning point. I have never known whether there was anything—whether this was kind of a false knowledge of FDR and really whether there was anything in that.

No, I don't think there's anything in that. And it's just so easy. Max Freedman[18] said to me the other night, "And when do you think the dedication started?" Well, that just irritated me so. It was always there. You know, the winter of his

---

16. On August 23, 1956, Jacqueline gave birth to her first baby, a daughter, who was stillborn. Her husband wanted a large family, and her difficulty producing children, especially in contrast to Kennedy sisters and wives who did so with little apparent effort, led to frustrations that inevitably affected her morale, her marriage, and her ability to make frequent trips with her husband during the 1960 presidential campaign and as First Lady. This made the stillbirth of their first child, three years into their marriage, and the death of the premature Patrick Bouvier Kennedy two days after his birth on August 7, 1963, all the harder for both Kennedys to bear.

17. The Kennedys bought the three-story Federal redbrick edifice at 3307 N Street in Georgetown (of which she said, "My sweet little house leans slightly to one side") and stayed there until they left for the White House.

18. MAX FREEDMAN (1914–1980) was Washington correspondent for the Manchester (England) *Guardian*.

back, which was awful, just to keep himself from going mad, lying there, aches and pains, and being moved over, side to side, every twenty minutes or something, or beginning to walk, and just as he was starting to walk on crutches, one of his crutches broke, so then he was back in. You know, then he started to write that book which he'd always had in his mind a long time—he'd had Edmund Ross—he talked to me about that a year or so before as the one classic example of profiles in courage.[19] And he'd always thought of writing an article or something on that, and then so that whole winter, he started to search out other people—enough to make a book. So, that wasn't any changing point. He was just going through that winter like he did everything—getting through an awful winter of sickness and doing the book.

The back had been an overhanging thing for some time before.

Yeah, with the back, it had just gotten worse and worse. I mean, the year before we were married, when he'd take me out, half the time it was on crutches. You know, when I went to watch him campaign, before we were married, he was on crutches. I can remember him on crutches more than not. And then, in our marriage, he'd be off it a lot, and then something would go wrong. It was really—I mean, the problem everyone found later—he didn't even need the operation. It was that he'd had a bad back since college, and then the war, and he'd had a disk operation that he never needed, so all those muscles had gotten weak, had gone into spasm, and that was what was giving him pain—the muscles. And so, then he'd go— I think if he went on crutches for four days, you know, he'd get everything better, but again that was only weakening it. And it wasn't until after his back operation that the poor doctor who'd been his medical man, Ephraim Shorr, said to him, "Now I think I am at liberty to tell you something which I wanted to tell you before, but I didn't think it was correct to do that to Dr. Wilson," who was the back surgeon.[20] This made me so mad how

---

19. EDMUND G. ROSS (1826–1907), Republican senator from Kansas, won his place in *Profiles in Courage* by casting the decisive vote in 1868 against President Andrew Johnson's impeachment, which cost Ross reelection.

20. EPHRAIM SHORR (1896–1956) was a New York Hospital endocrinologist. Philip Wilson (1886–1969) was chief surgeon at the city's Hospital for Special Surgery, where the operation was performed, and a Harvard classmate of JFK's father.

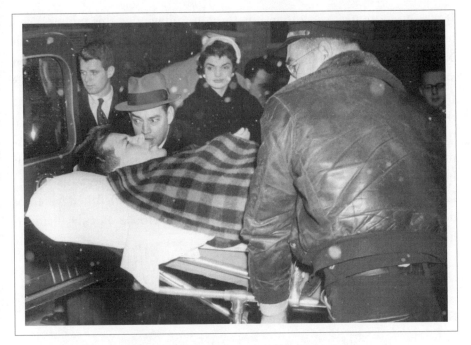

SENATOR KENNEDY ON STRETCHER ACCOMPANIED BY
ROBERT KENNEDY AND JACQUELINE KENNEDY, NEW YORK, DECEMBER 1954

doctors just let people suffer, and don't say anything to hurt the other eminent physicians' feelings. But then Dr. Shorr told him about Dr. Travell, who was a woman in New York, and lived down on 16th Street, and had been doing terrific things with muscles. And Jack went to see her. She put in this Novocain for spasms. Well, she could fix him. I mean, life just changed then.[21] Because, obviously, after a year of surgery and a year out, his back was weaker than ever. If you don't think that wasn't discouraging for him—to have been through that year and find that his back was worse, not better—

In other words, the operation of 1955 was not necessary?[22]

---

21. **JANET TRAVELL** (1901–1997) later became JFK's White House physician, the first woman to serve in that role.

22. JFK's double spinal fusion operation at the Hospital for Special Surgery in New York was actually on October 21, 1954, and included insertion of a metal plate to support the lumbar spine. That August, he had been warned by Lahey Clinic physicians that without such an operation, he might lose the use

It was no more necessary than it is for you to have one this minute. And it was just criminal. But, you know, all those bone surgeons look at X-rays—you see, Jack was being driven so crazy by this pain. They even said to him before it, "We can't tell if it will help or not." I remember his father and I and he talking, and he said, "I don't care. I can't go on like this." It was, you know, one chance in a million, but he was going to take it. And if it hadn't been for Dr. Travell—I mean, no one can underestimate her contribution then. Though later on, it was apparent that what he should be doing was build up his back with exercises. She was very reluctant to let him leave her Novocain treatments, which by then were not doing any good. This is once we're in the White House. But she changed his life then.

And she came on the scene when? 'Fifty-six?

No. When did he have his back?

'Fifty-five.

October—no, he had it October of '54.

The operation, it was the winter of '54–'55.

Yeah, and he came back to the Senate, June '55. So she must have come on the scene about June '55. He made a great effort to walk that day and walk around.

---

of his legs—and that for an Addison's disease patient like JFK, the surgery might produce an infection that could kill him. When the doctors operated, the latter occurred, leaving the senator in a coma. Last rites were administered. The following February, when doctors feared that the plate was infected and recommended another operation to remove it and perform a bone graft on his spinal column, Jackie wanted a second opinion, but doctors persuaded her not to seek it. The second surgery threw her husband into three months of agony and depression while recuperating in Palm Beach; she wished she had fought the doctors. After JFK's first operation, when he was on the brink of death, she had heard him calling for her but was barred from the room. She resolved never to let it happen again. Therefore on November 22, 1963, in Dallas, when a Parkland Hospital nurse tried to prevent her from entering the chamber where her husband was receiving desperate measures, Jackie told her, "I'm going to get in that room," and she did, which enabled her to be with him when he died.

But he'd come back, we stayed at the Capitol Arms Hotel[23] or something—right near the Capitol—he had a hospital bed there. He'd walk all around the Senate looking wonderful and tan in his gray suit, and then he'd come home and go in a hospital bed.

Oh, God, I think one of the most terrible sentences I've ever read was the one in Bobby's Introduction of Profiles in Courage[24]—*about "half his days on this earth spent in pain." Because, you know, around the White House, occasionally one could tell when he started to reach for something and then would stop or pull himself short, or he didn't want to stand too much. Yet I never—from what I saw of him, it was total stoicism about this. Did he ever mention it?*

He was never—when you think how many people are hypochondriacs, or complain, he never liked you to ask him how he felt. You could tell when he wasn't feeling well—you'd take care of him and put him to bed or something—but he was never irritable—he never liked to discuss it and he made a conscious effort to get his mind off it by having friends for dinner or talking about—you know, or going to see a movie, or—just to not let himself be sitting there having a pain.

And of course, this cut him off from sports, which must have been at one time—sailing—

Except—it's funny—because the month before we were married, we both went bareback riding in a field in Newport on two unbroken work horses and galloped all around the golf course. On our honeymoon, we'd played golf. It would cut him off for periods, but then he'd come back again. And then he played baseball all the time in Georgetown in the spring with the senators.[25] And he always would play touch football, but he couldn't run—I mean, he

---

23. The Carroll Arms Hotel was across the street from the Old (now Russell) Senate Office Building, in which JFK had his office.

24. RFK wrote the foreword to a memorial edition of his brother's book, which was published in 1964.

25. JFK played softball at a Georgetown park with Senate colleagues.

SENATOR KENNEDY RECUPERATES IN PALM BEACH, FLORIDA, 1955

could run enough, but he could never be the one to run for the touchdown. He would pass and catch and run around a little.

It would sort of come and go, would it?

Yeah.

I suppose when he was more tired, it would be worse. Or was it unpredictable?

It was unpredictable. Now that you know it's a spasm, I suppose it probably could come when he's tired. Or some thing might just put it out—something you wouldn't expect. He could go riding and nothing would happen. And some funny thing of dropping a pile of papers and stooping quickly to pick them up would set it off. But he wasn't in any way—I never think of being married to an invalid or a cripple, and I don't want it to look as if—because it hampered him so long.

That's the striking thing, because when I read that sentence of Bobby's—it is the last thing that one would think, having seen him off and on for many years, because he always seems to have had this extraordinary joy and vitality, and the fact that he had this, with this kind of business nagging at him—pain nagging at him—it was just a tremendous spiritual victory of some sort—a psychological victory.

Yeah. Oh, once I asked him—I think this is rather touching—if he could have one wish, what would it be? In other words, you know, looking back on his life, and he said, "I wish I had had more good times." And I thought that was such a touching thing to say because I always thought of him as this enormously glamorous figure whom I married when he was thirty-six. I thought he'd had millions of gay trips to Europe, girls, dances, everything. And, of course, and he had done a lot of that, but I suppose what he meant was that he had been in pain so much, and then hustling—well, then, those awful years campaigning, always with Frank Morrissey,[26] living on a milkshake and a hot dog. *[whispers about whether to discuss "stomach"]* He had also stomach trouble, which gave him a lot of pain sometimes, so it wasn't always his back. But all his family have it. It's just a Kennedy stomach. It obviously comes from nerves.

During campaigns and so on, did these things continue, and he just—

Oh, yeah. As I said, he was always campaigning on crutches. It was so pathetic to see him go up the steps of a plane, or the steps to a stage or something on his crutches, you know, because then he looked so vulnerable. And once he was up there and standing at the podium, then he looked so, you know, just in control of everything.

---

26. **FRANCIS X. MORRISSEY** (1911–2008) of Charlestown, Massachusetts, a dockworker's son who put himself through night law school, worked in JFK's campaigns for the House and Senate, and won appointment as a Boston municipal judge.

What did he make of sort of the Last Hurrah *world of Massachusetts?*[27] *Obviously he enjoyed it and got a great kick out of it.*

He enjoyed it the way he loves to hear Teddy tell stories about Honey Fitz.[28] He enjoyed stories about his grandfather. But he really wasn't— Kenny and Dave[29] and everyone, now that people are talking about writing books about Jack, they always say to me, "Why should Sorensen and Schlesinger write books? They won't be for the ones he belonged to. Why doesn't someone write a book for the three-deckers?"[30] *[Schlesinger laughs]* You know, and they think that Jack is theirs. But he wasn't, really. When I think now that he's dead and the different people who come to me—you'd think he belonged to so many people, and each one thought they had him completely, and he loved each one just the way love is infinite of a mother for her children. If you have eight children, it doesn't mean you love them any less than if you just have just two—that the love is diminished that much. So he loved the Irish, he loved his family, he loved people like you and Ken Galbraith.[31] He loved me and my sister in the world that had nothing to do with politics, that he looked to for pleasure and a letdown. He loved us all. And you know, I don't feel any jealousy. He had each of you. He really kept his life so in compartments, and the wonderful thing is

---

27. *The Last Hurrah* (1956) by the Boston novelist and newspaperman Edwin O'Connor re-created the old, dying Irish-American politics of his city and was made into a 1958 feature film starring Spencer Tracy.

28. JOHN FRANCIS FITZGERALD (1863–1950) was JFK's maternal grandfather and namesake, briefly a congressman from Massachusetts, then the first Irish-American mayor of Boston, known for his renditions of "Sweet Adeline." On the night in 1946 when JFK was elected to the House, "Honey Fitz" performed an Irish jig and forecast that his grandson would someday be President. Kennedy admired the upward mobility of his grandfather's political generation and enjoyed its folktales, but his own identity was so conspicuously different that some in his state called him "the first Irish Brahmin."

29. DAVID POWERS (1912–1998) was another Irish-American from Charlestown, jovial and unflappable, who started with JFK during that first House campaign and stayed with him for the rest of Kennedy's life, as friend, raconteur, traveling companion, and man-of-all-work.

30. The three-story Boston apartment houses known for housing newly arrived immigrants and factory workers and their descendants, especially Irish-American ones, such as Morrissey and Powers.

31. JOHN KENNETH GALBRAITH (1908–2006), born in Ontario, was a Harvard economist and liberal activist, best known in the late 1950s for his book *The Affluent Society*. He supported JFK in 1960 and became his ambassador to India.

PRESIDENT KENNEDY AND DAVE POWERS, 1961

that everyone in every one of those compartments was ready to die for him. And we all loved everyone else because they all liked me—because they knew I would. And I love Dave Powers, though I never saw him much before. It's just now that you see how Jack just knew in every side of his life what he wanted. He never wanted to have the people in the

THE KENNEDYS WITH BEN AND TONY BRADLEE
IN THE WEST SITTING HALL OF THE WHITE HOUSE

evening that he worked with in the daytime. And often I'd say, in the White House, "Why don't we have Ethel and Bobby for dinner?" because I thought Ethel's feelings might be getting hurt. But he never wanted to see Bobby, and Bobby didn't want to come either, because they'd worked all day. So you'd have people who were rather relaxing. You'd have Charlie Bartlett[32] and the Bradlees[33] a lot. It was sort of light—or I don't know—those parties that we used to have.

---

32. CHARLES BARTLETT (1921–) was a Washington columnist for the *Chattanooga Times*, later nationally syndicated, who, with his wife Martha, introduced JFK to Jacqueline in 1951 and remained a close friend of the President's. A fellow Catholic, Bartlett had served in naval intelligence in the Pacific during World War II. Mrs. Bartlett was godmother to John Kennedy, Jr.

33. BENJAMIN BRADLEE (1921–) was Washington bureau chief for *Newsweek*. He and his then wife Tony were Kennedy neighbors in Georgetown, became fast friends, and spent considerable leisure time with the Kennedys in the White House and other venues.

Best parties I've ever attended. Weren't they great? The greatest girls, the nicest times. Everyone was so much better than normal. Everyone was the gayest and prettiest and nicest.

And it was a mixture of cabinet and friends from New York, and young people. And I worked so hard on those parties because I felt once we were in the White House, I felt that I could get out, and I just can't tell you how oppressive the strain of the White House can be. I could go out and whenever Jack saw it was getting me down a little bit he'd really send me away—not exactly, but he'd say, "Why don't you go up to New York, or go see your sister in Italy?" And then he sent me to Greece, which was, you know, for a sad reason this year, but he thought I was getting depressed after losing Patrick.[34] I thought, I can go out, I can go to a restaurant in New York or walk down the street and look at an antique shop or go to a nightclub. You've heard of the Twist, or something—not that you care about nightclubs—and I don't want to go more than once a year—but Jack couldn't get out. So then I used to try to make these parties to bring gay, and new people, and music, and make it happy nights. And did he love them.

He loved them. Danced very rarely, but loved to—

Just walked around, puffing his cigar.

Talked to the girls—make Oleg dance the Twist. Or Steve or somebody.[35]

Yeah, then he'd move on very quickly. You know, to sort of see everyone.

---

34. Two months after losing her prematurely born second son in August 1963, Jacqueline and her sister Lee Radziwill sailed with Franklin Roosevelt, Jr., and his wife on the Aegean as guests of the Greek shipping magnate Aristotle Onassis.

35. OLEG CASSINI (1913–2006) was a New York couturier whom Jacqueline asked to design most of her White House wardrobe and who also participated in the Kennedys' social life. She wrote him that she wished to dress "as if Jack were President of FRANCE." She added, "Plan to stay for dinner every time you come to D.C. with sketches." "Steve" refers to Stephen Smith.

WEDDING OF JOHN FITZGERALD KENNEDY AND JACQUELINE LEE BOUVIER,
SEPTEMBER 12, 1953

He did have an extraordinary range of acquaintance and ability to enter in—to, sympathetically—to people of the whole range of the spectrum.

Yeah, that's so true, because the luckiest thing I used to think about him, you know, when we were early married and then later, was whatever you were interested in, Jack got interested in. When I started to be interested in French furniture, he got so interested in it, and then he'd be so proud, he'd go to Joe Alsop's[36] and recognize Louis XVI and Louis XV. And I started to collect drawings, and then he wanted to know about them. And he got interested in animals, or horses. Or then, when I was reading all this eighteenth century, he'd snatch a book from me and read and know all of Louis XV's mistresses before I would. So many of the senators, when we'd go out to dinner—senators and embassies this first year—all those men would ever talk to me about was themselves. And Jack was so interested—maybe it's Gemini, or what?[37] And once I asked him, the month before we were married in Newport, what he thought his best and his worst qualities were. And he thought his best quality was curiosity, which, I think he was right. He thought his worst was irritability, but, I mean, he was never irritable with me. I think by that he meant impatience. You know, he didn't like to be bored, and if someone was boring, he'd pick up the newspaper, but he certainly wasn't irritable to live with.

He was not irritable in the current White House sense.[38] No, I've just not seen anyone—from South Boston through Harvard to Palm Beach—he was at home in a greater variety of things and, as you say, made people from each of these kind of segments feel that he was with them. It was an extraordinary—

Yeah, then they'd all get interested in politics and things. You know,

---

36. **JOSEPH ALSOP** (1910–1989) was a Washington political columnist, Anglophile, Roosevelt cousin, and esteemed Georgetown host. He backed JFK in 1960 as "a Stevenson with balls." Alsop and his new wife Susan Mary, a descendant of John Jay, entertained a diverse mixture of guests during the Kennedy years, and theirs was one of the few private homes at which the President and First Lady dined while in the White House, which began with Kennedy's impromptu visit to Alsop late on his inaugural night.

37. Meaning JFK's sign of the zodiac.

38. Referring to reports of President Johnson's volcanic temper.

there's never been such a universal president before. It doesn't mean absolutely anything, but in the *Washington Post* the other day, I read the theater page—and Alain Delon, who's this little French "jeune premier" young movie star now, came to Washington. And so the drama critic went to interview him, and all he could talk about was Jack. And say, you know, how "all we young people"—well, I mean, there's a little sexy young French movie actor and he's so wounded by Jack. It's because Jack was young, and loved—you know—everything—elegance, girls, you know, in all the best senses of the word. It was like he had many things in common with that young man, the same way he'd have, you know, things in common with so many sides of you. Everyone found a part of him in Jack. Before that, politics was just left to all the corny old people who shouted on the Fourth of July—and you know, all the things that made me so bored with politics.

He gave youth and intellect and taste a world voice, which was felt all around the world, and he had this extraordinary combination of idealism and realism, which—

That's again—the Kennedys taught me all this—Jack, really—all this questioning, questioning. You know, if you didn't get on the offensive, they'd have you on the defensive all night. And so these questions he'd ask me or my sister—so once I asked him how he'd define himself, and he said, "An idealist without illusions."

Um-hmm. That's perfect.

Then once somebody asked me about him, and I said that—I saw that attributed to myself. But Jack said it.

In the senatorial years, whom would you see most of? In the Senate, I mean.

Well, in the senatorial years, when you think Jack was away every weekend, and so you'd have three or four days a week, two of which he'd be tired—but the ones we'd see—I remember little dinners—who would you have? The

Symingtons, Smatherses, Coopers—they were always—funnily enough, John Sherman Cooper and Lorraine.[39]

He's the nicest man in the Senate.

Yeah, I guess.

Not Hubert particularly?[40]

No, I never saw—the only ones I can remember having to dinner at our house the first year we lived on Dent Place—3327 Dent Place—we rented from the Childses[41]—I can remember having the Symingtons, Smatherses, and Coopers for dinner and—those are the only senators I can think of—oh, and Mansfield[42] sometimes. The year before, 1960, then you'd have others—I remember we had McCarthy—Eugene McCarthy[43] and a couple of others, I can't remember.

---

39. STUART SYMINGTON (1901–1988) was an Eastern-born patrician businessman, the first secretary of the air force, under Truman, and senator from Missouri from 1953 to 1976. Symington and his wife Evelyn lived four doors down from the Kennedys on N Street. John Sherman Cooper (1901–1991) was a Republican senator from Kentucky and had been Symington's classmate at Yale. Before both couples were married, Jacqueline and Jack had more than once gone out with the courtly Cooper and his wife Lorraine. John and Lorraine Cooper were also guests at the first dinner the Kennedys had at home after their honeymoon. George Smathers (1913–2007) was a conservative Democratic senator from Florida from 1951 to 1969.

40. HUBERT HUMPHREY (1911–1978), liberal senator from Minnesota, ran against JFK in the Wisconsin and West Virginia primaries of 1960 but pulled out after losing both. During the latter effort, he publicly carped about his campaign's relative poverty in contrast to what he thought to be the free-spending ways of Kennedy's side. After his withdrawal, Humphrey and JFK resumed their old friendliness.

41. Mr. and Mrs. Blair Childs. The address was actually 3321 Dent Place.

42. MIKE MANSFIELD (1903–2001) became Democratic senator from Montana in 1953, and served as majority leader from 1961 until 1977. The quiet, upright Mansfield had played softball with JFK and other senators in the early 1950s. One reason why Kennedy was glad to have Lyndon Johnson as vice president was that his Senate leader would not be the brash Texan but the loyal Mansfield. When Mansfield retired from the Senate, he said that of the presidents he had known, Kennedy was "the best of the lot." Honoring Mansfield's expertise on Asia, two presidents later made him ambassador to Japan.

43. EUGENE MCCARTHY (1916–2005) was senator from Minnesota from 1959 to 1971. He resented JFK, whom he considered his intellectual inferior, and, at the 1960 convention, gave an impassioned nominating speech for Stevenson. Kennedy suspected that McCarthy's real purpose was to stop his bandwagon so that Lyndon Johnson could win the prize.

Johnson, ever?[44]

Never.

You mentioned the Chicago convention—a couple of unsatisfactory conversations with Stevenson. Of course, the Stevenson-Kennedy relationship has always been a puzzle and slightly a sadness to me, because I think if the President ever saw Stevenson in a genuinely relaxed mood, he would have quite liked him, because he can be awfully engaging. But somehow, Stevenson would always freeze and become sort of prissy and so on with the President.

Well, this is all retrospect, but I always thought that every time Stevenson—Stevenson just let Jack down so many times. So, you know, Jack really worked hard for him and everything, and he wasn't nice to him at that convention. I remember he had a meeting with Stevenson before Stevenson threw it open—maybe the point of that meeting was—I don't know, I'm just thinking—was he hoping that Stevenson would ask him to be vice president, or what? Then I think—I don't know whether Stevenson—but I think this about so many people—Jack made them jealous.

I think eventually he made Stevenson deeply jealous because Stevenson saw the President taking away not only the nomination, but also many of his own supporters and doing really better than he had ever been able to, the kinds of things he most wanted to do. But in '56, I don't know—I think it's partly a generational thing, Stevenson was fifteen years older.[45]

Well, I see that with more people who were bitter about Jack while he was President. And then you hear about it. For instance, one is Scotty Reston.[46]

---

44. **LYNDON BAINES JOHNSON** (1908–1973) served as congressman, senator from Texas, and Senate majority leader before Kennedy placed him on his ticket in Los Angeles in 1960. On November 22, 1963, after President Kennedy's assassination, Johnson became the thirty-sixth president of the United States.

45. Actually seventeen.

46. **JAMES "SCOTTY" RESTON** (1909–1995) was a *New York Times* Washington columnist who did much to shape East Coast political opinion.

And someone very close to him told me it was a jealousy of generations. He couldn't bear to see someone younger, or maybe his age, come on. So Jack incited that—and Dean Acheson[47] the same way. And then there was also a jealousy of contemporaries, because someone who was just Jack's age, and sitting behind some little bank clerk's desk and hanging around the bar at Bailey's Beach[48] would just feel that he was a nothing when he saw all that Jack was doing. So he incited so many bitter jealousies, and they were the ones who'd say mean things about him. And I thought Stevenson was really horrible to Jack at the convention in 1960. When Jack asked him—was it in the Oregon primary?—to come out for him, or to pull out of it?[49] But he had been asking him things all spring, and Stevenson was just—Oh, I know what Stevenson said to him, that he couldn't do it because he couldn't be disloyal to Lyndon Johnson or something.

That's right. I was an intermediary. There were a number of intermediaries, I'm sure. But I talked to Stevenson a couple of times that winter and spring on the President's behalf—and Stevenson's answer was that he had told Lyndon Johnson in 1959 that he would remain neutral and would not come out for any candidate, and that he had to keep his word to Lyndon Johnson.

But then, I remember one night Jack coming home and rather—not rudely but with that sort of laugh he had, telling me that's what Stevenson had told him, and he thought that Stevenson was hoping to be named as running mate with Johnson. And then he told me something so insulting that Johnson had said to him the day before about Stevenson. You know, he was thinking, "How silly can this man be?" But Jack knew then, I think—I mean, he knew that he was going to get the nomination.

---

47. **DEAN ACHESON** (1893–1971) was Harry Truman's secretary of state, a towering figure in that era and a skeptic about JFK, sharing Truman's view that he was too callow and inexperienced to be president.

48. An exclusive Newport club, frequented by Jacqueline's mother and stepfather, which now represented to her a cloistered social world she had outgrown.

49. Hoping to be drafted for president at the 1960 convention, Stevenson had refused to say he would decline the nomination, if offered.

I think Stevenson, although he would not admit it to himself or to anybody else, was holding out for a deadlock in which he would be the presidential candidate. I doubt that he would have wanted to go on as a vice presidential candidate. But he wouldn't admit this, and so we people who had been for him in '52 and '56, as I had, would ask him whether he was a candidate. He would say he was not a candidate, and that released me, I felt, from any obligation. But in all this period, you know, if you've won twice, you keep hoping.

Yeah, oh, it's hard for him. But, you know, he just never had the breadth or depth that Jack did. You know, I just see it all now.

Someone once said that Stevenson was a Greek and Kennedy a Roman.

No. I think Kennedy was a Greek and Stevenson was a, well—

Kennedy was an Athenian and Stevenson from Thebes.[50] [laughs]

[laughs] Yes, I don't know, he was a little— He was all right, Stevenson. I mean, he was the first time anyone spoke anything in politics that you could listen—the first time anyone brought anything intellectual to politics.

He helped prepare the way. He helped open up the situation, and the President came along as a kind of climax.

But he couldn't make—I mean, there's no point to talk about Stevenson. Where he couldn't make decisions, or he'd go over his little papers, or he'd carefully take something typewritten and copy it in longhand because he was

---

50. In the spring of 1964, Jackie was reading and much influenced by Edith Hamilton's popular *The Greek Way*. The following spring, after examining the early version of Schlesinger's *A Thousand Days*, she wrote him in longhand, "You remember in my oral history—I disputed your remark that Adlai was a Greek + JFK a Roman. . . . Leaving Adlai out of it . . . I know what he brought to American politics in 1952—but he certainly showed many weaknesses + sad deficiencies of character later—you can make him sound as wonderful as you want—but just don't say that JFK was Roman. . . . Lyndon is really a Roman—a classic Emperor—maybe [Michigan Republican Governor George] Romney is one too. . . . Can't you make him Greek + Adlai Egyptian—or leave Adlai out + just make him Greek." After finishing her letter to Schlesinger, Mrs. Kennedy tore it in half and wrote him a milder one on the same theme.

so proud of everyone saying he wrote all his speeches—I don't know, poor man. It's sort of sad. You know, Jack achieved all he dreamed of in his life, and it must be sad not to have.[51]

It is sad. After the convention in '56, the President was quite relieved, was he— in not having got—immediately so—I know later, he would say often how pleased he was.

It's funny. There was just—I remember watching it with Michael Forrestal.[52] I'd gone to get a Coca-Cola or something, down underneath all those seats, and as I was coming back, suddenly that race started, and all the blackboards, the numbers started changing. I bumped into Michael Forrestal, and he grabbed me into a Westinghouse exhibit, and we watched the whole thing on television. And then we went to Jack's room at the Stockade Inn, or whatever it was?

Yes, Stockyards Inn.[53]

But he was just let down, like in any fight, and when he went on to say that— and do it so beautifully—just a little let down. Then we flew back—I can't remember if it was that afternoon or the next day—and then he wasn't anymore—he was just exhausted.

Do you remember who were the closest to him at that point at the convention? Torb and Bobby, and Ted Sorensen, I imagine.

---

51. During those years, Stevenson was able to build a decent rapport with the First Lady, which he never managed with the President, whom he resented for denying him what he considered his political birthright, starting with the presidency and the State Department. But by now, Jacqueline has adopted her husband's disdain for Stevenson.

52. MICHAEL FORRESTAL (1928–1989) was a family friend; son of the first secretary of defense, James Forrestal, for whom JFK had briefly worked in 1945; a New York lawyer; and later a staff member of Kennedy's National Security Council, specializing in Southeast Asia.

53. This traditional Chicago convention hotel was actually called the Stockyard Inn, and stood across the street from the International Amphitheatre, where the delegates were meeting.

Yeah, was he taking a bath over there and watching it on television? I guess, those three. They'd know what other people were. It was in that little room, you know, right out in back, and there was someone else there too—I have to think who—I can't remember.

And then, after '56, by the time he ran for the Senate in '58, he was quite clearly going to try for the presidency in 1960.

Well, he never once said to me in all his life, before we started the primary year, "I'm going to try for the presidency," or not. You know, it just went on. But of course he was, because then he came back— After the convention, he flew to Europe to stay with his father and just rest a few days in the South of France. And I lost the baby and he came back to Newport[54] a couple of weeks. Then we came down and lived at Hickory Hill that fall, while we were finding another house, but he was always on the move. And all that winter, he was on the move. And so, obviously, all that speaking, speaking, speaking, yes, he was aiming—yeah, I guess he did decide then.

I remember suddenly realizing it when he was so determined to win the Massachusetts senatorial race in '58 by the largest possible margin.[55] It was perfectly clear he was going to win, and therefore it wasn't very necessary for him to campaign, but he worked so hard in that campaign.

Yeah, I remember when we came back on the boat from Europe, someone met us with a poll of how Foster Furcolo[56] was doing. Would that be it? Jack's

---

54. Jacqueline's mother and stepfather spent summers at Hammersmith Farm in Newport. The Kennedys sometimes used the place, which was near a naval station and quieter than the Kennedy houses at Hyannis Port, as a summer White House.

55. JFK ran for reelection as senator in 1958. He was eager to win by a margin so impressive that it would give him a running start for the 1960 presidential race.

56. FOSTER FURCOLO (1911–1995) was the Democratic governor of Massachusetts from 1957 to 1961. Kennedy thought so little of him that if Furcolo should win the Democratic nomination against Republican senator Leverett Saltonstall in 1960 (as it happened, he lost), JFK planned to cast a quiet vote for the Republican. Some of the reasons Kennedy's poll ratings were down were his support for the St. Lawrence Seaway, which diverted jobs and commerce from Massachusetts; his work on labor reform, which outraged Teamsters and their allies; residual antagonisms from the

JOHN F. KENNEDY CAMPAIGNING FOR REELECTION TO THE SENATE
WITH JACQUELINE KENNEDY AND EDWARD M. KENNEDY

polls weren't so good. *[talk about tape recorder]* So then there was this major, frantic effort. Somehow that seems to me the hardest campaign of ever—that Senate campaign.

You mean, just the extent of more—

I mean just I never can remember sleeping at home for however many months it was. Two months, I guess. But you know, just running, running.

"Onions" Burke fight; and political quarrels with the Italian-American Furcolo, which, Republicans vainly hoped, might cause an Italian-American stampede toward Kennedy's little-known opponent, Vincent Celeste.

All those teas.

Mostly just endless cars. It was awful. Oh yeah, with Professor Burns,[57] and Jack telling him who to shake hands with on platforms, but all through the Berkshires, through Springfield, different hotels, you know.

Do you like campaigning?

I do—until you get exhausted. You know, about the fifth day out, it's just sheer exhaustion, and then, you know—I love it when it's going wonderfully—I love it when it's going wonderfully for Jack.

There's nothing more exciting than entering a crowded hall and watching the candidate come in, everyone going mad.

Yeah, well, all that part I loved, and towards the end, it was getting better and better.

---

57. JAMES MACGREGOR BURNS (1918–) was a Williams College political scientist, biographer of Franklin Roosevelt, and Democratic liberal activist who in 1958 ran unsuccessfully for the U.S. House from western Massachusetts.

The
SECOND
Conversation

*W*e ended up, I think, last time talking about the Senate, in which the President was reelected by this great majority and which, for the first time, made him sort of nationally spoken of as a possible contender for 1960. Did that—was it already—was that becoming, a kind of, do you think, a preoccupation in his own life, and yours and so on? Was everything sort of directed more and more to that?

Do you mean to being president?

Yeah.

Well, it was never spoken of out loud, but after election night in Boston[1]—I think we went somewhere in the sun or sometime, but then he started speaking all the time. Again, all those years before the White House—every weekend he was always traveling. You know, invitations from all over the country—and then they led up to the primaries, which were what, just 1960?

Nineteen-sixty.

It seems the thing went on forever.

---

1. JFK's Senate reelection victory of 1958, winning 73 percent of the vote.

During these times when he was out, like the 1958 campaign and so on, how did— he kept up reading and so on. How and when did he do that?

Well, he read in the strangest way. I mean, I could never read unless I'd have a rainy afternoon or a long evening in bed, or something. He'd read walk-

READING IN HYANNIS PORT, 1959

ing, he'd read at the table, at meals, he'd read after dinner, he'd read in the bathtub, he'd read—prop open a book on his desk—on his bureau—while he was doing his tie. You know, he'd just read in little, he'd open some book I'd be reading, you know, just devour it. He really read all the times you don't think you have time to read.

He'd read in short takes, and then remember it and come back and pick up a thread?

Anything he wanted to remember, he could always remember. You'd see things he'd use in his speeches. You'd be sitting next to him on some platform, and suddenly out would come a sentence that two weeks ago in Georgetown he would have read out loud to you one night, just because it interested him.

He had the most fantastic and maddening memory for quotes, because—while he remembered the quotes, but he couldn't always remember where they were from.

I remember the winter he was sick. His father had a whole shelf of books— *The World's Great Orations* or something that his father had given him and he'd read every single one of those books, and then I made—I asked his father to give them to him for Christmas, which, of course, he was delighted to do. But he'd been through every one of those. And he used to read me Edmund Burke's "To the"—what is it?

The address to—

"To the People of—"

Bristol.²

That's it, and well, all things through there, you know, he just—of course, that was a different winter. He'd just have days and days in bed to go through all that.

---

2. In his 1774 "Speech to the Electors of Bristol," the Anglo-Irish statesman-philosopher said, "Your representative owes you, not his industry only, but his judgement; and he betrays, instead of serving you, if he sacrifices it to your opinion."

You gather he'd done this as a child—been a great reader?

Yes, I know he'd read *Marlborough*[3] when he was about ten or eleven, because in his room at the Cape, which he's had since he was a boy, those books were in a little bookshelf by his bed—all old, sort of mauve backs. And he was always sick and in bed. He had scarlet fever. Then one year, he had some—either asthma or blood trouble—anemia or something, when he went out to Arizona.

That was when he left Princeton.[4]

Yeah. Then there was another summer—you know, he'd always been reading—all these things—and he used to give me books when we were going out before we were married. I remember the first one he gave me was Sam Houston by Marquis James—*The Raven*. Then he'd give me John Buchan—*Pilgrim's Way*—lots of John Buchan.[5] But he was just always reading, practically while driving a car.

Would he ever read novels besides thrillers?

Listen, the only thrillers he ever read were about three Ian Fleming books. No, I never saw him read a novel.

---

3. Winston Churchill's long biography of his best-known ancestor, John Churchill, the first Duke of Marlborough (1650-1722). In 1704, in the War of the Spanish Succession, Marlborough and his regiments defeated the French at Blenheim on the Danube, thwarting Louis XIV's campaign against Austria. Churchill's volumes are history as heroism, romance, and drama. JFK's lifelong interest in the book and its protagonist suggests one source of affinity with his wife, who used Churchillian language in a 1978 letter describing the "treasured friends, noble figures, shared moments, great endeavors" of her husband's presidency.

4. JFK had to leave Princeton at Christmas 1935, during his freshman year, to be hospitalized for chronic abdominal problems and a worrisome white blood cell count. On his release, he recuperated in Palm Beach, worked the summer of 1936 at an Arizona cattle ranch, and restarted his college career at Harvard that fall.

5. JOHN BUCHAN (1875–1940) was the first Baron Tweedsmuir, a prolific author of both fiction and nonfiction, and governor general of Canada from 1935 until his death. Kennedy loved Buchan's autobiography *Pilgrim's Way*, which he read on publication in 1940, and often cited Buchan's insistence that politics was "still the greatest and most honourable adventure."

Did he really like Ian Fleming much, or was that sort of a press—

Oh, well, it was sort of a press thing, because when they asked him his ten favorite books, he sort of made up a list, and he put in one sort of novel. You know, he liked Ian Fleming[6]—I mean, if you were in a plane or you're in a hotel room and there's three books on your bedside table—I mean, he'd sometimes grab something that way. There was one book he gave me to read—something about "time"—it was a novel where someone goes back in the eighteenth century and uncovers a mystery.[7] It was just a paperback book he'd found in some plane or something—the last two books he told me to read this fall—he was reading *The Fall of the Dynasties*[8] and—

Edmond Taylor.

And *Patriotic Gore*[9] he kept telling me to read—neither of which I've gotten around to.

Patriotic Gore, *particularly, is a marvelous book.*

I still haven't read it. But you know, he was reading all that in the White House, and I was growing illiterate there.

It is a matter of constant mystery, because he was surrounded by all these academics who supposedly read books all the time. None of us ever had time to read books,

---

6. IAN FLEMING (1908–1964) was the author of the thrillers starring James Bond, the British secret agent. The Kennedys met Fleming at a Georgetown dinner in 1960. The President enjoyed *From Russia with Love* in the White House theater shortly before his death.

7. *The Daughter of Time* by Josephine Tey (1951) has a Scotland Yard official investigating whether Richard III had killed the princes in the Tower of London.

8. Having been absorbed by Barbara Tuchman's book about the coming of World War I, *The Guns of August*, JFK sought out a broader treatment, Edmond Taylor's *The Fall of the Dynasties: The Collapse of the Old Order, 1905–1922*. It is not hard to imagine why Kennedy, having averted a nuclear war during the Cuban Missile Crisis the previous October, wanted to read it.

9. *Patriotic Gore*, the book on the Civil War by the critic Edmund Wilson, whom the Kennedys once invited to a White House dinner.

and he would say in a slightly accusatory way—ask us about books that had recently come out that none of us had read.

Every Sunday, he'd rip three pages out of the *Times* book section, with an "x" around what I was to get. You know, it'd be rather interesting to look over my bills from the Savile Book Shop, because all these things I'd order that Jack would say to get. And you know, on the weekends all the time, he'd be reading—

It would be fascinating. Are the bills somewhere?

I have all the bills. I suppose they're—and Savile Book Shop has a list. What else would he— For instance, at Camp David sometimes, if it was a rainy day or something, he'd stay in bed in the afternoon. Well, he'd go through two books.

He read very fast.

Yeah.

He did at one time take a fast-reading course. Did that make any difference?[10]

Well, that was so funny, because it was about like this tape recorder. Bobby came down with—Bobby had been over to Baltimore and gotten all this equipment with a little card you put in and the line runs down it. Well, we did it about once. You know, you're meant to speed up and answer questions about three crows—how many crows in the cabbage patch, or something. I think we did it twice one Christmas vacation in Florida, and then stopped. So he never really did that.

It was mostly history and biography.

Yeah.

---

10. While a senator, JFK had accompanied his brother several times to a speed-reading course in Baltimore but dropped out. After he became President, press accounts exaggerated the importance of this minor episode.

44

Why not novels, do you suppose?

I think he was always looking for something in books—he was looking for something about history, or something for a quote, or what. Oh, at Glen Ora, he was reading Mao Tse-tung, and he was quoting that to me.[11]

On guerrilla warfare?

Yeah. Then we started to make up all these little parables like "When an Army drinks, not it is thirsty," or something. He got terribly funny about it. But, you know, I think he was looking for something in his reading. He wasn't just reading for diversion. He didn't want to waste a single second.

Poetry the same—therefore wasn't—wouldn't read much. Would he read things you liked a lot?

Yes, he'd—this summer I was reading the Maréchal de Saxe.[12] I remember General Taylor[13] came out on the *Honey Fitz*[14] and I was asking him all about Saxe's battles. He was in Blenheim and everything, and I told Jack

---

11. The writings of the Chinese Communist leader (1893–1976) would have been of particular interest to JFK in the spring of 1961, when, with considerable foresight, he was considering how much effort, if any, he should make to seek a rapprochement with China (he pragmatically decided that was a project for a second term)—and when he was preparing for a summit with the man who had, until the recent schism between Moscow and Beijing, been Mao's chief world ally—the Soviet leader Nikita Khrushchev. And indeed during his private conversations with Khrushchev in June 1961, Kennedy quoted Mao's aphorism that power comes out the end of a rifle.

12. MAURICE DE SAXE (1696–1750), born a German, was a French marshal general and hero of the Battle of Fontenoy in 1745. He wrote a classic treatise, *Reveries on the Art of War*, that was posthumously published in 1757.

13. MAXWELL TAYLOR (1901–1987) was World War II commander of the 101st Airborne division and the first general of the Allied forces to ascend the French beaches on D-day. In 1959, he retired as President Eisenhower's army chief of staff, inveighing against what he thought to be Ike's overreliance on nuclear weapons—a complaint that he published in a book called *The Uncertain Trumpet*. Kennedy agreed with Taylor and cited his arguments during the 1960 campaign. Asked by JFK to investigate the Bay of Pigs failure, Taylor impressed him with his willingness to buck conventional wisdom. The President made Taylor his chief military adviser and then chairman of the Joint Chiefs.

14. One of the presidential yachts, which JFK had renamed for his grandfather.

what General Taylor said about him. I was halfway through that book, and Jack took it away from me, and read the whole thing. You know, if I'd ever say anything interesting in a book I was reading, he'd take it away and read it.

How about the theater?

Reading plays or going to them?

Going to them.

Well, we never had much time. When we were in New York, we'd go to a play once in a while, but he always liked light plays. You know, he wanted to sort of relax. He would rather go to a musical comedy or something than something heavy. But we used to play—when you say poetry—he didn't really read poetry—well, he loved to read sometimes Byron, you know, whatever was around he'd pick and read—bits of Shakespeare. But we had a John Gielgud record that we used to play over and over—"The Ages of Man"[15] or something. And then we had one this fall—what was it? Maybe it was Richard Burton—I don't know. He liked to play them sometimes at night. You know, when you'd be in bed you'd play records sometimes.

Mostly it was rather British history than American history. I have the impression—British and European history, is that right?

Yes, there was a lot of Civil War—was what interested him in American history. But there wasn't so much American history, really. Then I took a course on it one year by a fascinating man, who—I got to do some research for him later, Dr. Jules Davids.[16] But when I'd come home all excited—what I'd learned about the trustbusters or something, it really didn't seem to interest

---

15. Gielgud's recitings from Shakespeare (1958).

16. JULES DAVIDS (1920–1996), a gentle Georgetown University diplomatic historian who at the time was little known or published, performed research on five chapters of *Profiles in Courage*. His wife later noted that his honorarium of $700 was "a lot of money for us in those days."

him too much. He really was—it was British, really. He was sort of a Whig, wasn't he?[17]

He was. And was this the result of the time that he spent there when his father was ambassador? Did that sort of give him a—was it before that? It's an odd thing.

No, because he really spent very little time there, when you think he was finishing at Harvard, and he spent—what, maybe a summer, and his term or so at the London School of Economics. No, it was all his childhood—what he picked to read. You know, I keep saying *Marlborough*, but there were others which—well, I have all his books, that he always had, so when I get them out of crates, I just know—His mother can tell you some things about him—reading when he was six, asking some question—or seven, I guess. You know, some grown-up book that he'd found. It was just—I think his childhood reading.

Reading Marlborough *at the age of ten for example. So Churchill was always—at the end, a figure of meaning—*

I think *Marlborough* was more than Churchill. I think he found his heroes more in the past. I really don't think he admired—well, of course, he admired Churchill and he wanted to meet him. We did meet him one summer in the South of France but the poor man was rather, you know, a little bit gone by then. But he never had a hero worship of any contemporary—it was more in the past. What did he say once about the presidency? "These things have always been done by men, and they can be done now," when his father said, "Why do you want to run for president?" I'm not saying that he thought he was as great as Churchill, but he could see that he was up to coping with things and the failures of so many men who were alive now—and their short-comings. So, he was really looking for lessons in the past from history, but

---

17. The Whig party of the seventeenth through nineteenth centuries epitomized the British style of wealthy aristocrats standing for political office. The Whigs resisted a strong monarchy, just as their nineteenth-century American namesake party opposed powerful presidents such as their hated Andrew Jackson. Asked by James MacGregor Burns in 1959 about presidential power, JFK insisted, "I am no Whig!"

he did—no, you're right—he did admire Churchill's prose, and he read all those memoirs that came out.

I think that's right. I think he really sought—it was Churchill as a writer, more than—I mean, he admired Churchill as a statesman, but it was Churchill as a writer which really excited him and piqued his curiosity.

And I can remember him reading me out loud two things from that—the part where he describes the court of Charles II, which is wonderful sort of seraglio prose and everything—and then how he describes the civil war.[18] You know, he'd be reading, and he'd read aloud a lot.

Anyone in the American past whom he was particularly interested in? Hamilton, Jefferson, Jackson?

Well, Jefferson, I guess, and the one letter he wanted to buy so badly, but it was too expensive, and I was going to try and find and give it to him last Christmas was a letter that came up of Jefferson's, where he'd asked for four more gardeners for Monticello, but he wanted to be sure they knew how to play the violin, so that he could have chamber music concerts in the evening. That letter had come up at Parke-Bernet, and it would have been $6,000 or something, so he hadn't bid on it. You know, Webster.[19] He read all their things. I suppose Jefferson, really.[20]

What about—did he ever—Theodore Roosevelt, Wilson, FDR—?

---

18. In Churchill's four-volume *A History of the English-Speaking Peoples*. She means the English civil war of 1692–1696.

19. **DANIEL WEBSTER** (1782–1852), senator from Massachusetts, had his own chapter in *Profiles in Courage* for supporting the Compromise of 1850.

20. In 1970, Jacqueline wrote about her husband to Ted Kennedy, "He was the only president after Jefferson, to care about gardens—(A letter that came up at Parke-Bernet the fall of 1963, which he thought was too expensive to buy, I was going to try and give him for his birthday—Jefferson writes to France—for 4 gardeners—they would also play chamber music at Monticello in the evenings.) Like Jefferson, he cared about architecture—or rather the harmony of man in his environment."

Oh, then he was reading a book about Theodore Roosevelt this summer or winter.

Noel Busch—Alice Longworth[21] gave it to him.

Yeah, and he was saying to me, "Listen to how fatuous Teddy Roosevelt was," and he'd, "Look how—" and then he'd describe several—read me several things where Roosevelt describes what he does. Always in a sort of throwaway way—"And then I marched up San Juan Hill and killed five natives" —and rather apologetic about it. I think he saw through a lot of Theodore Roosevelt. Though he admired him too. But he read everything that came out by everyone.

What did he think of FDR? Did he ever know him at all?

Well, they all met him, because I remember Mrs. Kennedy telling me that I should think of all the children in the cabinet, because how nice President Roosevelt and Mrs. Roosevelt had been—all the Kennedy children met the Roosevelts.[22] But I don't think he thought he was any—he often thought he was rather a—charlatan is an unfair word—you know what I mean—a bit of a poseur, rather cleverly.[23] You know, that he did an awful lot for effect, and then

---

21. ALICE ROOSEVELT LONGWORTH (1884–1980), herself a landmark of Washington social life for most of the twentieth century, was Theodore Roosevelt's daughter by his first wife. Busch's book was *T.R.: The Story of Theodore Roosevelt and His Influence on Our Times* (1963).

22. This was in the 1930s, while Joseph Kennedy served FDR as chairman of the Securities Exchange Commission and ambassador to the Court of St. James's.

23. JFK's private coolness toward Franklin Roosevelt was almost unique among Democratic leaders of the 1960s, who usually regarded him as a household saint. It reflected Joseph Kennedy's painful break with FDR in 1941 over intervention in Europe, JFK's lingering resentment over Eleanor Roosevelt's hostility toward him before the 1960 Democratic convention, and his own lifelong aversion to almost all hero worship. Like many others, JFK was critical of what he considered to be FDR's over-tolerance of Soviet military power in Europe at the end of World War II, leaving the West at a military disadvantage in Berlin and the rest of Europe, which proved to be one of Kennedy's biggest troubles as President. Still JFK was not unwilling to recognize Roosevelt's qualities of greatness, especially in domestic affairs. In the Republican household of her early upbringing, Jacqueline's father used to jocu-larly quote from Peter Arno's famous *New Yorker* cartoon, "Let's go down to the Trans-Lux and hiss Roosevelt!"

he used to get furious—not furious, but irritated when people would tell him he should have fireside chats and things, and he found out how many Roosevelt had, which was something like—you know, very—

Thirteen or fourteen the whole time. I got the figures up for him.[24]

Yeah. Of course, he was interested in Roosevelt. He didn't have any—he wasn't patterning himself on him, or anything.

He didn't pattern himself on—

On anyone. I remember him telling me the time where Wilson had been wrong, or what their mistakes were, or how—but you know, all with hindsight. He was never arrogant. He just seemed to devour all of them and then, I suppose, it sifted around and came out—he used them all. That's what he did.

Now it always seemed to me quite extraordinary. Here are three men who lived about the same time—Winston Churchill, Franklin Roosevelt, and Joseph P. Kennedy, of whom the first two were in one sense or another great men and the third was a very successful man, a very talented man, but not a great man. And yet the children of Churchill and the children of Roosevelt have all been—in many cases, bright and talented, but somehow it all missed fire. And the Kennedy children have this extraordinary discipline.

I really think you have to give a lot of that credit to Mr. Kennedy, because Jack used to talk about that a lot. You know, he bent over backwards. When his children were doing something, he wrote them letters endlessly. Whenever they were doing anything important at school, he'd be there for it. The way he'd talk at the table. If you just go on being a great man, and your children are sort of shunted aside, you know—he watched—I always thought he was

---

24. Criticized for speaking too rarely to the American people on television, Kennedy was urged to follow the example of FDR's radio "fireside chats." He asked Schlesinger to find out exactly how many such chats Roosevelt had during twelve years as president to counter the popular impression that they were almost weekly. By contrast, President Kennedy had a press conference roughly every two weeks.

AMBASSADOR KENNEDY WITH JOE, BOBBY, AND JACK, 1938

the tiger mother. And Mrs. Kennedy,[25] poor little thing, was running around, trying to keep up with this demon of energy, seeing if she had enough place-mats in Palm Beach, or should she send the ones from Bronxville, or had she put the London ones in storage. You know, that's what—her little mind went to pieces, and it's Mr. Kennedy who—and she loves to say now how she sat around the table and talked to them about Plymouth Rock and molded their minds, but she was really saying, "Children, don't disturb your father!" He did all—he made this conscious effort about the family, and I don't think those other two men did. Oh, one other thing Jack told me about Roosevelt was how his foreign policy had been wrong and how he hadn't been good there—the mistakes he'd made there. I remember asking him once—

---

25. ROSE ELIZABETH FITZGERALD KENNEDY (1890–1995) was the President's mother, whom Jacque-line called "Belle Mère." At this point, she had an affectionate but somewhat distant relationship with her mother-in-law, especially in comparison to the instant connection she had felt on first meeting Joseph Kennedy. After the President's death, Rose and Jacqueline became closer.

In relation to the Soviet Union, I suppose.

I guess so, yeah. And how he underestimated or misestimated—whatever the word is—you know, the men he was dealing with. But perfectly, you know, just looking at it.

He had a great detachment about things because he had a great capacity to put himself in other people's positions and see what the problems were.

I always thought that of him, you know. Maybe that's what makes some people—like Jim Burns, who never knew him, but said he was detached and wondered if he had a heart.[26] Well, of course, he had the greatest heart when he cared. But he had this detachment. I always thought he would have been the greatest judge. Because he could take any case—it could involve himself, or me or something, where you—with anyone else, your emotions would be so involved—and look at it from all sides. I remember him speaking that way about General de Gaulle one time, when everyone was so mad at General de Gaulle last year.[27] I was so steamed up, and he was saying, "No, no, you must see his side." You know, he was nonetheless irritated.

---

26. Both Kennedys had resented the closing passage of Burns's 1960 book *John Kennedy: A Political Profile*, written with JFK's cooperation, which, while praising the Senator's talent and energy, questioned his emotional commitment to political goals. (In the final sentence of his book, Burns wrote that for Kennedy to bring "passion" to the presidency "would depend on his making a commitment not only of mind, but of heart, that until now he has never been required to make.") Jacqueline so vehemently objected to this that she wrote Burns a crisp rebuttal in longhand: "I think you underestimate him. Anyone sees he has the intelligence—magnetism and drive it takes to succeed in politics. I see, every succeeding week I am married to him, that he has what may be the single most important quality for a leader—an imperturbable self-confidence and sureness of his powers. . . . When you have someone like Jack, why write him off as a pathetic little string bean, groping and searching and somehow finding himself near the top, blinking in the sunlight?"

27. CHARLES-ANDRE-MARIE DE GAULLE (1890–1970), the Free French leader of World War II, served as French president from 1959 to 1969. In the mid-1950s, Jacqueline named her French poodle "de Gaulle." As an ardent Francophile in art, architecture, literature, history, and couture, she was all the more vexed, as the Kennedy years unfolded, by de Gaulle's willingness to poison his relations with JFK and the United States, as well as the rest of the Western alliance, by upholding his extreme standard of French pride and independence.

PRESIDENT KENNEDY AND PRESIDENT CHARLES DE GAULLE, PARIS, 1961

Well, that was the extraordinary thing. There are those who always see other people's sides to such an extent that it severs the nerve of action for themselves. It never did, in his case. He could see the point. He understood the political urgencies that drove other people doing mischievous things, but that—it never prevented him from reacting to it.

Yeah, I wish I'd given him a wristwatch with a tape recorder in it or something, because if you could hear him explaining de Gaulle to me—what de Gaulle's objectives were, and why he was so bitter. I mean, his analysis of that man—de Gaulle was my hero when I married Jack, and he really sunk down. Because I think he was so full of spite. And that's what Jack never was, and he always would say—I suppose women are terribly emotional, and you want to never speak to anyone again who said something mean against your husband—but Jack would always say, "You must always leave the way open for conciliation." You know, "Everything changes so in politics—your friends are your enemies next week, and vice versa."

Why was de Gaulle your hero?

He wasn't really my hero, but I sort of loved all that prose of some of his memoirs and thought this man who stayed away in the gloomy forest and came marching back, you know, being rather Francophile, just a vague sort of—

I agree. I thought, you know, at the funeral, that he was—in spite of all the mischief he has made—will make—an immensely touching and charming figure.

Yeah, of course he has two sides to him. That's what Jack would always say. You know, nobody's all black or all white. And he did, you know, realize what Jack was. I think he just felt guilty—I don't know— You know, he realized who Jack was, and that's why he came to the funeral. And I think that was an effort. He didn't need to do that.

He had a certain—the thing about de Gaulle and Churchill and the President and a few other people is that they had a sense of history, which produces sort of magnanimity of judgment. Although de Gaulle can be spiteful, he can also be very magnanimous and he recognized that the President— He saw him in the great stream of history, and that—of course, his memoirs are so marvelous in that respect because of the sense of the flow, the necessities which people have to respond to, and the wonderful prose.

Oh, yeah, when Jack made his announcement that he was going to run at the Senate—no, run for president—I'd been reading him the beginning things of de Gaulle's memoirs of how "I've always had a certain image of France" and he used part of that, paraphrased it for his own. Yes, you should look at that speech—"I have a certain vision of America" or something.[28] Another person he used to tell me a lot about was Randolph Churchill, Winston Churchill's father. "And I forgot about Goschen—" I remember he'd say that a lot of times, when someone resigned, and they found someone else to replace them. Do you know that story?

---

28. Announcing his presidential candidacy on January 2, 1960, JFK said, "I have developed an image of America as fulfilling a noble and historic role as the defender of freedom in a time of maximum peril. . . ."

No, I don't know that story.

There was some minister who resigned when Randolph Churchill was in the government, because he thought he was—it was on some point. Yeah, who was the one who resigned—of the Exchequer, a couple of years ago? On some little point of whether—some little thing with the budget?

He'd given information—

Not Thorneycroft—anyway, some man resigned and was immediately replaced, and this man thought that he couldn't be replaced, and they'd have to come around to do what he wanted, and right away, they appointed someone named Goschen. And the man—maybe it was even Randolph Churchill—said, "Oh, my God, I forgot about Goschen." *[Schlesinger laughs]* Which, you know, is a thing to show that anyone can be replaced.[29]

What did the President think, in 1959, about his contenders? Well, I guess he had Hubert, and he had Lyndon and Stevenson in the wings.

I don't know, exactly. You know, he liked Hubert before, but he always said when you get into a fight, it gets so bitter that you're just bound to sort of hate them at the end. It got very bitter, and he liked Hubert again afterwards. Lyndon sort of amused him. Well, Lyndon was so tricky and he'd come home and tell me things—when Lyndon made an announcement up at the Senate that he was fit to run—to all these reporters—that he could—I don't know—play squash and have sexual intercourse once a week. *[both laugh]* Lyndon—well, he'd just come over and—you know, he knew what he was dealing with there. I mean, he didn't ever admi—

---

29. In 1886, when Lord Randolph Churchill resigned as chancellor of the Exchequer, he presumed himself indispensable and was startled when Lord Salisbury quickly appointed George Goschen to succeed him, prompting Churchill to lament that he had "forgot Goschen." The more recent example she is thinking of was probably Peter Thorneycroft, who resigned in 1958 as chancellor of the Exchequer, along with two lesser officials, to protest increased public spending. Dismissing the resignations as "little local difficulties," Prime Minister Harold Macmillan quickly replaced them all.

THE DEMOCRATIC TICKET FOR 1960:
SENATOR LYNDON JOHNSON AND SENATOR KENNEDY IN HYANNIS PORT

He liked Lyndon. Lyndon was sort of—

He didn't particularly like him, but he could trade with him and not come off—
It was sort of, when you saw them together, it was really like fencing, in political things. And I always thought Lyndon was arguing with him or being rude, but Jack was sort of parrying with such amusement, and he always sort of bested him. Lyndon would give a big elephant-like grunt. But, you know, he didn't really—it wasn't anything personal.

I think he always felt—that he was amused, rather delighted by Johnson as a kind of American phenomenon, and at the same time, often quite irritated by a particular thing he would do at any point.

You know, Lyndon—I mean he just—what were his things—of Lyndon—Lyndon was the majority leader and he did get the position he wanted in the Senate, but I know he had to trade or really pester hard for that—for Foreign Relations and Labor. That's what he wanted so much. But in the primaries, it was more what you could do in Wisconsin, and who you could get to see, and then whether Hubert would go into West Virginia or not, more than the people. I told you last night how he'd get irritated with Stevenson. He never thought any of them were better than him, but, I mean, he wasn't ever conceited. I mean, if he could just get it—get over this Catholic hurdle and this youth hurdle and this rich—or whatever it was, you know, then everything would be fine. So, it was really overcoming those hurdles more than his opponents.

Do you think one of them worried him more than another, or were they all sort of equal?

I think it was Catholic and youth.[30] And I remember before he went out to Chicag—to California, I went with him to New York to see him off, and he made the speech—was it in Grand Central Station or the Biltmore?—about answering Truman's charges that he was too young.[31] But he did it without any bitterness.

And terrifically effective. At the end of '59, there is a—perhaps around Thanksgiving at Hyannis Port, there was sort of a meeting to plan strategy.

---

30. JFK hoped that his victory in heavily Protestant West Virginia would quash the Catholic issue for good, but it remained virulent enough that in September 1960, he felt compelled to appear before a group of Protestant ministers in Houston and reaffirm his strong support for separation of church from state, saying, "I am not the Catholic candidate for president. I am the Democratic party's candidate, who happens also to be a Catholic." Kennedy's youth was another obstacle: at 43, he would be the youngest man ever elected President.

31. In the most acute eruption of the youth issue all year, on July 2, 1960, appearing at the Truman Library in Independence, Missouri, former President Truman asked JFK, the front-runner for the Democratic nomination, to step aside on grounds that he was too young and inexperienced, and that the convention had been "rigged" in advance. Two days later, at the Hotel Roosevelt in New York, the candidate replied by saying that if "fourteen years in office is insufficient experience" (referring to his tenure in Congress but not his wartime naval years, which he elsewhere included in what he called his eighteen years of "service to the United States") that would rule out every twentieth-century president, including Truman himself. After making this statement, he flew to Los Angeles for his party's convention.

Oh, I remember that. We had one house there, and everybody was closeted for two days in Ethel and Bobby's, and all these men came up—Kenny, Larry, Bobby, everyone, and huddled away and planned. But, you know, when Jack would come home from something like that, I wouldn't ask him, "What did you plan here and there?" He'd come home, and then it would be fish chowder, or what would he like for dinner, or records, or then someone there to laugh. So that's—I mean, I would have been a terrible wife if I tried to pick his brains about that.

The last thing he would have wanted. I mean, he wanted other things. I think in a way, the great difference between—it was also true between Roosevelt and Truman, being—Kennedy and Johnson—is that both Roosevelt and Kennedy were master politicians, but politics was one part of their lives. It was something they enjoyed doing. It was an instrumentality they used to do other things. But then there were a lot of other things involved with life. I think with Truman, Johnson, politics is their whole world.

I know. And when you talk to either of them, it's all they can talk about. Every little metaphor—"my daddy down at the well."[32] Or Truman's fascinating about American history. You can just ask him anything. But you never can hear anything different from them. But, you know, Jack—well, I mean—I think a woman always adapts, and especially if you're very young when you get married and, you know, are unformed, you really become the kind of wife you can see that your husband wants. So, if he'd wanted—for instance, my sister's husband loves to bring his problems home, and they're all business, and Lee doesn't understand that.[33] But, you know, if Jack wanted to do that—and talk about things at home—then I'd be asking him questions. He didn't want to talk about the things that were bothering him. But other things of his life—I mean, it was always, you'd have to read the papers and everything. Because he'd be rather irritated if he'd say, "Did you see

---

32. One of LBJ's favorite sayings. To Johnson, a reliable friend was someone "you would go to the well with" in order to draw water, referring to the days when American Indians threatened settlers of European origin.

33. CAROLINE LEE BOUVIER CANFIELD RADZIWILL (1933–) was Jacqueline's younger sister.

Reston today?" And if you hadn't, you'd make sure you saw Reston the next day. Because if you'd say, "What did he say?" he'd say, "Well, you know, you should find that out yourself."

His staff were victims of the same. At this meeting, as I recall it, in Hyannis Port, was—the real thing, which kind of changed the whole place, in the sense that Ted,[34] who up to that time had been handling both, working both on the speeches and the political side—was taken out of the political side, and Bobby and Kenny and so on came in, and really took over the whole question of political—

Oh, yes, and I remember there was a rather bitter feeling for a while—or at least in Wisconsin, I think. Ted was bitter at Bobby. Ted didn't like whatever slot he'd been put into, and deprived—you know, there was a bit of friction there. But, you know, Jack could always trust Bobby. And, I suppose—I mean, he planned his campaign that way. He couldn't always trust Ted. You know, Ted had shown before that he wasn't—

You mean questions of judgment?

No. Questions of—well, yeah. But I mean that thing of *Profiles in Courage*. Jack behaved like a great gentleman to Ted then, because Ted didn't behave very well that year. I mean, I'm sure that's not why he gave Ted the speeches or something, but I must say, I couldn't look at Ted Sorensen for about two years after that.

Because Ted gave the impression he had written the book?

Written the book. Of course, the poor boy, he was just starting, he was new in Washington, but he used to really make a conscious effort to go around and take Jack pages, and things that he'd crossed out and added—you know, really to go out of his way to show them to people. And then, when Drew Pearson said it, then there was the lawsuit where Clark Clifford came and defended him—and, luckily, Jack had saved all these pages of yellow legal

---

34. Referring to Ted Sorensen.

TED SORENSEN AND SENATOR KENNEDY

pad that he'd written himself.[35] And, I guess, Jack loved Clark Clifford then, because when he asked Clark to defend him, I think Clark might have been under the impression that Ted really had written most of the book. But he never asked that question, and then Jack got all those yellow pages and

---

35. DREW PEARSON (1897–1969) was the foremost muckraking journalist of the day, with a widely syndicated column and weekly television program on ABC. Clark Clifford (1906–1998) was a St. Louis lawyer who was counsel and close adviser to President Harry Truman before starting a lucrative Washington law practice and earning a reputation as one of the "wise men" of Washington. During the 1950s, JFK was one of his clients. In 1957, Pearson charged on ABC that *Profiles in Courage* had actually been written by Sorensen. With Clifford's help, JFK forced Pearson to retract the allegation. During the 1960 campaign, Kennedy asked Clifford to start preparing for a potential transition to the White House. Through JFK's presidency, Clifford continued to advise both Kennedys on various matters private and public.

showed them to Clark, and Clark was just amazed and said, "These are the most valuable things you have. Lock them up. Everything." You know, and I saw Jack writing that book. So, you know, Ted would send down fifty books on Lucius Lamar—and everyone else—from the Library of Congress—and Jack would sketch it through. And Thaddeus Stevens, and all that. It was back and forth in the mail. You know, I really saw Jack writing that book. I never liked the way Ted behaved then. But you know, his life was all around himself, and, I think, just in the White House, he got to love one other person beside himself, which was Jack. So in the White House, he was fine.

As late as that? Because by the time—certainly Ted seemed to be the most devoted and selfless to the point of—

Let's see, *Profiles in Courage* would have been '55, '56? Well, I'd say, all through '56 and the beginning of '57. You know, Jack forgave so quickly, but I never forgave Ted Sorensen. I watched him like a hawk for a year or so. But then, as he had more to do, he didn't need to prove his little things. And then Jack gave him—again, don't you think this is a nice thing?—Jack gave him all the money from *Profiles in Courage*, because he felt Ted worked so hard—and he would work and stay up at night. As I said, he worked slowly—he always seemed to have to stay up until two or three in the morning to get something done. But don't you think—if everyone's saying that Ted wrote the book, for Jack then to give him the money from it—which he's made over a hundred thousand dollars—[36]

---

36. At this moment, Schlesinger was not averse to provoking Mrs. Kennedy against Sorensen. At the time of these oral history interviews, both men were rushing to complete rival books on President Kennedy, which for a time frayed their relations. In his 2007 autobiography (*Counselor: A Life at the Edge of History*), Sorensen notes Pearson's charge "that I had privately boasted or indirectly hinted that I had written much of the book (a charge that, I regret to say, may have been—it was all too long ago to remember—partly true)." He insists that "like JFK's speeches, *Profiles in Courage* was a collaboration, and not a particularly unusual one, inasmuch as our method of collaboration on the book was similar to the method we used in our speeches." Sorensen writes that in 1953, he and JFK agreed that on any outside published work on which they collaborated, Sorensen would receive at least half the fees or royalties. He adds that when *Profiles* became a major bestseller, generating royalties "far in excess of anything either of us had ever contemplated," JFK "unexpectedly and generously" gave him "a sum to be spread over several years, that I regarded as more than fair," and which, by 1961, still exceeded half the book's earnings. Despite her tart comments about Sorensen during these interviews, Jacqueline soon mended her differences with him and later, during her New York years, their friendship resumed.

Did Ted get all the royalties from Profiles in Courage*?*

Yeah, because then, you see—when it was published, Jack thought it would just be—

That's fantastic!

You know, just a little book that would make—I don't know—sell twenty-five thousand copies or something? But then it went zooming on to be a best-seller, bestseller, bestseller. Ted's gotten every bit of money from that book until the memorial edition with Bobby's preface came out. And then, from now on, it'll go to the Library. You know, so—

That's extraordinary! I never—Ted must have made hundreds of thousands of dollars.

I know he made at least a hundred. But you know, Jack wanted to give him something extra besides his salary because the boy did just live—and you know, and worked hard all night and everything—but Jack was such a gentleman. I just think that was such a nice thing to do.

Bobby was in Washington, in this period, all the time, but he really wasn't, until '59, sort of day-to-day involved.

Always when we were in Washington, we saw Bobby. It's funny. Just in the White House, we stopped seeing them in the evenings. When we went out, we saw Bobby. Before we were married, we always lived in Georgetown, we were at dinner with them once or twice a week. And then Bobby—they'd talk about the McClellan committee, the McCarthy committee—you know, all the things that Bobby was on.[37] But, I guess, then Bobby ran his Senate campaign—didn't he?

---

37. RFK had served as assistant counsel of Senator Joseph McCarthy's Subcommittee on Permanent Investigations before finally resigning in protest over McCarthy's excesses. From 1957 to 1959, he served as chief counsel for Senator John McClellan's committee on labor racketeering, a perch from which he relentlessly pursued Teamsters president James Hoffa.

Yes, he did.

In '52?

In '52, and Teddy, supposedly, in '58.[38]

But, you know, Bobby was always sort of—well, they were both so caring of what the other was doing. But then I guess—I suppose, at that Thanksgiving meeting, Bobby just gave up everything else and did everything for Jack from then on. I don't remember what Bobby was doing in '58 that he couldn't run the campaign. Are you sure he didn't run it?

My impression is that Teddy was nominally the campaign manager, but maybe not. The labor hearings were going on, I suppose, at that time.

Well, that's a major thing, I remember, in Jack's life, but I can't remember what year it was. But I can remember every morning for breakfast, Arthur Goldberg[39] would appear. Or George Meany,[40] and everyone—that was the year '57 when we moved in our house, because the first breakfast, I bought these creaky old dining room chairs, and at one of the first breakfasts, Jack and George Meany and someone else all went crashing to the floor. But all that year, you know, we were seeing people for the labor bill. He and Seymour Harris[41] that spring—

Much more labor than foreign policy at that point—

---

38. EDWARD MOORE KENNEDY (1932–2009) was the ninth Kennedy child. After Teddy's birth, Jack asked his parents, "Can I be godfather to the baby?" They agreed. Ted Kennedy was the campaign manager of record when JFK ran for a second term in the Senate, but as he was studying at the University of Virginia law school, he was not involved full-time. In 1962, Ted won his brother's old Senate seat and occupied it until his death.

39. ARTHUR GOLDBERG (1908–1990) of Chicago, son of Jewish immigrants from Poland and Ukraine, was general counsel to the AFL-CIO and United Steelworkers before JFK appointed him as labor secretary and then, in September 1962, to the Supreme Court.

40. GEORGE MEANY (1894–1980), a rough-hewn former Bronx plumber, was chief of the AFL-CIO.

41. SEYMOUR HARRIS (1897–1974) was a Harvard economist.

Well, it was to get through the labor bill. Was it against the Landrum-Griffin Bill?[42]

The Landrum-Griffin Bill came along as an—alternative, which was eventually passed as a result of Eisenhower's throwing himself into it.

Well, anyway, Jack had one whole spring working on that.

Spring of '59, I think. But at the same time, he would do things like give the speech on Algeria.[43]

Oh, yeah. Gosh, I had to be married for my contribution to that. Because the summer—that was the summer before we were married—he gave me all these French books, and asked me to translate them. And I was working for the *Times-Herald*,[44] living alone at my mother's house in Virginia. And I'd stay up all these hot nights, translating these books, and, as I couldn't tell what was important and what was not—

What sort of books?

I mean, all these—they were all in French on Algeria. No, no, this was Indochina. Sorry, Indochina. That's right.[45] That's what I did before I got married.

---

42. The Landrum-Griffin labor reform act of 1959 sought to regulate union practices to avoid the excesses that the Kennedy brothers had uncovered in their hearings. JFK wished to ensure that it did not also restrict honest union activity.

43. In 1957, the French were waging war against Algerians who wished to liberate their country from being a part of "metropolitan France." JFK gave a controversial speech denouncing French dominion over Algeria, taking the then-bold (and farsighted) view that it was in the American interest to side with anticolonial movements, both because it was right and because it would help the United States attract newly independent nations in which such movements had succeeded.

44. From 1951 to 1953, she was the "Inquiring Photographer" for the *Washington Times-Herald*, whose editor, Frank Waldrop, noted that Jackie "could see around corners." In that role, she covered the coronation of Elizabeth II.

45. In 1954, the French withdrew from Vietnam after an embarrassing defeat at Dien Bien Phu, and the United States was under severe pressure to replace them and pick up the struggle to keep the North Vietnamese leader, Ho Chi Minh (1890–1969), from seizing the entire country. JFK was skeptical and wished to learn more. With her excellent command of French, Jacqueline translated

That was '51–'52.

Yeah, translate all on Admiral D'Argenlieu, and Ho Chi Minh, and the Ammonites and the Mennonites.[46] I think I translated about ten books.

Ten whole books?

No, I mean really sort of skimming through the page, but—

Summarizing. Could he not read French?

Yeah, he could read French, but you know, but not enough to trust himself for a lot of facts and things. And then he would see—we were seeing a lot of French people then, and then they'd give some book. And the same—well, I did some for Algeria. But, you know—and the St. Lawrence Seaway, again I can remember that. You know, all those things were so brave.[47]

The Algeria speech was particularly so, because the whole Council on Foreign Relations crowd in this country were all outraged by it. I happened to be in Paris when the speech came out, and an old friend of mine, Jean-Jacques Servan-Schreiber of L'Express, was absolutely delighted by the speech and ran the full text and claims to be the first magazine in the world which put the President on the cover. And I remember writing to him from Paris, saying, "Pay no attention to these editorials from the New York Times saying how you shouldn't rock the boat. You are absolutely right. The people in France who care about it welcomed the speech."

Oh, yeah, I remember when he went to Poland, he wouldn't take me, because

---

books for him on the history and politics of French colonies in North Africa, the Middle East, and Southeast Asia and other subjects.

46. Georges d'Argenlieu was French colonial administrator in Indochina from 1945 to 1947. The Ammonites were Biblical seminomadic descendants of Lot. Swiss Mennonites emigrated to Algeria in the nineteenth century.

47. By voting for construction of the seaway, which would expand U.S. commerce at the expense of jobs in Massachusetts, Kennedy outraged many of his constituents, who complained that he was more concerned about the rest of the country than his own state.

he thought it wasn't serious to travel with your wife. But, you know, he was always more interested—well, so interested in foreign things. And then the minimum wage, I remember—whenever that was.[48] You know, all the things he cared about—I don't know what year. But, just as an example of him having a heart—I can remember him being so disgusted, because once we had dinner with my mother and my stepfather, and there sat my stepfather putting a great slab of paté de foie gras on his toast and saying it was simply appalling to think that the minimum wage should be a dollar twenty-five. And Jack saying to me when we went home, "Do you realize that those laundrywomen in the South get sixty cents an hour?" Or sixty cents a day, or whatever it was. And how horrified he was when he saw General Eisenhower—President Eisenhower—I guess, in their Camp David meeting before inauguration—and Eisenhower had said to him—they were talking about the Cuban refugees—and Eisenhower said, "Of course, they'd be so great if you could just ship a lot of them up in trucks from Miami and use 'em as servants for twenty dollars a month, but I suppose somebody'd raise a fuss if you tried to do that."[49] You know, again, so appalled at all these rich people just thinking of how can you live on— Not thinking how you can live just on twenty dollars a month, but just to use these people like slaves. He was just so hurt for them, though he'd say it in a sentence. That awful—Republican sort of— Look, oh and then, another time, when you were trying to raise money for the cultural center,[50] and a Republican friend of my stepfather said, "Why don't you get labor to do it? If you took a dollar a week out of all of labor's wages, you could have the money raised in no time at all." And he was just really sickened by that and said, "Can you think what a dollar a week out of their wages would mean to all those people?" So all those things show that he did have a heart, because he was really shocked by those things.

---

48. During their first debate in September 1960, JFK rebutted Nixon's charge that he was "too extreme" by complaining that Republicans were opposing an increase in the federal hourly minimum wage, then a dollar, to $1.25: "I don't think that's extreme at all."

49. Kennedy's meeting with Eisenhower was actually in April 1961, after the unsuccessful Bay of Pigs invasion.

50. This refers to the effort to build a National Cultural Center in Washington (later renamed the John F. Kennedy Center for the Performing Arts), finally opened in 1971.

Oh, I think the most—of course, he had a heart and he had a—in fact, you know, it wasn't on his sleeve, and people had been so used to a certain sentimental style of expression of that kind of thing. But he was deeply affected. But he was cool also. The fact that he was, is why someone like Hubert, whom I love, who is an admirable man—nonetheless can't connect with as many people as the President could, because Hubert is still—is in an earlier phase of reaction to this kind of thing. Did the President enjoy the primaries in 1960—apart from the fact it was a lot, and a great nuisance having to go through all this, but campaigning and so on?

You don't know the exhaustion of the primaries, and he often said that the four days we took in Jamaica between Wisconsin and West Virginia were what made it possible for him to be president. Because he just worked himself into exhaustion, and then the second wind and the third wind, and when you get that tired, you don't enjoy them. And sometimes, when we were in the White House, and he'd go on some long trip, he'd get tired—sort of a campaigning trip, and he'd come home and say, "Oh, my God, I just don't see how I got through those years." You know, "I just don't see how I did it." I suppose, when you stay that tired for that long—but then he'd lose his voice—I don't think anyone enjoys working out of sheer exhaustion. And in Wisconsin, we'd go into a ten-cent store or something, three people in it. They'd back against the back wall. They wouldn't want to shake your hand. You'd have to go up and just grab their hand and shake it. Or little rallies in a town, where you'd have a band and everything there and nobody'd show up. You know, they were really hard. Wisconsin was the worst.

Worse than West Virginia?

Because in West Virginia, I was so amazed. I thought everyone would be there staring at us like—

These "Papists"?

Yeah, and all that literature they were passing out about nuns and priests and everything. But the people were so friendly. There could be a mother with three blackened teeth, nursing a baby on a rotting front porch, but she'd smile and say, "Won't you come in?" In Wisconsin, those people would stare at you like sort of animals. Jack would say, "All this talk about the rural life is really"—you know—"overestimates it." Because the people are alone all winter long, and cold, and just with animals, and they're so suspicious. Maybe it's because they're Nordic too—I don't know. But they're suspicious people there. Eww!

You feel this was because he was a Catholic, or because he was an easterner, or were they equally suspicious of anybody—Hubert, or anybody?

I think that in Wisconsin, they're just suspicious of anyone sort of gregarious. I mean, I don't think they like someone coming up, or a band, or anything. And I think they were suspicious of him for all those reasons. Whereas in West Virginia, you know, they're a bit gayer, even though they're so poor. But I loved—I never met one person in West Virginia I didn't like, except for this strange man running around with his handbills wherever we spoke. And I never met one person in Wisconsin I did like, except for the people who were working for Jack.

When he was exhausted, he'd snap back quickly though, wouldn't he?

Oh, yeah, you'd stumble into some hotel bed and you'd get up at six in the morning. He could snap back. He could have a day home and just sleep all through it, and you'd get all his laundry done or something in the daytime, and pack him at night, and off he'd go or off we'd both go. And he could always sleep. He could sleep in the plane, almost like a soldier. I think that's—so many people's troubles are when they can't sleep.

Clem Norton[51]—I don't know if you've heard the tape of his—said Teddy has a street personality, the President didn't have a street personality.

That's true, he didn't. I mean, at the end, you know, he had that incredible

---

51. **CLEM NORTON** (1894–1979) was a crony of JFK's Fitzgerald grandfather who comes to life in Edwin O'Connor's *The Last Hurrah* as Charlie Hennessey, "a sallow, happy tub of a man in his fifties with bulging excited eyes." Norton had been superintendent of Commonwealth Pier and, campaigning from his own one-man sound truck, a perennial loser for mayor of Boston.

THE KENNEDYS CAMPAIGNING IN THE
WISCONSIN PRIMARY, 1960

thing.[52] But Teddy's more nineteenth century. He can go down and tell stories. He's more like Clem Norton, and more like Honey Fitz. But Jack never—he never said, "Hi, fella," or put his fat palm under your armpit, or, you know, any of that sort of business. It was embarrassing to him.

But he didn't actively dislike campaigning. He rather enjoyed it, didn't he?

Yeah, he enjoyed it. I mean, if you asked him his three favorite things he can

---

52. In June 1963, during a trip to Europe, JFK viewed the Berlin Wall and then gave a rousing speech (in what is now John F. Kennedy Platz) assuring free West Berliners that he would support them against Soviet threats to drive them from the city. When he spoke the words *"Ich bin ein Berliner!"* there was such an ovation that he later joked that he would offer three words of advice to later presidents at a moment of discouragement: "Go to Germany."

DURING THE NEW HAMPSHIRE PRIMARY CAMPAIGN

do in a day, I don't think he'd say campaigning.[53] But when he got caught up in it, and when it was going well, then he really liked it and responded. And the last—you know, as time went on, he was doing better and better. And he loved the people who really were glad to see him—the little old ladies, or children, or what.

I always felt that when he went out as President on a trip and saw crowds, he'd really come back very refreshed. Didn't you feel him filled with new energy and confidence—

Yes, it was so good for him. And he'd say how good it was to get out of Washington, where it's this little group that just writes—in and in and in— you know, little correspondents hashing others. It was so good for him to get away and to see that he was adored. You know, it was great whenever he did that. And when he went to Europe this June.

---

53. By contrast, Robert Kennedy was shocked in 1964 when LBJ told him that of all the things in life, he liked campaigning the best.

The

THIRD

Conversation

WEDNESDAY, MARCH 4

1964

L ast time, we started talking about the convention, and the months before the convention in 1960, and the President's view of his various opponents and problems, and one of the things that always surprised me was the way in which liberals—the arguments I used to have to have with some of the older liberals and academics and so on, about the President. It sounds very odd now, because no one obviously has done more for intellectuals in the White House since Jefferson. I suppose one of the big reasons for it was the whole McCarthy business. How—you knew McCarthy?[1]

No, I didn't know him. I just went to see one of the hearings once. But Jack was sick at the time of the McCarthy thing, wasn't he?

Yes, he was.

And then they knew that his father had been a friend, or hadn't he been to the Cape once? I don't know.

He'd apparently been to the Cape once or twice and—

---

1. When JFK entered the Senate in 1953, his Republican colleague Joseph McCarthy was using the Senate's Subcommittee on Permanent Investigations to pursue supposed hidden Communists in the U.S. government, damaging innocent lives in the process. Caught between the many Massachusetts voters (especially Irish-Americans) who loved McCarthy and the liberal Democrats who abhorred him, Kennedy was criticized by some for failing to publicly denounce the Wisconsin demagogue. In December 1954, when the Senate voted to censure McCarthy, JFK was recovering from his near fatal back operation and was the only Democratic member not to participate.

Never when we were there.

But he wasn't in any sense a pal or chum or anything like that—

Oh, no, never! I just went out of complete curiosity once to see those hearings, and saw that man, who was rather frightening. But I suppose they all thought that because of Mr.—again, I suppose the liberals all attributed it to Jack being his father's son or something like that?

I think that was part of it and also the fact that he didn't attack McCarthy, though, as a matter of fact, very few members of the Senate, including people like Hubert Humphrey and Paul Douglas, attacked McCarthy.[2] What do you suppose he thought of him?

You know, I think he thought it was awful. You know, the way he was flailing around and handling everything? And then he did make some statement either from the hospital, or was it just before his operation, or he would've voted to censure him but he wasn't there, was that it?

Yes. A speech was prepared for delivery before he went to the hospital. The speech was never delivered and indicated that he was for censure. I think when the actual vote came, he was pretty sick and I don't think any statement was issued at that time.

He thought of McCarthy—well, you know, poor McC—I mean, if you saw McCarthy, then you'd see a man in his last—I remember, I think he was coming in and out of the elevator when I was standing there—well, the man was just gone. He smelled of drink and his eyes looked awful. You know, I think Jack thought just what everyone thought of McCarthy. But again he was never anyone to run in a pack against— And then, of course, I suppose he had partly the political problem at home, didn't he?

Yes.

---

2. PAUL DOUGLAS (1892–1976) was a liberal Democratic senator from Illinois.

Every single one of his voters in Boston—anyone whose name was McAnything they thought was wonderful. But I think he did that quite well.

Most of them or a lot of them thought McCarthy was probably a Democrat. No, I can remember at times when I—do you remember the old John Fox—not the good John Fox, not Judge Fox, but—

Oh, the one who owned a paper?

Owned the Boston Post.[3] *At one time he started an attack on Communists at Harvard, particularly on me.* [Jacqueline laughs] *And Jack was in town and went up and explained to him that I probably wasn't a Communist, and I shouldn't be attacked. And later, he told me about it and said as a consequence of that he decided that John Fox probably thought that* he *was a Communist!*

Yeah, then Bobby was against McCarthy, wasn't he, or was that later? When was Bobby's thing with Roy Cohn?[4]

Bobby, well, that was about this time—

Was Bobby working for McCarthy then?

Bobby originally—Bobby was minority counsel. He was counsel for the Democrats on the committee but he had originally—he and Roy Cohn had worked with McCarthy and then he couldn't stand Cohn's methods—and then he was associated

---

3. JOHN FOX (1906–1985) bought the *Boston Post* in 1952 for $6 million (including a loan of $500,000 from Joseph Kennedy, for which Fox expressed his thanks by renouncing his endorsement of Henry Cabot Lodge in favor of JFK for the Senate). Fox made the paper shrill and McCarthyite, and deployed it in strong support of "Onions" Burke in the spring of 1956. Later that year it went bankrupt. Fox ultimately died penniless.

4. In January 1953, Robert Kennedy started work for McCarthy's committee as an assistant counsel under McCarthy's abrasive and unscrupulous counsel, Roy Cohn. The animosity between the two men over matters great and small at one point almost led to a fistfight. By the summer, Robert had moved to the Democratic side of the committee staff, then quit altogether.

with Symington, Jackson, and the opponents.[5] He apparently was a friend of the ambassador's at some point.

Yes, not a great friend. You know, again, Mr. Kennedy was so loyal. There seems to be all these Irish—they always seem to have a sort of persecution thing about them, don't they? I notice the way Mrs. Kennedy speaks even now about—not even now but, you know we—"Is someone a Catholic?" or "Are they Irish?" As if it's—you know, I guess they've had such persecution.

Mrs. Kennedy can remember what it was like to grow up in Boston—

Yeah, but she even will say now when you say you know someone or someone's coming for dinner—"Is he a Catholic?" or "Is she a Catholic?"—as if that will make them nicer. It's really a timidity. So, I'm sure Mr. Kennedy was rather conservative—you know, he might have just liked Joe McCarthy out of—this was before everything bad happened—because he was Irish, because he was Catholic, and because everyone else was down on him. But you know, never going into anything deep in it. Because they never talked about him at home. And he certainly never told Jack—you know, to be for or against him. It was a messy situation Jack was in—putting out a censure and everything, and they hated it in Boston.

Yeah. It was a very difficult local situation on it. What about the Nixons? Did you ever see the Nixons in the senatorial days?

No. Oh, well, I used to see her at bandage rolling. You know, the Senate wives have to go roll bandages every Tuesday and the vice president's wife is always the chairman of it. She's dressed in a white nurse's uniform. That's the only time I ever saw her.

I think she'd be perfect at bandage—bandage rolling. Well, it's about 1960, the primaries, and you remember the Wisconsin primaries being the hardest. Did the

---

5. **HENRY "SCOOP" JACKSON** (1912–1983) was a Democratic senator from Washington whom JFK seriously considered for vice president in 1960.

President ever, at any point, seem worried about the outcome or was he too absorbed from day to day to have feelings? Was he up and down or was it a fairly—

Well, you just had to work so hard. You know, when you're really in a campaign, you don't almost have time to think of the outcome, though he'd be going over polls and the this and the that district. But I remember election—primary night in the Hotel Pfister in Milwaukee. You know, that was awful. It was so funny. We were all on—just like on nails. And then it came out sort of a draw. Well, it was just so awful because there everybody had put all they had into a fight and you were just left exhausted. And you saw it had proved nothing. And you'd have to start again. Oh, and I remember that awful man, Miles McMillin, who wrote for the paper in Madison, who is married to—the girl he's married to, Rockefeller, was married to Proxmire.[6] Well, he used to write all these anonymous letters to the paper, saying scurrilous things about Jack. He was a terrible man. Again, a wild-eyed liberal creature.[7] He came cruising through the apartment that night when we were all in there counting the returns and—oh, it was awful of me—I walked by him twice without saying hello—cutting him dead. *[laughs]* And Jack— I mean, I was so mad at him. Jack was polite.

West Virginia, like you said, was more agreeable.

Well, the people were just nicer there. And you know, you went slugging along again, but—oh, and then there, for the first time, we separated, and I'd go off with someone on my own little tour—you know, in and out of little shops or a little bar or all those little mining towns. And the people were all so nice to me. You know, just tiny, little—never more than ten or twenty people.

---

6. MILES MCMILLIN (1923–1982) was a reporter and later publisher of the *Capital Times* of Madison, Wisconsin. His wife Elsie Rockefeller McMillin (1924–1982) had been married to the state's new senator, William Proxmire. JFK thought McMillin was anti-Catholic.

7. In 1964, Mrs. Kennedy still thought of liberals as people who gave Jack trouble—as did, on occasion, her husband. Members of the group that JFK called "professional liberals" had mistrusted him since he first ran for the House in 1946 because of his conservative father. Once he was President, they charged that he was a militant Cold Warrior and too intimidated by conservative southern Democratic congressional committee chairmen to vigorously pursue the liberal agenda on civil rights, education, labor, health, poverty, and other domestic issues.

SENATOR KENNEDY TALKS TO COAL MINERS
DURING THE WEST VIRGINIA PRIMARY

Would you speak, or just—

I'd just say hello to them all, and talk to them. You know, and tell them who I was, and I'd have someone with me. Who was it? Did I go with Franklin?[8] Because he was usually with Jack. Then every night, we'd be at some big rally, where Franklin would talk. But then, you see, in the middle of that campaign, I started to have John. So then I was sort of—rather sent home a bit. I just was there about the first half.

Had Franklin been an old friend, or did he become a particular friend in West Virginia?

No, he'd been a friend of Jack in Congress. You know, they—they were always running around and busy and everything, but they'd always liked each other. And then—I guess we saw them a few times when we were married. Yeah, we used to see Franklin. So he always was a friend. Not constant. But you could always laugh with him and he—you know, he amused me and he and Jack amused each other. So that's—and I went off with Franklin in Wisconsin, I remember. We went all through one colored district together and all through supermarkets where no one looked up at us. That's when he became—in Wisconsin, he helped there too. But West Virginia is where we saw the most of him and from then on, he was a very good friend.

West Virginia began to get a little bitter. I guess it was pretty bitter in Wisconsin with Hubert.

Yeah. I guess it did because what were they saying? Oh, just as Jack said, a fight always gets bitter. The Humphrey people were saying the Kennedys were buying the election and the Kennedy people—Humphrey had

---

8. FRANKLIN ROOSEVELT, JR. (1914–1988) served in Congress with JFK from 1949 to 1955. Kennedy especially valued his endorsement in 1960 because it offset the pre-convention opposition of his mother, Eleanor, who much preferred her close friend Stevenson. After failing to find him a suitable position in his government (he asked McNamara to appoint him secretary or assistant secretary of the navy, as his father had been under Wilson, but the new Pentagon chief refused), the President made him undersecretary of commerce in 1963.

not been—had any military service, and I forget what else it was.[9] But, you know, Jack didn't say any of that. He was mostly trying to prove why he wasn't dangerous as a Catholic.

Which he did—completely, of course. He won in West Virginia three to one, as I recall. Something like that. And then after that, did—

Oh, do you want to know something interesting about the night that we won there? I guess that night was just too frightening. You know, we didn't want another night like the Hotel Pfister. So he came back to Washington and we went—we had dinner at home with the Bradlees and we went to a movie.

What was the movie, do you remember?

We had been going to some movie at the Trans-Lux, but it was half over, so we went to some strange movie on New York Avenue. Just the only movie that was sort of open that we could get in. It was some awful, sordid thing about some murder in California—really, I mean, just morbid.[10] And then we came home to our house, terribly depressed by this movie, and waited for the phone to ring. And I was in the pantry getting some ice cubes and suddenly I heard this war whoop of joy! And they'd called Jack and it was, well, you know, just fantastic in West Virginia, so then we all got in a plane and flew down there, and got there in the middle of the night. But you know, he was so nervous about it, he just didn't want to be there. So we had this strange little evening of not wanting to be by the radio, the phone, anything.

---

9. Campaigning for JFK in West Virginia, Roosevelt told reporters that Humphrey was "a good Democrat, but I don't know where he was in World War II." In fact, the Minnesotan had tried to enter the wartime military but was rejected because of a hernia.

10. This melodrama was *Private Property*, by director Leslie Stevens, so low budget that it was filmed in Stevens's Hollywood Hills home, starring his wife, Kate Manx. It portrays a housewife taking up with hoodlums, with scenes of rape and murder. By Bradlee's recollection, JFK speculated (correctly) that *Private Property* was on the Catholic Church's index of prohibited films, and joked that it would have helped him with some of West Virginia's Catholic-hating voters, had they known he would be watching it.

Is that the—that's the only election you ever did that, isn't it? Most of the other times you were always there.

Yeah. The other times we were always there, yeah.

This was really so much a make-or-break thing. And after this, did it seem to be clear sailing?

Well, I guess it did to Jack. Because then it was to really go around and talk to people, wasn't it, and keep speaking. Well, what month would that have been?

Well, that was May, and then in June there was President Truman's attack. Remember that?

Oh, yeah.

On experience. Did that upset him much or—

Well, you know, it irri— I mean, it was just one more thing to, you know, swat down like a buzzing fly. But I remember when he answered that, because that was on his way out to the convention. So June and July, what did he do? Well, then there was the long session of the Senate.

That was after the convention.

Was that after the convention? Were June and July—I guess he was mostly in Washington, wasn't he? Wasn't the Senate still in session then?

Yes, the convention was in July. It was earlier because the Democrats were out of office and then he came back and the special session began in August.

Then whenever he'd come up to the Cape for a weekend—oh, or a day—you should have seen our little house. There'd be fifty Lithuanians arriving with folk dolls for Caroline or something at eleven in the morning, then they'd go. Then, I don't know, then Tom Mboya[11] would come, and then Governor Stevenson, then Norman Mailer, then—just in and out of our house. And everyone on the street outside—I'd started to build a stockade at the convention, but I only had it half finished—that split fence. So, Lee and Stas[12] were staying with us and everyone could see them getting in and out of the bathtub because they had a room on the street. It was rather close living that summer.

About the convention, were you or the President ever alarmed by the way things were going at the convention? For example, all the Johnson efforts or the Stevenson picket line, or anything like that?

You see, I was at home at the Cape with my mother and stepfather and Janet. I was the only person in the whole compound because I was having John.[13] And I was panic-struck, reading the papers. Well, Jack would always call me up, usually terribly late at night, or say something would be all right, or not to worry, or this or that. I suppose he was worried about me worrying, having a baby. Oh, but I was panic-struck watching it. But I guess they weren't as worried out there, because Bobby told me that once he got to the convention, he knew they'd get—you know, he'd get the nomination.

The President would call you every day—and Bobby, would he call you?

No, no, Bobby told me that later. No, Bobby didn't call me.

---

11. TOM MBOYA (1930–1969) was a young Kenyan nationalist leader who, during their July 26, 1960, meeting in Hyannis Port, convinced JFK, chairman of the Senate subcommittee on Africa, to have the Kennedy family foundation support the effort by Mboya's Airlift Africa to place Kenyan students in American universities. One young Kenyan studying in America was Barack Obama, Sr., an Mboya friend and supporter who had arrived in 1959.

12. STANISLAS ALBERT RADZIWILL (1914–1976), known as Stas, was an exiled Polish prince and London real estate investor who was the second husband of Jacqueline's sister Lee. He campaigned among Polish voters for JFK in 1960 and was John's godfather.

13. Although it was not publicly advertised at the time, Mrs. Kennedy was suffering through a difficult pregnancy. She had been asked by doctors to stay as quiet as possible until the expected birth in December. "Janet" refers to her half-sister, Janet Auchincloss.

JACQUELINE BEING INTERVIEWED IN HYANNIS PORT, 1960

So you missed, of course, the sort of business of the great Stevenson act—[14]

Yeah, I just saw it on television.

And Lyndon saying—you saw things like the debate between the President and Lyndon. You missed Lyndon's people going around saying—talking about Addison's disease and—[15]

Oh, I remember that because when Lyndon Johnson came after the convention to our house at the Cape, we moved out of our bedroom—it was a very small house there—so that he and Lady Bird could have that room. We were

---

14. Referring to the Illinoisan's encouragement of a Stevenson draft movement in Los Angeles.

15. Before the convention in Los Angeles, operatives for Lyndon Johnson had cast grim forebodings about Senator Kennedy's health.

sort of sleeping in a single bed in this tiny little guest room. And then we had to go over to Mr. Kennedy's, which was where all the press would meet the next day, and Lyndon plunked himself down in Mr. Kennedy's chair. I was just thinking, "Do you know what chair you're sitting in after the things you said about that man?"[16] And anytime Lyndon would talk that night, Lady Bird would get out a little notebook—I've never seen a husband and a wife so—she was sort of like a trained hunting dog. He'd say something as innocent as—I don't know—"Does your sister live in London?"—and Lady Bird would write down Lee's name and "London." Just everything. I mean, she had every name, phone number—it was a—ewww—sort of a funny kind of way of operating.[17]

They were like a hockey team.

Yeah, well, you know, just—she always had these three green notebooks just filled with everything.

We talked about this the other day but it was not on the tape so you were—about the problem of Lyndon's going on the ticket.

Oh, well, I think everyone was disappointed because of all the people, they liked Lyndon Johnson the least, and I must say, Symington behaved awfully nicely there, didn't he?[18]

---

16. In Los Angeles, LBJ had castigated Joseph Kennedy (with whom he had previously been quite amicable and who had quietly urged him to run for president in 1956 with Jack as running mate) for his pessimism before World War II about Britain's chances against Nazi Germany. Johnson said, "*I never thought Hitler was right.*"

17. Off the tape, Jacqueline told Schlesinger that during the visit, she had asked Lady Bird what she had been doing since the convention, expecting her to say something like she had been "resting up since that madhouse." Instead Mrs. Johnson replied that she had been sending notes to all those people who had been so kind to her husband in Los Angeles.

18. On the day of his nomination, Kennedy had told Symington's close Missouri friend Clark Clifford that he intended to make Symington—who had run his own desultory presidential campaign, hoping to be chosen after a convention deadlock—his running mate. Symington thereupon started writing his acceptance speech. But the next day, JFK told Clifford that, having been persuaded during the night that he couldn't win without Lyndon, he would have to "renege on an offer made in good faith." Jacqueline wrote to Eve Symington that it would have been "such fun if it had been you and Stu."

Yes.

You never thought he was any great statesman or anything, but he was just such a gentleman the way he did that. And I know that made Jack sad. I even wrote Symington a letter—which I asked him to burn. *[laughs]* And he wrote me back that he burned it—saying I wish he had been the vice president. But I know Jack had to do it because—have Lyndon as his running mate—to annul him as majority leader because here this man with this enormous ego would have been just enraged and blocking Jack in every way and yes—you know, and keeping everything in. I know he kept that session in before the convention.[19]

I think he called it before the convention.

Yeah, that was it, so Jack couldn't get out and campaign and do more things. I mean, he'd done something before to really make things difficult for him.

I recall it was called before the convention but took place after.

Well, he certainly didn't make—If you'd had him up there with that enormous ego, and thwarted and bitter—so nobody was happy about it. Everyone was even amazed that he accepted. Well, some other people can tell you

---

19. LBJ had called an extraordinary post-convention session of the Senate. Jacqueline had always liked Johnson—he felt she was "nicer" to him than anyone else in the Kennedy entourage, but this passage suggests some disenchantment with the new president. Two days before Christmas 1963, LBJ demonstrated his tendency to overreach. He telephoned Mrs. Kennedy to wish her a happy holiday ("How's my little girl?") without telling her that he had reporters listening in so that he could show off his closeness to the revered widow. And Robert Kennedy, who detested Johnson, had regaled her with such tales as LBJ's hasty request of JFK's personal secretary on the morning after the assassination to vacate her West Wing office "so I can get my girls in" and his reversal of various Kennedy appointments, policies, and intentions. But, although unsettled by Johnson's periodic gaucheries and his negation of a number of JFK policies, Mrs. Kennedy liked LBJ and had great fondness and admiration for Lady Bird, who had often filled in for her as First Lady. Jacqueline was also grateful to her successor for pledging to complete her White House restoration designs and to preserve the White House Historical Association and her other improvements intended to ensure that the mansion would remain a museum-quality showcase of American history and culture.

about it, going down into his room and everything—*[whispers]* and I guess he was drunk, wasn't he?

Phil Graham was a great go-between and told me—I have notes somewhere—that the Friday I went out and had dinner with Phil, he gave me a great account of his role as kingmaker-intermediary. I think Joe Alsop also thinks that he was responsible for getting Lyndon on the ticket.[20]

Gosh, I don't know. I suppose Bobby could really tell you all of that.

Bobby was against it.

But, I mean, Bobby knows. All I know is that a call was placed at something like eight o'clock in the morning and Lady Bird answered. And Lyndon was still asleep. And then Jack went down. Lyndon said he'd come up but Jack said no, he'd go down to his apartment and Lyndon just accepted right away. But I don't know what had gone back and forth, and they all were rather surprised. So, I don't know if all these people were kingmakers or not.

Joe and Phil waited on Senator Kennedy on the Tuesday and said he had to put Johnson on the ticket. The President said nothing. But then subsequently, according to Phil, the President called him and I forget where this—and asked him about calling—what he should do about calling—said, "I want to go ahead with Lyndon." And I think then the President called Lyndon directly. Lyndon was asleep and then all this business started. Then later the thing seemed to get off the tracks and Phil was called in to kind of put it together.

---

20. **PHILIP GRAHAM (1915–1963)** was publisher of the *Washington Post* and a close Johnson ally who, in the habit of many newspaper proprietors of the time, liked to be involved in politics behind the scenes. But in his posthumously published memorandum on his role in LBJ's selection, he in no way suggests that he was anything close to a kingmaker. Nor does Alsop in his memoirs. By Graham's account, his own role was limited to urging both men to run together and then—after JFK went down to Johnson's Biltmore Hotel suite and made the deal with him—encouraging LBJ not to bolt the ticket when angry liberals threatened a floor fight. RFK, who even in 1960 disliked the Texan, much later insisted that his brother's offer of the vice presidency had been merely pro forma, and that Johnson had "grabbed" it. Graham, Alsop, and others insisted that JFK had planned in advance of his nomination to make a serious offer to Johnson in order to carry important southern states and thus win the presidency. There is unlikely to ever be a definitive verdict on how much Kennedy really wanted Johnson on his ticket.

I see. Oh, what else was I just thinking of? Can't remember.

Before the President went to Los Angeles, did he talk very much about—did he speculate about the vice presidency?

No, he really didn't. He was at the Cape and I flew down with him to New York and we stayed—did we stay the night at that Idlewild[21] hotel?—or else I just saw him off and went back to the Cape—you know, and said goodbye to him. I guess we did stay the night because the Truman thing was sometime. He really didn't. You know, it was more just to get it himself. So, that all obviously happened in those four or five days there.

Did he ever get permanently mad at people?

Never! And then I used to say to him sometimes—you know, it was so funny in politics—it was all everyone talked about, every night. And I'd hear him speaking nicely about someone and I'd say, "What? Are you saying nice things about X? But I've been hating him for three weeks." You know, if I saw him in the street I was going to make a point to just glare at him and cross over to avoid him and Jack would say, "No, no, that was three weeks ago. Now he's done x, y." You know, I mean, in politics things do change so quickly and Jack would never—he'd often say that—never get in anything so deep that you've lost all chance of conciliation. I mean, he never treated it—what did he say? "In politics you don't have friends or enemies, you have colleagues"? That isn't quite the right—

Interests. Palmerston used to say there are no permanent friendships or alliances, there are only permanent interests. Something like that.

Yeah, but he never got—I mean, I'd get terribly emotional about anyone, whether it was a politician or a newspaper person who would be unfair, but he always treated it so objectively, as if they were people on a chess board— which is right. I mean, how could you if you—if he'd gotten so mad at all

---

21. Now John F. Kennedy International Airport in New York.

those people, then you may need to work with them again later. So, it's the only way to be effective—which is one reason I think women should never be in politics. We're just not suited to it.

Yeah. He was a great realist in that way, because I remember in Los Angeles, everyone felt as soon as Lyndon attacked the ambassador, that this finished him.[22] That's because of the theory that developed of sort of Irish feuding. Too many people had seen John Ford films, which I didn't—[23]

John Connally was the one who was going around about saying Mr. Ken— about Addison's disease too. And then, you know, the day before Jack died in Texas, I said to him, "I just can't stand Governor Connally. I can't stand his soft mouth." He was so pleased with himself and he'd spend all our times in the car telling Jack, I guess, how far he'd run ahead of him in Texas. So, I'd say, "What's he trying to tell you? It seems so rude what he's saying to you all the time." And Jack said, "Oh, well, he's been making up with a lot of businessmen down here and gotten a lot of support he didn't have before. That's what he's telling me."[24] But Jack would just sort of take it— you know, "yaaah"—and then when I said that, that I hated Connally, Jack was so sweet. He sort of rubbed my back—it was as we were going to bed—and said, "You mustn't say that, you mustn't say that." He said, "If you start to say or think that you hate someone, then the next day you'll act as if you hated him," and then, "We've come down here to Texas to heal everything up and you'll make it all impossible." Nellie Connally was refusing to ride with Yarborough—everybody was refusing to ride with Yarborough—everybody was refusing to ride. And there were two people

---

22. Meaning JFK's father, the former envoy to the Court of St. James's.

23. Referring to the director, who made pictures such as *The Informer* (1935), about an Irish rebel who betrays a comrade.

24. JOHN CONNALLY (1917–1993) was a lawyer and Texas crony of Lyndon Johnson's. At a press conference before the balloting in Los Angeles in 1960, Connally had demanded a medical evaluation of whether Kennedy was healthy enough to serve as president. Nevertheless, JFK made him secretary of the navy. Elected governor of his state in 1962, Connally and his wife Nellie rode with the Kennedys through four Texas cities on November 21 and 22, 1963. During the Dallas motorcade, in the last words they spoke, Connally, a conservative Democrat, told the President of a soon-to-be-published poll that showed him running ahead of JFK in Texas in 1964. Kennedy replied, "That doesn't surprise me."

named Yarborough and, I don't know.[25] Everybody was hating everyone. And you know, Jack said just, "You know, you mustn't think that about people." He said it so kindly.

And the same way with the Stevenson people. When you think that the top people on the Stevenson drive at Los Angeles were George Ball, Bill Wirtz, and Tom Finletter. All of whom were immediately—[26]

Oh, yeah, I know. I think it's so good to be able to forgive quickly. That's a quality that Jack liked in me, being married—that if ever there'd be a slight little cloud, I'd always be the—I'd rush and say, "Oh, dear, did I upset you? Did I say something wrong?" Or "I'm so sorry." And he loved that, because I think it's hard for men to make up first in a family, in a rather intimate way. But he did that same thing—I can't do it in my life outside marriage, but he did that same thing outside.

Would he ever get depressed or was his temperament just terribly equable?

Oh, his temperament was terribly even, except when he'd be in pain for a long period of time—for instance, his back—and when he'd done the three or four usual things, which is go stay on crutches four days—if that doesn't work, go to bed for two days, or have a hot pack or something. And if it just seemed to stay on and on, he couldn't shake it, then he'd get very low, but just because of that. But if he had something to do, he'd get up and do it. And then eventually it would get better. But, in the beginning years of our marriage, ill health was—just seeing Jack in pain used to make me so sad all the time,

---

25. One of the purposes of the Texas trip of November 1963 was to resolve an intra-party feud in that state which pitted Johnson and Connally against their political nemesis, Texas senator Ralph Yarborough. Connally refused to ride in the presidential motorcades with Yarborough. Yarborough refused to ride with Johnson. In Fort Worth that final morning, JFK had been compelled to tell Yarborough, "For Christ's sake, Ralph, cut it out!" The other politician with the same name was liberal Don Yarborough (no relation), who had almost defeated Connally for the Democratic nomination for governor of Texas in 1962.

26. WILLARD WIRTZ (1912–2010) was Kennedy's undersecretary of labor before moving to the top spot in 1962. George Ball (1909–1994) was his undersecretary of state for economic affairs. Thomas Finletter (1893–1980) was his ambassador to NATO. All three men had been ardent Stevensonians.

but really after—when? I guess, after the Senate thing, it didn't seem to be as much of a problem anymore.

In 1960, his back didn't trouble him much, did it—during the campaign?

No, I mean, he had the best health in the world. I think one reason was he was doing so much, too much. When he got in the White House, he took this nap every day—it was just forty-five minutes. He'd come—who could be bothered to get in your pajamas for forty-five minutes? —and he'd hit that pillow and go to sleep and wake up again. I mean, I couldn't sleep—it would take me forty-five minutes to doze off, but it was so good for him. Then all his back and his stomach and everything weren't always plaguing him. He just always overtaxed himself. And so he never was in better health or spirits than all his White House years.

Did he ever have trouble sleeping?

No.

Never took sleeping pills? Never—just always—

Sometimes, in a campaign, he would take one tiny little sleeping pill. If you got in late and you had to get up early and you were in some awful smelly hotel bedroom. I remember once there was a whiskey bottle under the mattress because the American Legion had had a convention in that hotel there before and there were whiskey bottles under all our mattresses. Well, you know, just to make sure he got to sleep so he'd be awake the next day. But, a little tiny thing, and then he wouldn't the rest of the time. Because you needed your sleep—my gosh, you only got about four hours. I remember I tried not to take any, and you'd toss and turn, so then I'd borrow one of his sometimes.

You were in Hyannis Port all the summer of '60, during the special session.

That's right.

And then, of course, you were there all autumn.

Let's see, I did a lot of things in the spring in Georgetown, and then I went to New York for that ticker-tape parade. The first debate I saw in my house in Hyannis and had people down from Boston. The second one—whichever one was in New York, I was there for. And the third one I was in Washington for—the third or the fourth.

Do you remember how he felt when the whole question of debates came up?

Oh, well, I remember the one in New York, which was the one I was with him for—how he just had piles of briefing books and he had sort of a busy day, but then he'd sit in a room for two or three hours and he had about five people there giving him every conceivable awful question you could think of. I mean, he really prepared for it—like sort of an exam. And, you know, was so confident—no, not so confident—but you know, he wasn't moaning or groaning or worried or anything. And then when he called me up at the one in Washington the minute it was over, that was—I guess maybe it was the second one in Washington—because he said on the phone they had the temperature here down to thirty degrees below zero, or something, because I guess Nixon had perspired in the first one—sort of laughing. But he really was quite confident.

What did you think during the first debate?

Oh, well, I thought what everyone else did. I just couldn't believe it. You know, it was so obvious. It was just so clear. That really changed everything. Jack always told me the thing that changed his '52 campaign—this was before we were married—was his appearance on *Meet the Press* with Lodge.[27] He said that that was the hump and then everything started to go his way. Well, that first debate was—I always thought it—but I was so glad that it was just

---

27. **HENRY CABOT LODGE, JR.** (1902–1985) was a Republican senator from Massachusetts and namesake grandson of the Brahmin senator who killed Woodrow Wilson's dream of American membership in the post–World War I League of Nations. Appearing alongside the well-respected Lodge gave JFK a boost similar to that of appearing with the vice president of the United States in debate. After losing to Kennedy, Lodge served as Eisenhower's ambassador to the United Nations before joining Richard Nixon's losing ticket in 1960.

SENATOR KENNEDY IN THE FIRST DEBATE AGAINST
VICE PRESIDENT RICHARD NIXON, SEPTEMBER 26, 1960

so obvious. Because you could just see he'd won it, and hear it in the street
and everywhere.

*Was there any talk before that about the—I mean, the President obviously thought
that the debate would be a great opportunity, if he could get it, but didn't suppose
that Nixon would go along. Do you remember any of that?*

Not really. I remember sort of talk on and off all spring about the debates.
No, I don't know what made Nixon finally decide to—

This was his great miscalculation. And I think he did it because he'd been a champion debater at Whittier College and thought that he could win. I'm sure there was no—I think he thought that this would make the experience for him, if he would get up there with this young kid.

But I remember the talk in evenings of which debate would be—wasn't one foreign policy, one domestic?—I remember all those evenings when they were hashing out—a lot of people would come and they'd decide how the debates would be made up. But I don't really remember the leading-up-to-it part.

I know you weren't, because of John, weren't around, along, all the time on the campaign. Do you have any impression on whom the President relied particularly in campaign strategy and the like?

Well, himself really. Because whenever he was home you'd hear him calling and I mean, he'd be telling people what to do. I suppose he did rely on Bobby—didn't he?—most of all. Bobby—

And he always checked his judgment with Bobby. Didn't always take it, as in the case of Lyndon Johnson, but I think he always wanted to see what Bobby reacted—how Bobby would react.

Then his father was always—you know, I was so glad Mr. Kennedy had a chance to do something. But he would be taking Billy Green to Pavillon or something—or maybe that was all before.[28] But he'd talk to his father too, but more to hear what his father reported. You know, all those old men—

John Bailey, did he matter?[29]

---

28. WILLIAM GREEN (1910–1963) was a congressman from Philadelphia and the city's Democratic chairman. Jacqueline's description here of Joseph Kennedy's efforts for his son's campaign is minimalist.

29. JOHN BAILEY (1904–1975) was chief of Connecticut Democrats and an early Kennedy supporter whom the President appointed as Democratic national chairman.

Oh, yeah, well, John Bailey—I don't really know—

He was the chairman of the committee—

Yeah. We always loved John Bailey. That's the first place we ever went when we were married, and Jack made a speech in Connecticut. But no, I don't think he was calling up John Bailey for advice.

As far as whatever I saw, it seemed to me he was really running the whole show himself.

Yeah. And then he'd say, and Bobby would say, and everyone—you know, "Nobody must ever get mad at the candidate." So that's where Bobby was sort of the buffer. And everyone who had a fight or then somebody hated Ted Sorensen in some state, and somebody else—there'd be two chairmen and which one would be the one. All those things Bobby would have to do, so that those people wouldn't get mad at Jack. You know, which Bobby gladly did. That's another reason—he got the sort of image of being someone people disliked, but he had to be so tough for Jack. And Bobby said that to me the other day—you know, it's so nice to have someone for you who can fight your fight—I mean, be the one that people get mad at—not at you. Just the way Frank Morrissey used to tell me that the candidate could never be the one to leave the room, so Frank Morrissey would have to haul him out. And he'd always be protesting, "No, Frank, I don't want to go yet." *[Schlesinger laughs]* But you always had people to protect you and do that for you.

Tell me, tell us, about the last day before the election.

Well, everybody was at the Cape. Oh, no—

You went to Boston—

Yeah, we woke up in Boston so we must have slept there the night before.

There was a big rally at the Boston Garden the night before. I think you were there, weren't you?

No, I wasn't. I was at the Cape, so I must have gotten up very early and been driven to 122 Bowdoin Street[30] and from there we went to the voting place. Then we flew down to the Cape in the *Caroline*,[31] and then that long day started. I remember we had fish chowder. You could still sit outside. And it's so funny, talking about the longest day, who should come running out from the garage in sort of a servant's part but Cornelius Ryan, who had written *The Longest Day*, with a print of a picture.[32] We both said, "What are you doing here?" We didn't really know him—he introduced himself. So then Jack started questioning him all about *The Longest Day* and the this and the that part of it. And you should ask Ryan about that—and I guess he'd gotten in it through Pierre.[33] Then you'd take walks and you'd go over to his father's house, to Bobby's house.

What kind of a day was it?

It was a cold, fall Cape day—very clear. But I know we lay out on the porch with blankets on us, sort of in the afternoon in the sun. Then he'd go over— Bobby's house had been turned into just a, you know, command post—I mean, radios, telephones, boards, workers. But Jack kind of stayed away from that. And then dinner—

How did he seem—

Sort of restless, but quiet. He'd go over there, then he'd try to take a nap.

He wouldn't speculate about things anymore—

---

30. The modest apartment some distance beyond the gold-domed Boston State House that JFK had taken in 1946 to establish residency for his first campaign for Congress, which by 1960 served as his and Jackie's voting address.

31. The Convair plane bought by the Kennedy family for JFK to use in the 1960 campaign.

32. CORNELIUS RYAN (1920–1974) was the Irish-born author of *The Longest Day: June 6, 1944*, a 1959 bestseller made into a feature film by Darryl F. Zanuck at Twentieth Century Fox.

33. JFK's press secretary, Pierre Salinger.

Oh, no, he wouldn't talk about it. I mean, it was—you had what he loves—his fish chowder—and then he was picking Cornelius Ryan's brains about *The Longest Day.* That poor man was so amazed. Then we'd take a little walk because you knew that the really bad part wasn't going to get until night. And then—I forget which house we had dinner at, but afterwards we were all watching it in our house. I remember Connecticut came charging in. And I said to Jack, "Oh, you know, now you're President now," and he said, "No, no" very quietly. So I watched until, I guess, about 11:30 or twelve and then everyone knew that it would be an all-night thing. So then I was sent up to bed. And all the—it was so sweet—Jack came up and sort of kissed me goodnight—and then all the Kennedy girls came up, and one by one we just sort of hugged each other, and they were all going to wait up all night. And Jack slept in the next room that night. So when I woke up in the morning, I went flying into his room to see—just to hear the good news—to hear that he'd heard sometime while he'd been awake—and no, there wasn't anything.

He had gone to bed, eventually.

Yes, he went to bed I think about four or something, and this was about a quarter of nine or eight thirty.

Was he still sleeping when you came in?

Yes. *[laughs]*

You woke him up?

Sprang him—and there was nothing, so then I woke the poor man up. Then you'd get up and then everybody walked around—you've seen those pictures—in raincoats. Up and down. Then the press people were sort of gathering and I guess it was about noon or one o'clock that the word finally came.

Nixon finally conceded then.

And then—oh, then I had to see the press in Ethel's house—all those

PRESIDENT-ELECT JOHN F. KENNEDY (CARRYING CAROLINE) AND THE FIRST LADY-TO-BE,
HYANNIS PORT, THE MORNING AFTER THE 1960 ELECTION

women saying, "What kind of First Lady will you be?" Those horrible women. And then we all had our pictures taken together in the big house. Then we were all going to go down to the Armory and Mr. Kennedy didn't want to come. So sweet, he always tried to stay in the background. I remember just grabbing him and saying, "You have to come now." He was so sweet. And we all went down to the Armory.

[John Kennedy, Jr., enters the room.]

John, can you talk? Hold it a little farther away from there—like that. John, you went to the airport today.

JOHN: Yeah.

Did you like it?

JOHN: Yes.

John, what happened to your father?

JOHN: Well, he's gone to Heaven.

He's gone to Heaven?

JOHN: Yeah.

Do you remember him?

JOHN: Yeah.

What do you remember?

JOHN: *[mischievously]* I don't remember *any*-thing!

You don't remember anything? Remember when you used to come and run into his office?

JOHN: Yeah.

And he'd play with you?

JOHN: Yeah. Can you put John on?[34]

O.K., we'll put John on.

[John leaves the room.]

Do you remember when the President knew he was going to be President? Did he say anything or did he just sort of take it in his stride?

Well, I think we were all out somewhere and someone yelled, "Nixon's conceded!" I think by then you sort of knew, by the votes, that it was bound—it was just sort of waiting for Nixon to concede, wasn't it?

Yes.

So, well, when it came, what could you do? I mean, you know, we hugged each other.

Would you say he was a religious man?

Oh, yes. Well, I mean, he never missed church one Sunday that we were married or all that—but you could see partly—I often used to think whether it was superstition or not—I mean he wasn't quite sure, but if it was that way, he wanted to have that on his side.

_____

34. Meaning on the tape recording.

PRESIDENT KENNEDY AND JOHN IN THE WEST WING COLONNADE

Pascal's wager.[35]

But I remember once he said to me something Somerset Maugham said: "Suffering doesn't ennoble, it embitters." So I don't know whether—he ever—must have had a few talks with God—I don't know if he did—just thinking, "Why does all this have to happen to me?" But he never said that. I think you couldn't be brought up the way he was without just thinking—

Well, obviously he accepted the religious sort of structure of existence and belief in a God and he believed that—he liked his children to be raised as good Catholics, and believed in Sunday Mass, and so on.

I mean, I know he wasn't an atheist or an agnostic or anything. No, he did believe in God but he didn't—You know, like all of us, you don't really start to think about those things until something terrible happens to you. And, you know, I think God's unjust now and I think he must have thought that along— He used to say his prayers—really—

He'd say prayers every night?

Yeah, but he'd do it so quickly it was really a little ritualistic thing. He'd come in and kneel on the edge of the bed—kneel on top of the bed and say them, you know. Take about three seconds—cross himself. That was—I don't remember him doing that in the White House. But, you know, it was obviously—it was just like a little childish mannerism, I suppose like brushing your teeth or something. It's just a habit. But I thought that was so sweet. It used to amuse me so—standing there.

Did he ever have any close friends in the clergy?

Not really his friends. I know Bishop Hannan he saw, but I guess that was

---

35. The seventeenth-century philosopher Blaise Pascal argued that even though God's existence could not be proven by reason, one should behave as if He did exist because there was nothing to lose by living in a God-fearing manner—and potentially everything to gain.

more because of politics and everything down here—that's the one he always liked the most. Oh, and then Father Cavanaugh was a great friend of his father's and, you know, was a rather liberal priest.[36] He liked him.

Bishop Wright in Worcester?

Oh, yes, he liked him very much. And of course, he loved Cardinal Spellman[37] after—

He really liked—I didn't—really?

In the beginning when we got married, I know they were having a big fight, but by the time he was President he liked him.

Did he?

What Cardinal Spellman did—you know, he was just so for Jack, and then he made all those speeches about—he really changed. Because he'd been such a conservative churchman. Kenny O'Donnell told me that Cardinal Cushing[38] used to make speeches—"Any boy who doesn't go to a Catholic college . . ."

---

36. **PHILIP HANNAN** (1913–) was auxiliary bishop of Washington, a World War II Army chaplain who parachuted into the Ardennes and helped to liberate a concentration camp, with whom JFK had maintained an unpublicized, quiet running conversation about religion and politics during his presidency, and who officiated at his funeral. John Cavanaugh (1899–1979) was a priest who was president of Notre Dame from 1946 to 1952.

37. **FRANCIS CARDINAL SPELLMAN** (1889–1967) was archbishop of New York from 1939 until his death. Although he had officiated at the weddings of Robert and Edward Kennedy, he strongly supported Richard Nixon in 1960, disdaining JFK's opposition—in his ardor to demonstrate fealty to the separation of church and state—to federal money for parochial schools and to the appointment of a U.S. ambassador to the Vatican. In 1945, Spellman launched the annual white-tie Alfred E. Smith Memorial Foundation Dinner, a fund-raiser for Catholic charities which, in presidential election years, usually features jocular speeches by both candidates, as it did in 1960.

38. **RICHARD CARDINAL CUSHING** (1895–1970) was archbishop of Boston from 1944 until the year of his death. Son of an Irish immigrant blacksmith, the gravel-voiced Cushing, who had originally wished to be a politician, was a Kennedy family intimate who presided over JFK's wedding to Jackie, prayed at both JFK's inauguration and funeral, and strongly supported the widow when she was remarried in 1968 to Aristotle Onassis.

and point his finger at Kenny, who was in his parish, because Kenny went to Harvard. Then Cardinal Cushing changed and when all those—

Oh, you mean Cush—I thought you were talking about Spellman—

Oh, did I say Spellman?

Yes.

Oh, my goodness!

That's why I was surprised.

[laughs] Oh, no, I meant Cushing—I couldn't have said Spellman. Oh, no.

Well, of course he changed. Absolutely.

Yeah, and he said all the things—the right things—what a Catholic should be saying. And he did not like Cardinal Spellman.

No, that was my impression because I significantly recall hearing him on Cardinal Spellman. No, Cushing was very loyal. Cushing has a sort of exuberance of temperament, doesn't he?

Yeah, and he's very funny—I mean, he's sort of *Last Hurrah*-ish and the crusty way he speaks. So I'd say he was devoted to Cushing and Cushing to him.

But this came on along later, didn't it, because as you say at the beginning Cushing was not that way. Remember Monsignor Lally of the Boston Pilot? *Was he ever—?*

I don't remember him—or even his name.

And what about Spellman?

Oh, Mr. Kennedy—why didn't he like Spellman? Didn't he have Nixon to the Al Smith dinner? You know, he so obviously was against Jack. How could you like him? And his little mincing ways. You know, he really was trying to just slit Jack's throat all the time and wouldn't be a help. Wasn't the Puerto Rican bishops or something—[39]

Yes.

Put out a big—Cushing would make the right statement and answer to that, but Spellman never would. So many of the Catholics were so to the right—to the right of Goldwater. Spellman was one of them. And now he's left in the backwash—in the new wave of the Church.[40] I'm so pleased!

Such a shame that the President and Pope John never met.

I know.

What happened at confessional?

Oh, well, when Jack would go to confession, there'd be long lines at Christmas and Easter, and he'd have a Secret Service man go stand in line for him. You'd have to stand about an hour, then he'd come over and just slip in the line, so nobody really knew who he was. The priest never knew. That was in Florida, at Christmas and Easter. It would be at a little church in West Palm Beach—not the church that we usually went to on Sundays. So he went to confession—you know, like anyone would.

It's amazing how it was done without—

---

39. In October 1960, three Catholic bishops in Puerto Rico declared it a sin for Catholics to vote for any candidate opposed by the Church, which gave ammunition to those charging that no Catholic should be elected president. Delighted to do damage to JFK just before the balloting, Cardinal Spellman publicly endorsed the bishops' edict. Cardinal Cushing opposed it.

40. Spellman found himself on the losing side of the debate over the progressive reforms initiated by Pope John XXIII at the Second Vatican Council in 1962.

Once he told me, as a joke, that sometimes priests would make you go to confession right before a communion breakfast, and he'd always say, "I forgot my noon prayers," and "I missed Mass on Wednesday," as his sins because—you wouldn't want some men in front of the whole room. But, I mean, he was so funny about it. But he really cared. He always did that. Again, was it superstition, or training, or what? I mean, lots of times I wouldn't go.

It always seemed to me that Bobby was more religious than the President.

Oh yes. Much. I mean, you know, go to things like First Friday, or Ethel would.[41]

---

41. She refers to the Catholic custom of prayer and Holy Communion on the first Friday of nine successive months.

The

FOURTH

Conversation

MONDAY, MARCH 23

1964

I think we stopped last time at Hyannis Port on the day of the election. You stayed there for a couple of days, as I recall. I know Marian and I came down for luncheon on the Friday after the election.

Oh, yeah. I didn't realize that was after the election.

And then, I think, on that afternoon you went to Palm Beach.

I guess Jack went to Palm Beach and I went back to Washington because I was going to have John any minute.

That's right.

So he must have gone to Florida for a couple of days for a rest, then he'd come back to Washington. Yes, and then when he came back Thanksgiving—he was back and forth all the time—and then Thanksgiving he came back. We drove all down to the country that day around Middleburg[1] to look for a house to rent and then he went back that evening and I had John late that night.

What was the date of John?

---

1. Middleburg, Virginia, was the de facto capital of that state's "Hunt Country." They were looking for a weekend place that would allow their family to escape the city and Jacqueline to go riding and fox hunting.

It was November 25—it was Thanksgiving Day. So then he came back that night—just turned around his plane—and then he stayed at our house in Georgetown all the time, sort of forming his cabinet and everything and marching over to the hospital about three times a day.[2]

What do you remember about the formation of the cabinet?

Well, it's rather difficult because I was in the hospital all the time, so I'd just see all those people—pictures of them all, standing in the snow outside our house, and then he'd come over and tell me about some of them— McNamara[3] and everyone. I remember when we went down to Florida, December 20, Dean Rusk[4] came that first night. We had dinner—it was just Jack and I there then. We had dinner alone with him. And then, I think, Jack was either trying to get him then—or had Dean Rusk accepted and they were talking?

The President was for a long time uncertain as between Rusk and Bill Fulbright.

That's right. I remember. Then that conference in Florida, where Caroline

---

2. The Kennedys had planned for Jacqueline to give birth in New York Hospital, as with Caroline, in mid-December. But on November 24, 1960, while the President-elect was flying to Palm Beach, a radioed message told him that she had gone into premature labor and been taken by ambulance to Georgetown University Hospital. When she arrived, she asked, "Will I lose my baby?" After midnight, John F. Kennedy, Jr., was born by caesarean section.

3. ROBERT MCNAMARA (1916–2009), born in San Francisco, son of a shoe store manager, was a Harvard Business School professor with a devout faith in the value of statistical analysis. After World War II, during which he analyzed the effectiveness of U.S. bombing forays in Asia, he rose through the ranks of the Ford Motor Company, becoming president in 1960, two days after JFK's election. Eager for at least one big business Republican in his cabinet, Kennedy met him at his Georgetown home and offered Treasury or Defense. McNamara accepted the latter, provided that he could appoint his own people. Kennedy agreed, impressed with his toughness. Later McNamara was the architect of President Johnson's escalation in Vietnam, until his resignation in 1968.

4. DEAN RUSK (1909–1994) of Cherokee County, Georgia, was a Rhodes Scholar who had been Truman's assistant secretary of state for the Far East, and then president of the Rockefeller Foundation. When other possibilities for the State Department did not pan out, Kennedy turned to the mild but tenacious Rusk, whom he had not known, consoling himself with the notion that he planned to be his own secretary of state anyway.

THE CABINET IS SWORN IN BY CHIEF JUSTICE EARL WARREN, JANUARY 21, 1961

walked in with her shoes on. That was when Senator Fulbright[5] was there, I suppose, to tell him he couldn't be or something?

I think that Bobby was opposed to Fulbright on the ground that Fulbright, because of his position on segregation, wouldn't be, you know, hot for Africa.

Oh, what do you think? Do you think it's too bad that Fulbright wasn't chosen?

---

5. J. WILLIAM FULBRIGHT (1905–1995) was a Rhodes Scholar who was Democratic senator from Arkansas from 1945 to 1975. As a member of the Senate Foreign Relations Committee, which Fulbright chaired, JFK had admired his allergy to conventional wisdom, but knew that as secretary of state, the Arkansan would have been doomed by his opposition to civil rights and his outspoken support for the Arab states, which would have hampered his ability to deal with African countries and Israel, not to mention alienating African-American and Jewish voters at home. "Caroline walked in" refers to the occasion when the President-elect and Fulbright were meeting reporters behind the Kennedy house in Palm Beach, and the three-year-old Caroline tottered into the scene, wearing her mother's high-heeled shoes.

My personal view is yes.

Me too.

How did Rusk strike you? The President had not known Rusk before.

No. Well, he was very quiet—you know, they were talking. I just sort of stayed for dinner and then went back to bed. You see, that's a time that I won't be very good on because I was really quite weak and we had one little bedroom in the back of the house—and then the Kennedys all came back and then it was just a madhouse. So I'd really see Jack in our room and—I was really in bed most of the time. Dean Rusk, you know, I thought he was—he seems to be a rather compassionate man. I've always thought that about him and—I don't know. When you meet him, you think much more of him than when you know things he could have done and isn't doing.

That's absolutely right because he gives the impression of great intelligence and he's always awfully good in defining a situation. He's much less good in saying what should be done about it.

He's terribly scared to make a decision. I think what you really need is a strong secretary of state. I can't remember, we did speak about that in the tape before—but how it used to drive Jack crazy in the White House—how he'd ask for some routine answer to something the Russians had done. I think this was after Vienna.[6] It was taking six weeks to get it out or eleven drafts

---

6. At the end of May 1961, the Kennedys went to Vienna, where the President met for two days with the Soviet leader Nikita Sergeyevich Khrushchev (1894–1971). The two men had only met once, briefly at the Capitol in September 1959, when JFK was a senator and Khrushchev had come to the United States to meet with President Eisenhower at Camp David. Now that Kennedy was in power, each wanted to take the other's measure. Kennedy hoped that behind closed doors, without the need to posture for the public, he and Khrushchev could reach some kind of worldly modus vivendi about Berlin, Cuba, Southeast Asia, and other Cold War powder kegs. Khrushchev, who had risen to power under Stalin, interpreted Kennedy's private willingness to deal as political weakness. Knowing that the Soviets had many fewer nuclear-tipped missiles than the United States, Khrushchev aimed to overcome that military weakness by impressing his ferocity on the new American President, telling him, "If you want war, that's your problem." Kennedy left Vienna feeling shaken, saying, "Roughest thing in my life." Khrushchev told his aides that Kennedy was "too intelligent and too weak." His underestima-

and he used to say, "Bundy[7] and I do more work in the White House in one day than they do over there in six months." And Dean Rusk seemed to be overtaken by that apathy and fear of making the wrong decision that so many people in the State Department have. So he really turned out not to be so satisfactory. But Jack—he was loyal and, you know, Jack just felt a terrible guilt—I mean, he wondered—I know I told you this before—of how he could get him out the next time without hurting him.

No, but you told me—but not on the tape, so go ahead.

Well, he was always wondering who he could have as secretary of state the next time. He was toying with so many people in his head. McNamara was one, but that wasn't really definite—Bundy?—but just someone strong there. And then he would feel so badly about Dean Rusk and I'd say, "Couldn't he go back to the Rockefeller Foundation?" and Jack would say, "No, no" — you know—"he's really cut his bridges there." He was so kind. He didn't want to hurt the man, but he just knew something had to be done there. And now I keep reading in the papers—I don't know if it's true or not—that Lyndon loves Dean Rusk.

I think Johnson will find the same thing and that—the trouble is the contrast between Rusk and McNamara, because McNamara always has the capacity, first, to control his own department and then to make recommendations, and speak about things with clarity, come up with ideas and get things done. I think the President used to feel: if only he had a McNamara instinct.

---

tion of the President in Vienna was one factor in his decision to challenge Kennedy in 1962 by slipping offensive missiles into Cuba.

7. MCGEORGE BUNDY (1919–1996), an Eisenhower Republican, was the son of a Boston Brahmin mother and a diplomat from Grand Rapids, Michigan, known as "the brightest boy at Yale." Fluent in French, he collaborated at age twenty-six on the memoirs of his father's friend Henry Stimson, FDR's wartime secretary of war, and became the youngest dean of the faculty ever appointed by Harvard. JFK appointed him as national security adviser, which until that time had been something of a clerk's position. After the Bay of Pigs, with his shrewd and gentlemanly instinct for power, Bundy convinced Kennedy that it should be much enhanced, so that the President would have a full-time in-house counselor to protect him against future bad cabinet advice—a redefinition of the job that has prevailed ever since. He also felt such an affinity with the President that he changed his registration to Democratic.

Yeah. Oh, there were so many things he was going to do. I was just thinking. He was going to get rid of J. Edgar Hoover—who's just been signed up again.[8] The next tape we do, I'll have a list because I wrote them down the other night of—about five, six things he was going to do this time.

Oh, was he?

And you know, they've all been done the wrong way.

Um-hmm. McNamara was absolutely new, you figure. I don't think the President ever had met him—had he before?

No, and he told me McNamara asked him one thing. They came in for their little conference in our tiny Georgetown house, and the first thing McNamara asked him was, "Did you really write *Profiles in Courage?*" and Jack said he had. And which again shows—that's why I told you I was so angry at Ted Sorensen—that just seed of doubt. And then McNamara really had this worship for Jack, and then he said, well fine, that he'd love to be it.

He was offered the Treasury, I think, originally.

Was he? I know that Lovett was offered his choice between State, Defense, and Treasury, and he couldn't take either, and Jack said, "You know, that

---

8. J. EDGAR HOOVER (1895–1972) was the first director of the Federal Bureau of Investigation, which he helped to create, and its predecessor agency, from 1924 until his death. Hoover's admirers cited his success in pursuing criminals and Communists. His detractors noted Hoover's metastasizing hatreds (for example, Martin Luther King and the few journalists and politicians who dared to criticize him), eccentricities (after an automobile mishap while making a left turn, he ordered his driver to abjure all future left turns), abuse of civil liberties, and Napoleonic tendencies. All agreed that Hoover spent his FBI years amassing unprecedented and largely unaccountable power, with his files of potentially damaging information on those who might stop him. In 1960, the newly elected JFK felt that, especially with his narrow margin, he had little choice but to immediately reappoint Hoover. But unlike his predecessors, Kennedy required the old man to deal with the President through the attorney general—in this case, Robert Kennedy, whom Hoover predictably detested—and hoped that resounding reelection to a second term would allow him to fire the FBI director and replace him with someone more cognizant of civil liberties. By contrast, President Lyndon Johnson made Hoover virtually director-for-life.

really is quite a tribute to a man to think that he could have any of those three, but he just was too sick."[9] And then the big thing with Governor Stevenson wanting State but telling him that he had to have the UN. That was rather—I can remember Jack telling me about that.

How did it—did that give him a lot of difficulty—the President—or was he rather amused by it all?

You know, it was unpleasant. I mean, he didn't like having to do it or anything, but he wasn't going to give him the State Department. I remember the earliest times when we spoke of it, you knew that Governor Stevenson would get the UN and not State, which he wanted. But it's sort of unpleasant to have to tell someone that. And I remember their conference on the doorstep was rather vague or Stevenson said he didn't have anything to say, or something funny. You can go back and find out what it was.[10]

Why do you suppose he decided not—against Stevenson for State?

Well, why should he give him—Stevenson had never lifted one finger to help him. But yet, it wasn't just bitterness or that, because look at all the people Jack took who had been against him or for someone else. He thought that man had a real disease of being unable to make up his mind and Stevenson irritated him. I don't think he could have borne to have him around every day coming in complaining as secretary of state about something. I mean, it would have been an awfully difficult relationship, and I think it would have just driven Jack crazy and—I really don't think Stevenson would have been

---

9. ROBERT LOVETT (1895–1986) was a Wall Street investment banker and Truman's final secretary of defense. JFK was eager to show continuity with the previous Democratic government by appointing a well-respected figure, but Lovett declined any appointment for reasons of health.

10. When he went to Kennedy's Georgetown house to learn about his future, Stevenson was nonplussed when the President-elect offered him not secretary of state but ambassador to the UN. After their meeting, on his doorstep in the cold, Kennedy told reporters that he had asked Stevenson to go to the UN and the Illinoisan declared that he would have to think about it. Stevenson's diffidence was understandable, but at a time when others were happily accepting presidential appointments, Kennedy was annoyed to be so publicly rebuffed. Stevenson's friends persuaded him that if he turned down the UN, Americans would forget about him. Thus Stevenson grudgingly accepted the job.

as good as Fulbright. I don't think he'd have been terribly different from Dean Rusk. Maybe he would have.

I think also—I think one thing that was in his mind was the purpose of having people who'd be—who have strength on the Hill for the measures. And I think that's one reason why Fulbright appealed to him because he thought the fact that the Senate knew Fulbright would mean that they'd have confidence.

Oh, yeah. Oh, poor Fulbright. If only he'd been picked—yeah, then Lyndon would like him and everything. And Fulbright was—yes, he was right. I remember he was the one—practically the only person who agreed with Jack—or who was against the Bay of Pigs?[11]

That's right. Um-hmm. The only one who spoke out against it firmly in one of the meetings.

Yeah. Though apparently at the second meeting he thought it might be all right, but you know, he sort of agreed at the end. But still—I think a lot of Fulbright.

When did Dillon[12] come into the picture?

Well, sometime around then—but again, I was in the hospital.

But you'd known the Dillons in Washington.

Oh, yes.

But not terribly well, I gather.

---

11. In April 1961, JFK approved a revised version of an existing secret plan left by Eisenhower to launch CIA-backed Cuban exiles in an invasion of Cuba to overthrow the government of Fidel Castro. When the landing, on Cuba's Bay of Pigs, failed, causing the President a mammoth embarrassment less than three months into his term, Kennedy publicly took responsibility.

12. C. DOUGLAS DILLON (1909–2003) was a Republican investment banking heir who served as Eisenhower's ambassador to France and undersecretary of state before JFK appointed him as his treasury secretary.

Not terribly well, but as well as we knew anyone. I mean, we'd been to their house for dinner a few times and I knew Phyllis Dillon. So they were one of the few people whose house we went to dinner to—occasionally, as sort of a friend, but never terribly close. And now I'd say of all the cabinet once we were in the White House, they were really our best friends. The only ones we really saw in the evening or at our private parties were them and Mc-Namara—the McNamaras. But the Dillons were the only ones we ever had dinner with just the four of us. The McNamaras and the Dillons would come to the private parties—those dances and things.

Did putting Bobby in the cabinet cause a lot of—

Oh, that was awful because—I suppose that was Mr. Kennedy completely. Bobby told me that once, after November, the weeks before we left the White House. He said it was Mr. Kennedy who really did it—and he said Bobby didn't think it would be good for Jack and Jack could see the problems it presented, though he never would say that to Bobby. And Bobby really went into this sort of slump that people say he was in since Jack's death. He didn't know what he wanted to do and again he wanted to go away and teach. He just didn't want it and finally—you know, he'd keep saying no or, he hadn't decided, or this or that, and finally one day Jack just called him in and said, "Well, you have to," or something, and it was decided. That shows you what Bobby is like and how he was just doing everything he could to get out of it, whereas Eunice was pestering Jack to death to make Sargent head of HEW because she wanted to be a cabinet wife.[13] You know, it shows you some people are ambitious for themselves and Bobby wasn't.

What do you think the President would have had in mind for Bobby, if not the Justice—bringing him into the White House in some way or—

---

13. **ROBERT SARGENT SHRIVER** (1915–2011) was working for Joseph Kennedy at the family-owned Merchandise Mart in Chicago when he met his boss's daughter Eunice and married her in 1953. During the interregnum, he served as the President-elect's highly effective chief talent scout. Kennedy made him the first head of his new Peace Corps. Later Shriver commanded President Johnson's War on Poverty, served as U.S. ambassador to France, and ran as Democratic nominee for vice president in 1972.

ATTORNEY GENERAL ROBERT KENNEDY AND PRESIDENT KENNEDY
IN THE OVAL OFFICE, APRIL 1962

I don't know. But he was so used to working with Bobby and having him to sound out decisions with, so I suppose it might have been that domestic— sort of like Bundy, only not. I don't know. I think he always wanted Bundy for Bundy's job, didn't he? Or did he decide that after?

I think he must have always had it in mind. He decided it sort of in December. He was absolutely definite that he wanted Mac down with him and I think in the course of December down in Palm Beach he decided that he would be the man for that job.

And—oh, but that job really changed completely, the way, what Jack and Bundy made of it, didn't it?

Yes, it was much more. It had been a rather routine job with people like Gordon Gray[14] and so on and it became, partly because of Mac's ability and partly because of Rusk's weakness, it became—

Jack saw he needed that?

It became much more of a job.

And just the way he saw he needed to get General Taylor there after the Bay of Pigs. He sort of created this job. Oh, one other thing I was going to tell you—the cabinet, what was it? God, my mind's gone blank.

Mac? Or?

Oh, one thing in Florida that I can remember about the interregnum that was rather a painful day. It was when Franklin Roosevelt, Jr., came down and Franklin told me Mr. Kennedy met him at the airport and said, "If it wasn't for some Italian in New York, we'd all be working for you now," meaning Carmine.[15] You know, again Mr. Kennedy's charm—oh, no, no, no, that was

---

14. GORDON GRAY (1909–1992) held the post at the end of the Eisenhower years.

15. CARMINE DE SAPIO (1908–2004) was the Tammany Hall boss who had blocked FDR, Jr.'s, dream of becoming governor of New York.

before West Virginia—sorry. That's what he said to Franklin to get him to help in West Virginia. But, Franklin wanted to be secretary of the navy and McNamara said that he couldn't have him. Franklin always thinks that Henry Ford told McNamara he couldn't have him—some convoluted reasoning there. I forget what it is. So it was very hard for Franklin—you know, to tell him that. But he took it so sweetly.[16]

I wonder why Bob had that feeling?

I do think it might have been—either Henry Ford or McNamara had a meeting with Franklin. His mind was sort of set against him a bit before. I think Franklin would have been all right.

I think Franklin would have been a very good secretary of the navy.

Yeah.

Franklin is bright and he's capable of hard work and I think he's been—all I hear of him is the good job in Commerce.

So Jack felt terribly about Franklin. He offered him ambassador to Canada, ambassador to Italy, every time anything—this was in the months after the presidency and before, anytime he could think of anything, because he knew he really owed so much to Franklin, and Franklin said, no, he just would use these years to make some money and keep his Fiat—and then one—I guess it was last winter—we were at the Roosevelts for dinner and I guess this undersecretary of commerce job had come up because after dinner Franklin and Jack disappeared into an upstairs bedroom about an hour and a half, and Franklin had been, I guess, telling Jack how much he wanted it. So, on the way home in the car, Jack was so happy to see—you know, at last there was something Franklin wanted. And then he was made it.

---

16. JFK gave FDR, Jr., substantial credit for helping him win the pivotal West Virginia primary, reassuring many voters who worried about his Catholicism but who venerated President Roosevelt for saving their homes and jobs during the Great Depression.

How about Udall?[17] Had you known him at all?

Not really. You know, just the way I knew all the senators. I think he was always the one Jack wanted for that, don't you?

Yes.

Jack owed him a lot for Arizona, which he took away from Lyndon and brought to Jack. And he was bright and he really was—I mean, Jack said he's one of the best secretaries of the interior. You know, he really cares about conservation and all that. So I knew he was always planned and—who was it for Agriculture? There were three people—Herschel, does that make sense?

Herschel Newson?

Herschel or somebody, and Docking, was it?

Docking was the governor of Kansas.

Yeah, we knew him, we'd stayed with them. And some Her—well, Herschel Loveless, is it?

Herschel Loveless, yes, the former governor of Iowa.

Yeah. But Jack didn't like him much, I don't think? Anyway, he made things rather difficult. When Jack interviewed him, I guess he just had no ideas or was just—I know Jack was really depressed after that. And he loved Orville Freeman.[18] I don't know if he was always wanting Orville Freeman or how Orville Freeman came up.

---

17. STEWART UDALL (1920–2010) was a Democratic congressman from Arizona when JFK made him secretary of the interior.

18. ORVILLE FREEMAN (1918–2003) was governor of Minnesota before he became Kennedy's secretary of agriculture. He was a former Marine who, like the President, had won a Purple Heart for valor in the South Pacific during World War II. Freeman gave JFK's nominating speech at Los Angeles in 1960.

Orville gave the nominating speech in Los Angeles.

Yeah, but I mean, I wonder why Jack just didn't make him that in the beginning.

Orville didn't want it. Orville wanted to be attorney general.

I see.

Or to be secretary of the army, for some reason, and he just had a sense that the agricultural problem was insoluble and I think that was—my recollection is that, that was the last cabinet office filled.

I know at the convention, Jack was promising everyone Agriculture, wasn't he? I mean, a couple of people like Loveless and—

I think yes—particularly Middle Westerners.

Yeah.

To sort of flourish before them. Hodges?

Well, I don't remember any problem or anyone else they were considering besides Hodges.[19] Who found Hodges? I think it was Sargent. And I don't know, it didn't set your mind aflame. I think maybe Jack thought he needed someone older.

Nice old man, a southerner—

A southerner business would trust, or something. I can't remember any comments he ever made and what kind of secretary of commerce Hodges was.

19. **LUTHER HODGES** (1898–1974) was a one-term North Carolina governor who had swung his state to JFK for vice president in 1956. The President-elect, who needed at least one southerner in his cabinet, made him secretary of commerce.

And then Ed Day as postmaster general.[20]

Oh, yeah. I don't know why he was chosen either, do you?

They wanted a Californian.

Oh, yeah. Well, he was the one cabinet member I really thought was third rate. I mean, I don't know about being postmaster general, but just corny and just—I don't know. I never thought much of him.

Now all the members of the cabinet, really the only ones whom the President knew moderately before, besides Bobby, were Douglas, and I guess, and Stewart Udall.

And Freeman.

And Freeman. But Rusk and McNamara and Hodges and Day, of course, Arthur Goldberg, we forgot.

Oh, yeah.

Goldberg was an old friend.

Yes, and he knew Goldberg—I mean, there was never any doubt in his mind that he wanted Arthur for that job. And I remember how sad he was when the appointment came in the Supreme Court, though he thought Wirtz was wonderful—a wonderful man. You know, it was sort of the way McNamara and Gilpatric[21] worked together in Defense. You know, he really hated to lose Arthur in Labor but he really cared about his appointments to the Supreme Court. He said, "Oh, God, I'll hate to lose him." And now Arthur just thinks he's—I don't know—just the way all the Supreme Court justices get to think

---

20. J. EDWARD DAY (1914–1996) had been Illinois insurance commissioner under Governor Adlai Stevenson before serving as an insurance executive in California.

21. ROSWELL GILPATRIC (1906–1996) was a Wall Street lawyer who served under McNamara as undersecretary of defense.

of themselves. I was so amazed that Arthur would rule that way and—that thing they just passed, where you can write anything about people in public office. And Arthur would even say you could do it with deliberate malice.[22] He was one of the three who were for that. When you think, ads like that in the paper was partly what killed Jack.[23] They get so detached from life up in the Supreme Court. There's this atmosphere of just reverence. But still, Arthur Goldberg's brilliant. But he talks more about himself than any man I've ever met in my life.

Has that always been so or is it—

Well, in the early days when he used to come for breakfast all the time, for the labor bill—they were obviously talking about the labor bill. But I really started to see much of Arthur Goldberg after the presidency. And I was really horrified. But, I mean, I know he's brilliant. I just think it's such a shame to be so pleased with yourself.

Apart from Rusk and from Day, the President was fairly well satisfied with the cabinet. Did you think?

Yeah, I don't think he cared about Day one way or the other because I don't know—I mean, is the Post Office Department a big problem?

No, I think Day ran it perfectly competently.

Yeah, Day was just sort of a—I don't know—he was always being in little skits at the multiple sclerosis ball. I just thought he was silly. But, that was

---

22. *New York Times v. Sullivan*, March 9, 1964, which decreed that a plaintiff in a defamation or libel case must prove that the defendant's statement was made with actual malice, in full knowledge or reckless disregard of its falsity. This ruling granted new license for publication of vicious comments about presidents and other public figures. Goldberg felt it would never be possible to firmly establish a defendant's motive, so he preferred a wider berth for the press.

23. Referring to a full-page extreme right-wing advertisement in the *Dallas Morning News* on JFK's last morning, accusing the President of treason, which had moved him to warn Jacqueline that Dallas, bastion of the radical right, was "nut country."

me and I never really discussed him with Jack. But I don't think he thought much of him.

One of the interesting things is the President's instinct for people because his capacity to pick people whom he knew rather slightly—even Lovett and McCloy,[24] for example. He hadn't known them much before, had he?

I don't think so. I mean, he'd obviously known them, but not terribly well. He could tell so much by talking to them, though I guess, with Dean Rusk, he made a mistake, but as you say, Dean Rusk comes over so marvelously when you're talking to him. You think he can save the world.

That would be his—how would he go about sizing them up? He'd talk to them— that'd be the main thing, of course, then he'd get a lot of reports from Sarge.[25]

Yeah. He'd have all these reports and things, and things that other people would say about them and then they'd come. It's like an interview if you're going to be accepted in a school or something. I mean, he'd be in that living room with them for a couple of hours and they'd just talk.

Did he ever describe what he talked about?

Well, it was such a hard time for him, those busy days. And then when he'd come over to see me in the hospital, he would— Later I told you what he said about McNamara and I know how disillusioned he was with Loveless—just certain, who had no solution to the farm problem, and no original thoughts. The others—I should have asked him all that, but when you live with a man who's so busy and everything, you don't want to just question him, question him, at the end of the day. So you pick it up by what he's telling someone else or what he wants to tell you—though I might have been dying to know. I'll

---

24. JOHN MCCLOY (1895–1989) was a wartime aide to FDR's war secretary, Henry Stimson, as well as a Republican Wall Street lawyer known as "Chairman of the Establishment." He advised JFK on disarmament.

25. Sargent Shriver, who was performing reconnaissance on potential appointees.

remember more later. Now my mind has gone so blank about so many things that I know I remembered before.

It'll come back. What gave him the most trouble besides Franklin and Stevenson in that period? Do you remember anything else in which he seems [to have had a] problem?

No. I remember—did I say it before—about him getting Clark Clifford to do that reorganization thing? It wasn't trouble. That was something he was very pleased with. Did I say that in the tape before?

No, you haven't.

Well, right after he was elected, he got Clark Clifford. I think he'd asked Clark way before election, saying, "If I get elected you must be prepared right away to do this transition thing." So, Clark had been looking into it, you know, making great things, so that everybody who was appointed to something spent those months between November and January literally at the desk of the man they would succeed. And he said there'd never been such a, you know, well-done transition. But he was thinking about that way before he was even elected.

What were your own thoughts about getting in the White House?

It's funny. I used to worry about going into the White House.[26] This was before the campaign started or it got so close—you know, thinking all the things anyone thinks. It'll be a goldfish bowl, the Secret Service, I'll never see my husband. Then once Jack was nominated and everything, then you were so happy for him. And then once you got in it, I mean, you were just so happy for him, then you found out that it was really the happiest time of my life. It was when we were the closest—I didn't realize the physical closeness of having his office in the same building and seeing him so many times a day.

---

26. After the election, JFK found that the prospect so depressed his wife that he asked FDR, Jr., to reassure her.

There was always a great tension living there, but I used to—I remember thinking in the White House, "What was the matter with me that I spent so much time worrying, would it ruin our marriage to get in the White House?" And here it was so happy. And then I thought, you never can know what will be the best for you.[27] Then once we were in the White House, I used to worry all the time about getting out of it. And I used to think, what will you do with Jack, who will be fifty-one or something when he leaves? This caged tiger who's such a young age, still able to do so much. And sometimes I used to ask him about that and be worried. And he'd always soothe me and say, "You know, it won't be a problem when it happens."

What did—did he ever talk about what he might do after the presidency?

Yes. In the beginning, he used to sort of treat it as a joke and didn't like to talk about it, and he'll say, "Oh, I'll be an ambassador to Italy," or something. And that would get—but he was just teasing. And then I'd say, "Oh, you have to run for the Senate." And—again, this shows something wonderful about Bobby. Once I told Bobby that I was so worried and that if only Jack could run for the Senate, you know, have Teddy's seat, because Jack said they wouldn't take two brothers from there. So Bobby went and spoke to Teddy and came back and told me that Teddy said that he would not run when Johnny—that's what the brothers always called him—was out, which is so touching because that was the highest thing that I think Teddy could ever have hoped for. And anyway, I told Jack that because I always remember him saying how John Quincy Adams—

Yeah.

—came back and was a congressman all his life, and I thought he could be a senator and have a base and do all his other things from there. And Jack was really wounded when I told him that. And he was touched that I cared so much to be so worried, but he said, "No, I never, never would do that. And

---

27. In June 1962, Jacqueline wrote her friend William Walton, "My life here which I dreaded & which at first overwhelmed me—is now under control and the happiest time I have ever known—not for the position—but for the closeness of one's family. The last thing I expected to find in the W. House."

take that from Teddy? How could you think I'd do such a thing? So you go back to Bobby and tell him." But I think that shows something so close about those three brothers.

Yes.

That each would—there is Bobby making Teddy give up his prize, which Teddy does gladly, and then Jack refusing. They all worked with such love for each other. And just towards the end, Jack was thinking about being either publisher of a great paper or—I don't know. Bundy said to me the other night that he thought he might have ended up in television or something. I think he would have had to do something. He was getting rather excited about it. Sometimes he talked to Ben Bradlee about it—"Think we could buy the *Washington Post?*"—or something, rather jovially, but you could always tell when he was toying with an idea that pleased him in his mind. I think he would have gone around the world, written a book, done something with his library, and then really entered into that.

Where would you—where would you have lived, do you suppose?

Well, I just assumed we'd have lived in Cambridge, but maybe we wouldn't have. Or then I thought we should still live in Washington, but now I know that would have been completely wrong. And Jack always said we shouldn't live in Washington. He was right. It would be too hard for an ex-president to live in this city, which is so oriented to the new president. So maybe we'd have lived in—

He spoke to me about living in Cambridge part of the time. I got the impression that he would spend three or four months a year there and whether—

Sort of Cambridge, New York. I think that's what it sort of would have been.

The newspaper too he also—

You know, that would have been—

JACK, BOBBY, AND TEDDY, HYANNIS PORT, 1960

Considered as a possibility.

Yeah, that would have been such a full-time job with him. And Bundy said to me the other night—It just made me so sad, because Jack could have had his happiest years later. He said he sort of would have been the "President of the West." And you know, anywhere he went, he would have been—and anything he said people would have listened to so. And then Bundy said—I don't know if it's true or not—that after a while there would have been such a demand for him to come back that they might have had to do something about seeing if you could have a third term—you know, not in succession, but later. I used to say, "If only they could make a rule to keep you here forever"—because the one thing, when you leave the White House—and Jack always used to say this—is that you just have a cold fear going over you every day when you pick up the morning papers because you know how close it is—how some man far down can make a blunder, like Skybolt[28] or something, and everything can blow up. And the president just has to be watching everyone, everywhere, which only someone young and brilliant like Jack can do. So you'd have been just scared all the time, and knowing you had no power to do anything. But Jack always said, "Oh my God, no, I'd never. Eight years is enough in this place." Then you could see that it really did—it is the burdens, the way you look at Lincoln's pictures, over the years, and how much tireder and older he got. You can see that in Jack's pictures. Though he never spoke about—he would sometimes speak of the cares of it, but he'd never, you know, moan or feel sorry for himself. But he'd just say, like a, you know, a prisoner thinking of getting out—"Oh, no, eight years is enough in this place."

When you—when did you begin to think about restoring the White House? Was that before?

---

28. In 1962, the United States abruptly cancelled its program to build Skybolt missiles, including some promised to British prime minister Harold Macmillan as an incentive to shut down his own surface-to-air missile program. Washington's seemingly cavalier treatment of its British ally nicked Macmillan's prestige in his own country.

Yeah, I think once Jack was elected, or maybe whenever I thought I might be the president's wife. I just so knew that that had to be done. And then in Florida, between Christmas and inauguration, I had them send me a lot of books and things from the Library of Congress. And then once I was in there, I was in bed for about a week in the Queen's Room after inauguration, but I can remember seeing David Finley in bed and maybe John Walker,[29] so it started right away. Because just to look at that place! Maybe just because I'd been to the White House obviously, for some congressional receptions, and my little tour around with Mrs. Eisenhower.

How was that?

Well, this might be rather interesting, but—I'd read in the paper that it was customary for the first lady to show the new one around. And it was the last thing I wanted because, as I say, I was about to have this child. So I asked Tish[30] to get in touch with Mary Jane McCaffrey, Mrs. Eisenhower's secretary. Mrs. Eisenhower told Mrs. McCaffrey not to give our people any help.

What?

But Tish knew her or somehow, so she used to meet Mary Jane, sneak away for lunch somewhere. And Tish liked Mary Jane very much, and she'd tell her, you know, things that you ought to know. And so when I asked if I

---

29. DAVID FINLEY (1890–1977) was the first director of the National Gallery of Art; first chairman of the White House Historical Association, founded by Mrs. Kennedy; member of her White House Fine Arts Committee (he refused unwanted gifts on the committee's behalf); and, from 1950 to 1963, chair of the U.S. Commission of Fine Arts, which oversaw the design of federal buildings and monuments in the capital. As Jacqueline wrote another official, Bernard Boutin, she found Finley "a most cultured man + preservationist—but if only he would act more forcefully—so much could have been saved." John Walker III (1906–1995) was director of the National Gallery from 1956 to 1969. After the inauguration, she was still recovering from John's traumatic birth.

30. LETITIA BALDRIGE (1925–), tall, energetic, and intense, had preceded Jacqueline at Farmington and Vassar and was a family friend of the Auchinclosses. She served in two American embassies in Europe and had resigned as a Tiffany executive to start her own public relations business in Milan when, in July 1960, Jackie called her and asked her to be White House social secretary "if Jack makes it." When Baldrige left her job in the spring of 1963, JFK told her she was the most "emotional" woman he had ever met.

have to, you know, "If it's something Mrs. Eisenhower's going to do, could I do it soon, because I don't know when I'm going to have this baby?" And apparently when Mrs. McCaffrey gave Mrs. Eisenhower that message, she hit the ceiling and said, "This is my house, and nobody's going to see it"—and all of that. So the message was given back to me, and I was just filled with relief because how could I see anyway, make sense of walking around that enormous house, you know, in half an hour and a cup of tea? I was so glad I wouldn't have to do it. So then I was in the hospital and I had John and it was all rather dramatic. And then, I think, the press started building up on Mrs. Eisenhower. So she kept pestering Tish and everyone: Could I come and see it before we went to Florida that day? And I got out of the hospital about noon and we were to leave, I think, at two-thirty for Florida. And I didn't want to go. I'd never done anything but walk around the room and, just to be boring, after a caesarean it's very hard to walk and all that for a while. Like a fool, I said I'd go. I wish I hadn't. And then they said they'd have a wheelchair and everything. And there was never any wheelchair and you just were dragged around every floor, and not even asked to sit down, and brought in and out of the—past all the press. And when I got back, I really had a weeping fit and I couldn't stop crying for about two days. It was something that takes away your last strength when you don't have any left. So that wasn't very nice of Mrs. Eisenhower.[31]

A terrible thing. But why, do you suppose?

She was very funny. She always referred to it as "my house" and "my carpets," and I guess—didn't President Eisenhower say during the campaign, "Whenever Mamie thinks of that girl being in the White House she goes s-s-s-s-s"—or a raspberry or some charming sound? You know, there was this sort of venom or something there. And then, I guess, people used to say she'd go crazy when she'd hear all the things that we were doing. I suppose it's never that nice to hear about a new first lady who's doing things that you should have done, or something. "But I hear the Red Room is purple," she'd

---

31. She was later informed that Mamie Eisenhower had told her staff to keep a wheelchair behind an ornamental screen but only bring it out if Mrs. Kennedy specifically asked for it. After flying to Palm Beach, Jacqueline spent the next fortnight in bed.

PRESIDENT EISENHOWER MEETS WITH PRESIDENT-ELECT KENNEDY IN THE OVAL OFFICE

say. I don't blame her for that, but you'd think she might have been a little sympathetic before.

Yes. How did the President and President Eisenhower—

I guess President Eisenhower was fine when they went—the first meeting. I don't know what they talked about, but Eisenhower said, "And then I want to show you how quickly the helicopters can come here to get you away." And he pressed a button and they were there in three minutes and we flew away. So Eisenhower was fine with him.

What did the President think of Eisenhower?

Well, not much. You know, what did Joe Alsop say to me once—to us both?

"Eisenhower would be the worst president of the United States with the possible exception of James Buchanan." You know, Jack saw that all that could have been done, I mean, how really he kept us standing still and gave away—I don't think he thought much of him. But he used to say, "Look at that man's health. His cheeks were as pink as a something, and he's smiling and chuckling away." Oh, another thing we noticed that was really funny. In the White House, in the door of Jack's—the sill to Jack's office in his bedroom—we thought there were termites. They were just riddled with little holes. And so I asked the usher, Mr. West,[32] because I thought, is the White House going to fall down again like it did under Truman? It was the cleats from his golf shoes. You just wouldn't believe! I guess he must have just walked all around the White House in them.

The same thing in the President's office.

Yeah. Now they're worn away. You don't notice it as much.

Do you remember anything about Nixon's visit to Palm Beach? Didn't he come down in interregnum?

Oh, did Jack go to see him?

No, that's right. He was nearby in Florida.

In some hotel.[33]

That's right. The President went over to see him.

I think that must have been when I was either in the hospital or— That must have been before, right after the election.

---

32. **J. BERNARD WEST** (1912–1983), who served as chief usher from 1957 to 1969, directing the household staff of the White House, had a close and productive relationship with Mrs. Kennedy. He welcomed and provided crucial aid to her efforts to restore the White House.

33. The two men met in an oceanside villa near the Key Biscayne Hotel.

Lincolns Bedroom— the only room
in the whole place I like — we
cant change it — wouldnt want to

ROOM 223
1960

opposite end of hall from us —
guest rooms open off it —
Dont care about it —

EAST HALL
1960

JACQUELINE KENNEDY'S PRE-INAUGURAL NOTES ABOUT THE
LINCOLN BEDROOM (TOP) AND EAST HALL (BOTTOM)

UNVEILING THE FIRST WHITE HOUSE GUIDEBOOK—
THE WHITE HOUSE: A HISTORIC GUIDE

THE VIEW FROM PRESIDENT KENNEDY'S DESK IN THE OVAL OFFICE

That's right. I guess before your baby had come.

Yeah, when I was staying in Washington. I don't remember anything about—Did Smathers[34] go with Jack? Or did Smathers go another time and say how exhausted Mrs. Nixon was and that she was just lying like a cadaver in, you know, this chair, just not moving, with this bitter, desperate face and how terribly bitter she was. Somebody told Jack that. That, you know, she'd say the most terrible things and, "Let's have a recount!" and everything. I don't really remember about his conversation with Nixon. I mean, I remember him telling me about it, but now I can't remember what he said. Mrs. Kennedy told me to write everything down the first year I was married and I did, which is all just nothing—what Arthur Krock said to Dean Acheson, or something. And all the years when I should have been writing things down, I wasn't.

How did the President feel about the restoration?

The restoration?

Of the White House.

He was interested in it. He'd always get so interested in anything that I cared about, but then he was nervous about it. I mean, he wanted to be sure it was done the right way, so he sent Clark Clifford to see me. And Clark Clifford was really nervous because he tried to persuade me not to do it, which Jack never—

Why? On the grounds of politics?

He said, "You just can't touch the White House." He said, "It's so strange. Everyone, America feels so strangely about it, and look at the Truman Balcony. And if you try to make any changes, it will just be like that." And I

---

34. George Smathers, Democratic senator from Florida.

said, "It won't be like the Truman Balcony,"[35] and then I told him all about Harry du Pont[36] and all the people we hoped to get. And when I had to make my little pilgrimage to Harry du Pont. So as it went along bit by bit, and how you'd set this committee up and certain legal things and—then Clark was very good about setting up the guidebook.[37] So once Jack saw it was going along with sort of good counsel, I mean, he was so excited about it.

He was terribly proud of it. He used to love to take people around and show—

Yeah, when I found him that desk so early?[38] Well, that was about the first

---

35. President Truman had been denounced in 1947 for his apostasy in adding a second-floor balcony to the mansion's south front. In March 1963, Jacqueline wrote David Finley, whose job it was to rebut complaints about some of her innovations, "The President told me you were the only person who stood by President Truman on his balcony problem!—I didn't know that—but I should have—because it is so like you." The South Carolinian replied, "I must be quite honest. . . . I agreed with the other members of the Commission that an eighteenth century Georgian house, such as the White House, should not have the line of columns broken by a balcony, as was done in the nineteenth century plantation houses." But the president had taken his objection kindly, and "Mr. Truman and I were friends." Replying to Finley's notice that he would leave the Fine Arts Commission that year, Mrs. Kennedy wrote him one of the emotive longhand notes that won loyalty and affection from so many with whom she worked: "I never dreamed that such a terrible thing could happen—while I was alive— It is inconceivable to think of existing without you—What will I do? . . . I could never find words to express all the gratitude and affection and indebtedness I will feel for you until my dying day."

36. HENRY DU PONT (1880–1969), the Republican heir to a famous fortune, was a well-respected expert on American art, furniture, and horticulture, and had done much to reshape Winterthur, his family's old 900-acre Delaware estate, opened to the public in 1951, with period rooms and gardens. Du Pont chaired Mrs. Kennedy's bipartisan Fine Arts Committee of prominent Americans advising her on the White House restoration. As an Americanist, du Pont was sometimes distressed by the French-inspired improvisations of Stéphane Boudin. On some of his visits, du Pont would rearrange White House furniture, after which Jacqueline would discreetly have it moved back. When du Pont was trying to block one of Boudin's designs for the Green Room, she wrote J. B. West, "Please enclose this humble letter soliciting his approval. If we don't get it he will have the shock of me doing it anyway!"

37. Clifford also helped Mrs. Kennedy establish the White House Historical Association, which to this day supports the upkeep of the mansion's public rooms, helps first families to acquire paintings and furniture, and publishes contemporary versions of the guidebook, *The White House: An Historic Guide,* and books on presidents, first ladies, and the White House gardens, all launched by Jacqueline Kennedy. The guidebook was purchased by a half million readers during its first six months, swelling the coffers of the new association.

38. Among neglected White House treasures, Jacqueline discovered the Victorian desk made from the H.M.S. *Resolute* that became famous in JFK's Oval Office and has been used by every president but one since Gerald Ford.

MRS. KENNEDY DURING HER TELEVISED TOUR OF THE WHITE HOUSE

thing and then—but he was riveted—and, oh, the White House television tour [39]—he used to watch all the time. He was so sweet, the way he was proud of me. And then the guidebook was another thing. You saw that you could never get enough money to do it. You know, people weren't going to give up good pieces of furniture, or you'd have ninety-nine cups of tea with some old lady and she'd give you fifty dollars. So, I'd always been trying to write this guidebook. But the curator would never sit and work on it—Mrs. Pearce. She

---

39. In February 1962, Jacqueline's hour-long tour of the White House restoration was seen by 56 million television viewers and won her an honorary Emmy.

PRESIDENT AND MRS. KENNEDY IN THE WHITE HOUSE

liked to have tea with other curators. It was very hard, but we got that written. But then Jack McNally in Jack's—who was sort of this happy little Irishman who was in charge of taking people through the White House and the tours— said it would be an absolute outrage and desecrate our nation's—you know, the White House—to have money exchanging hands there and everything. And a lot of people said that you couldn't sell a guidebook there. And I said you could because it would be one of such quality. And so, when I told Jack that, you know, he'd had more opinions saying not to do it, but he listened to me and said, "All right, go ahead." Which was nice of him and then it did turn out to be all right.

Was there ever any criticism of the things that you did in the White House in these years?

Never—no, the most incredible interest. And then the tours would start going. And every night he'd come home saying, "We had more people today"— this would be after you'd found the Monroe pier table or something—"than the Eisenhowers had in their first two years." And oftentimes he—and then the guidebook was selling a lot—he'd always be teasing McNally about it. So he was just so proud. I was so happy that I had—could do something that made him proud of me. Because I'll tell you one wonderful thing about him. I was really—I was never any different once I was in the White House than I was before, but the press made you different. Suddenly, everything that'd been a liability before—your hair, that you spoke French, that you didn't just adore to campaign, and you didn't bake bread with flour up to your arms— you know, everyone thought I was a snob and hated politics. Well, Jack never made me feel that I was a liability to him, but I was. And then I was having a baby and couldn't campaign. And when we got in the White House all the things that I'd always done suddenly became wonderful because anything the First Lady does that's different, everyone seizes on—and I was so happy for Jack, especially now that it was only three years together that he could be proud of me then.[40] Because it made him so happy—it made me so happy. So those were our happiest years.

---

40. Mrs. Kennedy is being modest here. From the time of their grand trip to Paris of May 1961 and, especially, her vastly popular televised tour of the White House, she was not only no longer a political liability but would have been a major asset to the President when he ran for reelection in 1964. Knowing

HEAD OF A YOUNG BOY AND A FIGURE OF HERAKLES—
ROMAN SCULPTURES PURCHASED BY JOHN F. KENNEDY DURING
HIS VISIT TO ROME IN 1963 AS GIFTS FOR HIS WIFE

He was terribly proud. And, he was proud of the knowledge that he got from you. He liked to sort of talk about furniture and paintings, which are things that he didn't—had not known a great deal about at one point in his life.

I know, and he really started to know about them. He got interested in sculpture. I forget how. Oh, Stas had given Lee a Roman head one Christmas. And then it was the first thing he saw that he really started to care about him-

this, JFK used strong persuasion to have her agree to accompany him on planned trips to Texas and California that were to be the forerunner of that campaign. In her presence at the Rice Hotel in Houston on their final evening together, the President asked Dave Powers to compare the crowd that had greeted them that day to the one when he had come to Houston alone the previous year. Kennedy beamed when Powers said it was about the same, "but there were about a hundred thousand more for Jackie."

self. And he used to go into Klejman, opposite Parke-Bernet in New York—opposite the Carlyle,[41] whenever he was there—and look, and he started to buy all the Greek sculpture that you see in this room—all the Egyptian sculpture. And then he really knew his field. Of course, he loved it because anything that old he'd say, "Think, this is 500 B.C." But he had such an eye. A thing about his taste—when Boudin, the French—much more than decorator—he's really a scholar, from Jansen would be around, so many things that he'd say how to arrange a room or hang pictures,[42] I'd be in doubt about. Then I'd ask Jack what he thought without telling him what Boudin thought. And Jack, about five or six different times, which I have written down, would say the same as Boudin. He had—I was so disappointed in the Blue Room when I first saw it. I thought it was too much.[43] You know, Jack liked it. He really had this eye and he'd pick out the best things. He just had taste in every facet of his character—for people, for books, for sculpture, for furniture, for rooms, for houses. He bought our house in Georgetown because the doorknob was old, which he liked, and he liked the sort of old look of it. For our tenth anniversary, he was so sweet. You know, after dinner was the time for present giving. And suddenly into the room comes Provi, our little maid, with about thirty different boxes. They were all from Klejman, except for one—he knew I used to collect drawings so he had gotten a couple of drawings

41. During the White House years, the Kennedys kept an apartment at the Carlyle Hotel in New York. Parke-Bernet was an auction house and J. J. Klejman an antiquities dealer.

42. STÉPHANE BOUDIN (1888–1967), president of the Paris design firm Maison Jansen, who had advised on restoration at Versailles, Malmaison, Leeds Castle, and other historical monuments, was quietly secured by Mrs. Kennedy to guide her on her White House project. She told one of her aides, "I've learned more about architecture from Boudin than from all the books I could have read." To avoid public controversy about employing a non-American, her staff took pains, with Boudin's consent, to keep him in the background. But privately Jacqueline thought it completely appropriate that she consult a Frenchman, because of French contributions to the American Revolution, the French talent for using architecture and the arts to convey national glory, and because, as she considered how the White House should look, she was captivated by the sensibilities of Presidents Jefferson and Monroe, both former ambassadors to Paris, who adorned the mansion with French and French-inspired artifacts, painting, and furniture.

43. She feared a public outcry against the room's new design, which was no longer dominated by blue. But by 1980, she considered the chamber "Boudin's masterpiece," with its "sense of state, ceremony, arrival and grandeur."

EGYPTIAN SNAKE BRACELET JOHN F. KENNEDY GAVE
TO JACQUELINE ON THEIR TENTH WEDDING ANNIVERSARY

from Wildenstein.[44] And when I think that when we were first married, he always used to give me things he liked, like a letter of Byron or a letter of John Quincy Adams or something, which was fine. And I could see the present that he wanted me to choose the most was this Alexandrian bracelet. It's terribly simple, gold, sort of a snake. And it was the simplest thing of all and I could just see how he loved it. He'd just hold it in his hand. So, you know, that was a special present and he wouldn't say which one he wanted to give me, but I could tell so I chose it.

How would he have selected those? Catalogue? He wouldn't—

Oh, well, I think he had Klejman send him—he'd talk to him on the phone and had him send up a lot of things. And then he had about fifty things up in his room because he'd been through—all through dinner, he was locked in his room. And he sifted out about the fifteen he thought I'd like. And one of them was an Assyrian horse bit because it so fascinated him that—that had been used in the, I don't know, the wars against the Persians or something—

---

44. Wildenstein & Company was a Manhattan art gallery.

Persian horse bit, maybe. Sylvia Whitehouse[45] was there that evening and she laughed. It was so sweet to see how Jack loved it, and she said, "I do think we might have something a bit more sentimental for your tenth anniversary." But he wanted to take it down and try it on Caroline's pony the next day to see if it really worked. *[Schlesinger laughs]*

Do you remember anything about your first day in the White House?

Yes, I do. Didn't I tell you about it?

Not on the tape.

Oh. With Dr. [Travell]—well, the next morning I was just laid out in the Queen's bed. We were living at that end of the house then because our end was being painted.

This is Inauguration Day—or day after?

The day after Inauguration. And she had my leg up in the air trying to get some kink out of it. I just couldn't walk. And who burst in the door but Jack and President Truman, and poor President Truman just turned scarlet. I don't think he'd ever seen a woman but his wife in bed in a nightgown before. And so they burst out and then Jack stuck his head in and said, "Can I bring him in?" And, you know, then we had a very jolly talk there. Then he also brought Robert Frost in that day. And then at night, we'd have supper always in the little Lincoln Sitting Room on trays. You know, I loved those days.

What about Inauguration Day? Do you remember anything about the few days before Inauguration—about the speech and so on? Was the President worried about that?

---

45. SYLVIA WHITEHOUSE BLAKE (1930–) had been Jacqueline's Vassar classmate and one of her bridesmaids. Her husband, Robert, was an American diplomat.

A HANDWRITTEN DRAFT OF THE INAUGURAL ADDRESS

Oh, well, I can remember him writing his speech in Florida.[46] You know, all different yellow pages and then bringing in and reading you parts of it and crossing out other parts. I never heard him really read the whole thing until Inauguration Day, but each part I remember listening, knowing that I'd heard it before. We had this small bedroom in Florida and there were so many people

---

46. In the ground-floor corner bedroom of his parents' house in Palm Beach.

146

in the other part of the house—I was in bed most of the time. And Jack would come in with his cigar, you know, puffing away, with a big pad of yellow pages and he'd be sitting—and he'd sit on the edge of my bed and he'd read me some things he'd written and then he'd flip them over, scribble something, and then he'd pile it on his desk, which was just overflowing with papers, and papers were just all around that room. Then he'd go out and have a meeting or sometimes he'd play golf. He was just so happy then—he looked so well, you know, they were such happy days for him.

Did he worry at all in the interregnum about anything, as far as you could see?

No, what he was doing then is solving everything that was coming up, he was dealing with it. And that was always when he was the happiest. He never was worried because he always said, "Someone has to do this job" —what is it?— "and it's always been done with humans." There's a very good quote of his there somewhere.[47] But he knew he could do it as well as anyone else. And so he was just delighted at last to be being able to. But then at night, we'd get up for supper and then he might read some part in the library or ask his—the rest of his family or whoever was there.

Who were around then?

Well, Mr. and Mrs. Kennedy. And I suppose Bobby must have come in and out a couple of times. There was always someone—then Sam Rayburn[48] and Lyndon and Lady Bird came down once. I tell you, you'd go in the bathroom and you'd forget to bring your wrapper and you couldn't get out because Pierre Salinger[49] would be having a press briefing in your bedroom. You'd just go mad. So then Jack would grab up those big pages and stuff them in his briefcase, I guess, when he went back to Washington. I don't know when it was written.

---

47. In what he came to call his "peace speech" at American University in June 1963, Kennedy said, "These problems are man-made. Therefore they can be solved by man. And man can be as big as he wants."

48. SAMUEL RAYBURN (1882–1961) was speaker of the house until 1961 and a mentor to the young congressman Lyndon Johnson.

49. PIERRE SALINGER (1925–2004) of San Francisco, bon vivant, former journalist and aide to Robert Kennedy, served as press secretary during the 1960 campaign and White House years.

He came back early that week, as I recall, and you came up on Wednesday, probably.

Yes, I came up the day of the gala, whichever day that was.

The day was Thursday.

That's right.

How did you like the gala?[50]

Oh, it was all right. You know, it was such a festive evening and I thought that snow was so pretty. The gala—I didn't really—and I had to leave—halfway through it. I remember one—parts of it I liked—I remember one thing I thought was so awful, it was a man named—Alan King? He was telling all these horrible jokes about marriage—I mean, the wife is a shrew, and the—I just thought that's so sad when comedians do that. But otherwise, you know, everyone was excited. And then—

Where'd you sleep on Wednesday night?

At our house, 3307 N. And then the next morning—

Was that hard? Were you all excited?

Oh, yes!

Did you sleep all right that night?

Well, it was like children waiting for Christmas or something that night. Because I was awake when Jack came home. And I think there'd been a dinner that his father had organized at Paul Young's[51] or something, later? But you

---

50. **FRANK SINATRA** (1915–1998), singer and JFK friend, had organized a pre-inaugural gala featuring Hollywood performers such as singer Nat King Cole and comedian Alan King.

51. A Washington restaurant.

know, I couldn't go to sleep, I was awake when he came home. It was just such a night to share together because that night we were, you know, in the same bed. Then the next morning getting up and getting dressed, and the snowstorm—all the excitement, leaving our house. I never thought then that I was leaving it for the last time. I mean, I never thought of sort of saying goodbye to it. And then going to the White House, and we all had coffee in the Red Room before. I remember sitting on that sofa next to Mrs. Nixon, who looked really pretty that day. You could see she could really be rather New York chic when she wanted, in sort of a black Persian lamb coat and hat. And Mrs. Eisenhower—it was very nice, you know, everybody was there drinking coffee and things. And as we left, I rode with Styles Bridges[52] and Mamie Eisenhower to the Capitol. And as I was sitting in the car, President Eisenhower and Jack came out afterwards or something and she said, "Look at Ike in his top hat. He looks just like Paddy the Irishman!"[53] And then I think she reali— And then on the way to the Capitol, she said that it would be the first time in her life, tonight, when she would dial her own telephone number because she'd had a switchboard for thirty years. I kept thinking how those people have been taken care of all their lives—but anyway. You know, it was rather making conversation up there. Then, all the inauguration and Cardinal Cushing and the lectern burning, and then poor Robert Frost.[54]

There's a marvelous picture with the expression of anxiety on your face in solicitude for Robert Frost. What happened there?

Oh, yeah. Well, you could see him, it was such a glare from the snow that he really couldn't see what was written on the paper. And then Lyndon got up and held his hat over it, but the poor man still couldn't see. And he looked like he was going to cry, he just sounded so sad, but then, thank heavens,

---

52. **STYLES BRIDGES** (1898–1961) was a Republican New Hampshire senator and one of those responsible for inaugural arrangements.

53. Not the most diplomatic comment Mrs. Eisenhower could have made sitting beside the wife of the man who was now the nation's most prominent Irish-American.

54. During Cushing's very long invocation, smoke curled up from the lectern, due to an electrical malfunction, and when the aged poet rose to read a poem he had written for the occasion, he was blinded by sunlight and so instead recited his classic "The Gift Outright."

PRESIDENT KENNEDY DELIVERING HIS INAUGURAL ADDRESS

MRS. KENNEDY GREETS HER HUSBAND FOR THE FIRST TIME AS PRESIDENT

he knew "The Gift Outright." And oh, and watching Jack when he said that and everything. And then I never had a chance—as I was sitting about three away and everyone says, "Why didn't Jack kiss you after?"—which of course, he would never do there. But you had to march out in such order that I was about eight behind him—with women, or something. And I so badly wanted to see him before the lunch, just to see him alone. I went to a room with all the ladies, where they had sherry and coffee, and he was with the men. And I caught up to him in the Capitol and, oh, I was just so proud of him. And there's a picture where I have my hand on his chin and he's just looking at me and there really were tears in his eyes. Suddenly a flash came because I didn't think there was anyone there. In the papers it said, "Wife chucks him under chin." I mean, that was so much more emotional than any kiss because his eyes really did fill with tears. *[whispers]* Just say, "Oh, Jack"—you know—"what a day!" And then the lunch in the old Supreme Court chamber in the Capitol. I remember everybody was sending their little menu card around to be autographed, it was very jolly. With Truman—I sat next to Warren.[55] Then we got in the car for that parade, sort of not quite knowing how to wave. And then when we got to the White House, I guess we went in for a minute and walked out to the stand. Oh, Jack was just so happy. They had hot soup or something in that stand, and he wanted to see every single bit of that parade. He was just so proud and he was—they'd keep telling us how it would be running late and I left after a couple of hours because again, I was really so tired that day. And, but he stayed until just nightfall—I think he was the last person there, you know, and came in and there was a big reception downstairs. Again I was in bed. And that night, he was to go to a dinner for all the cabinet at Jane Wheeler's[56] and I was to stay and have dinner in bed and everything, and he would come back and pick me up to go to the first ball. And about 9 o'clock or something, when it was time to start getting dressed, again I couldn't get out of bed. I just couldn't move. And so I called up Dr. Travell just frantic and she came running over. And she had two pills, a green one and an orange one, and she told me to take the orange one. So I did and I said, "What is it?" And then she told me it was Dexadrine, which I'd never taken in my life—and that I never have again. But thank God, it really did its trick because then you could get dressed. And then Jack came, and he came upstairs and he brought me down to the Red Room. There were a few people—the Foleys,[57] I remember. We all had a toast of champagne and he did—he liked how I looked and he said something so nice and we went off to that ball. It

---

55. EARL WARREN (1891–1974) was the governor of California whom Eisenhower had appointed as chief justice in 1953. Although a Republican, Warren had been glad to swear in Kennedy, rather than Nixon, who was a political enemy.

56. JANE WHEELER (1921–2008) was a Washington hostess and early Kennedy supporter.

57. EDWARD FOLEY (1906–1982) was a well-known Washington lawyer, former undersecretary of the treasury under Truman, and chairman of JFK's inaugural committee.

PRESIDENT AND MRS. KENNEDY ATTENDING THE FIRST INAUGURAL BALL AT THE NATIONAL GUARD ARMORY, WASHINGTON, D.C.

was so funny with the aides, because the old aide, the head of the White House aides, kept trying to be with Jack all evening and the other three were jumping in and out. And then to come into that ball, that was exciting. And there's that wonderful picture of him sort of pointing. Then we went to one at the Mayflower where Lyndon was right next to us at that one. And then we went to a third one at the Wardman Park and just on the way, it was like Cinderella and the clock striking midnight, I guess that pill wore off because I just couldn't get out of the car. And so Jack said, "You go home now," and he sent me home with that aide. And I guess he went on to all the other balls, and then to Joe Alsop's.

I was staying with Joe then.

And I was so happy. Sometimes I thought later I wish I'd been able to sort of share all that night with him. But he had such a wonderful time, and then he must have gotten home about three or four, but he came in and woke me up. And I slept in the Queen's room. He slept in the Lincoln Room then, so that was his first night in Lincoln's bed. And—well, he was just so happy. Then the next morning when he woke up, very early, well, I was awake too, and so I went in that room and it's the sunniest room. You know, we both sat on that bed. I mean, you did again feel like two children. Think of yourselves sitting in Lincoln's bed! And he went off with that wonderful springing step to his office and then again, I told you, he'd come crashing back with Truman and Robert Frost. They were such happy days for him. And he couldn't wait to get the children back. And all that end smelled so of paint, but he'd keep saying, "You've got to bring them back soon." He really missed them. I guess they came back about two weeks later.

What was your theory of sort of relaxation and entertainment at the beginning at the White House?

Well, it was really what it had always been. Jack was so like his father in that he hated to leave his house, whether it was Georgetown, the Cape, whether we had my mother's house in Newport, and even in the White House, he hated to go out.

He always hated to go out?

Yeah, his father loved to stay home and he thought he had the best food and everything that's best in your house. So Jack was brought up—you know, as long as everything was nice at home. He loved to go to Joe's[58] because the food was always so good. So, it was exactly as it'd been in the past. You'd have the Bartletts, or David Gore, who was around just after inauguration. He wasn't ambassador yet. Or Max Freedman once, or it was just suppers on trays then. Or if any of his family were down or—

You went out more that first winter than later.

We only went out about twice that first winter—three times. Once to Lorraine Cooper's because Jack—it was the first time we ever went out and Jack loved Cooper. He didn't really want to go to that dinner because Lorraine's dinners were always so big. It really wasn't much fun for him. And then, we went once to Joe's when Jack—and once to Rowlie's. Jock Whitney was at Rowlie's and everybody—they found out about that because the snowplows came and scraped off Rowlie's street before or something.[59] So, because those three things caused such commotion—you'd think we went out every night—those were the only three times. And I forget what we went to Joe's for. Then we really stopped—oh, maybe once in the spring again, we went to Joe's. But we hardly ever went out after—you know, it proved such a production and everything. It was really more fun to have people come to you. He'd always work very late and you'd always have to juggle the children's naps or something so they'd be there when he came home. He liked to see them for about a half an hour before dinner. And, well, if you were going out and you want to take a bath and change and leave, it was just a nuisance. So, that's one thing that you never missed, being in the White House.

---

58. Refers to the Alsop house.

59. ROWLAND EVANS (1921–2001) was a Washington reporter for the *New York Herald Tribune*. John Hay "Jock" Whitney (1904–1982) was the paper's owner and publisher.

How about—how often would you have movies, for example?

Not very often. Gosh, we didn't—I don't know, maybe four times a year or something? I think—

Oh, more than that, surely.

Well, the first winter we might have had a few. Really, not very many because I can only think of about four or five that we saw the whole time there. I think in the summer he might have some.

It seems to me, I'm sure I've seen that many with you or him.

You think?

None of which he ever stayed for more than about half an hour, though.

I remember the French—oh, *The Last Year at Marienbad*—oh, he hated that. Yeah, or sometimes there'd be a USIA thing he'd want me to see or something, you know, something he'd done. But really not so many.

How would he begin the day? What time would he get up?

He'd get up a quarter of eight and George[60] would come knock on our bedroom door and then he'd get up and go into his bedroom and have breakfast there. I'd ring for breakfast at the same time or I'd sleep a little later. And then the children would come in and it was so incredible because they'd rush to turn on the television set and you'd hear this roar, full blast, of cartoons or that exercise man. And Jack would be sitting there—he had breakfast in a chair with a tray in front of him, you know, reading the fifty morning papers or sheafs of all those briefing books to go over with Bundy, and this racket around. Then he'd take a bath. And I always thought it was so funny

---

60. **GEORGE THOMAS** (1908–1980) was an African-American from Berryville, Virginia, who was JFK's longtime valet and lived on the third floor of the White House.

for people who used his bathroom—guests—it was the bathroom that men could use after dinner. Because all along his tub were all these little floating animals, ducks and pink pigs and things. Because he said, "Give me something to do to amuse John while I'm in my bath." So John would float all these things around. And, he just could have those children tumbling around him. And then he'd always come in before he went over to the office—come into my room—I mean, I'd only be half asleep or else I'd be having breakfast—and see me. And he used to take Caroline over to the office with him every day—

That would be about 9:30.

Yeah. Quarter of eight—yeah, maybe a little earlier, I suppose. He'd be, I guess, over an hour having breakfast, reading the papers and taking a bath. And later on, it used to be John's treat to walk to the office with him every day.

Had George always been in the White House or did you—had he always been with the President or what?

George had been with Jack when he first came to Congress.

Oh, he came in—

He found him. He was with Arthur Krock[61] before and Arthur told Jack about him. Then he left for a couple of years and worked for Ethel's mother. Then he came back to us—he wasn't with us at Hickory Hill—he came back '57 and he was with us ever since.

Where is he now?

---

61. ARTHUR KROCK (1886–1974) was a conservative *New York Times* columnist. Krock had once been a close friend of Joseph Kennedy's and adviser to Jack while writing *Why England Slept*, but had broken with them in 1960 over JFK's growing liberalism while seeking the presidency. An old friend of Jacqueline's grandfather, John V. Bouvier, Jr., and her stepfather, Hugh Auchincloss, Krock had helped her get her job on the *Washington Times-Herald*.

PRESIDENT KENNEDY PLAYING WITH CAROLINE AND JOHN ON HIS WAY TO THE OVAL OFFICE

He's somewhere. I mean, he lives where he—in Washington. He comes to see us a lot. I mean, we'll always take care of him. But poor George, he really got the shakes—I mean, he couldn't—I asked him if he wanted to work here, but he's just too old, he dropped—and in the White House, all he'd do that used to amuse Jack so. He'd open the door so that some other slave could carry in Jack's breakfast tray. The only thing he did was pull open the curtains and then turn on the bath, and then he'd go up and all the little White House Mess boys were shining his shoes and everything.

Then the President would always come back for lunch.

Yeah.

I don't think he ever had lunch in his office, did he?

Never, unless he had a business lunch, you know, in the family dining room downstairs. He always kept our floor—we put in the dining room—he'd keep all his business lunches downstairs. And he knew that that was our private place. It's so different from now, where everyone gets the tour of the bathrooms and things.[62] Maybe because Jack had young children.

And he very rarely liked to have—he didn't like business lunches, did he? It seemed to me that he was very—he much preferred to see people in his office rather than have luncheons.

Yeah, they were really heavy. Then he'd come up, you know, they were hard for him. And you're always awfully tired at the end of one of those White House mornings in your office and your nerves are on edge. So to have to go through a long lunch and wine and everything. And then he'd come up afterwards and still try to take whatever little nap he could. He never took a nap before, but in the White House, I think he made up his mind he would because it was so good for his health. Something was always

---

62. Referring to the exuberant tours of the White House given by Lyndon Johnson since becoming president.

cracking up before. And he'd always said that Winston Churchill used to do it and he'd often say how much more, you know, staying power it gave him. But his naps, my Lord, did I tell you about them?

No.

Well, it'd be forty-five minutes and he'd get completely undressed and into his pajamas and into bed and go to sleep and then wake up again. And I often used to—

And he could go to sleep—put himself to sleep, could he?

Yeah. I used to think, for a forty-five-minute nap, would you bother to take off all your clothes? It would take me forty-five minutes to just snuggle down and start to doze off. Sometimes when he had lunch in his room, in bed he'd have it. I'd have lunch in there with him and then I'd close the curtains and open the window for his nap and then I'd wake him up from it. And then I'd sit around while he got dressed. That was my hour instead of the children's. It would just be like clockwork—forty-five minutes and he'd be back in his office. And then he'd always work until, well, after eight at night.

Would he swim every day or was that only the later part after—

He came to the White House in the best physical condition that he was ever in in his life. He had muscles and everything. He played golf, sort of eighteen holes—all these things he hadn't been able to do for a long time. And then he sat in his desk, without moving, for six weeks. He didn't walk around the driveway, he didn't swim, and suddenly his back went bad. He'd lost all the muscle tone. So then it was awful because he was really in pain. Dr. Travell would come and pump him full with Novocain and finally we got— *[to John]* Oh, out!

JOHN: **Why?** [John leaves.]

Really the fact he wasn't exercising—

Yes, you see, he'd never done much exercise anyway, but as he said, the campaign of jumping in and out of cars, walking, you know, kept him fit. And then for the first time in his life, he'd really had from election to inauguration a lot of it in Florida, to play golf—I don't know, twice a week or three times—to swim, to walk on the beach. He never had such a long period of daily some kind of exercise. And he just lost it all sitting in his desk. And then he went back to Dr. Travell, but all that Novocain, it didn't do any good anymore. You know, it wasn't until the next October—I got so mad at her because then other doctors were trying to bring in Hans Kraus, who could build you up through exercises.[63] Well, all these doctors are so jealous of each other and she wouldn't let Kraus come in. And finally, I'd sat by so many times while doctors did things to Jack—well, doctors just pushed Jack all over the place—that I really got mad and got in there and got the back surgeon and the other—everybody and just forced her to have—him to have Kraus. And Kraus started these series of exercises which he did every evening with the navy chief. You know, like lift—trying to touch your toes or lying on your stomach and trying to raise one leg. And you could just see—I mean, he still was in pain a lot that winter—oh, and it went out really badly, you remember, in May in Canada. But by the next October, when he started to do these, after a while—

But he was weak before he went to Canada? In other words, it wasn't the planting the tree in Canada which caused it all, it was really the lack of exercise that really did it.

Yeah. And—

---

63. **HANS KRAUS (1905–1995)**, an Austrian-born mountain climber, was an orthopedic expert who extolled exercise as a remedy for back injuries. When JFK's back problems grew worse in 1961, he consulted Kraus, who agreed to take on the case as long as Dr. Travell was removed from the President's case and that Kraus would be able to reach Kennedy at any time by direct telephone. Aghast that Travell had simply cured the President's pain with Novocain and let the President's chest, abdominal, and back muscles atrophy, Dr. Kraus warned him that he would soon need a wheelchair unless he began a strict regimen. Under Kraus's care, JFK was telling friends by 1963 that he had never felt better and felt hearty enough to resume golf. Dr. Travell, who was well-known to the public as the first female White House doctor, was allowed to keep her title and observe at least the fiction that she was still caring for the President.

How long a day would he exercise?

Oh, well, these exercises with the chief would just take about fifteen minutes. You know, sort of sitting-up exercises or then they'd hold your legs so you'd have to try to lift it up against it. But you know, Jack could never touch his toes. He couldn't get his hands down any farther than his knees standing up. He couldn't put on his shoes before—sort of bend over that far.

Oh, really?

Well, he could if he'd lift his foot in his lap, or something. So, as I say, he wasn't a cripple—that sounds funny—he could do everything, but you'd just notice when you'd see him trying to reach for something he'd dropped on the floor, how stiff he was. My Lord, at the end, in a couple of months, he could touch his toes, he could do all these things he'd never been able to do—knee bends— So then once Kraus started—then that was, you know, encouraging, because he'd get so discouraged. That's when you'd see him in black periods. Well, he'd tried and he had every doctor and Dr. Travell had given him the tenth treatment and before she always helped. And now there didn't seem to be any answer. So then Kraus then helped him and that cheered him up.

Your White House parties—the best parties I've ever gone to—were they—

Well, I'll tell you why I thought of having them. The one thing I noticed was that I could get away from the White House and I could go to New York and see a play or go to a restaurant. Jack never liked to go out before, when he was in his home, but he had liked to stop in New York a couple of days, see a play, go to Pavillon[64]—see some different people. I mean, we were young and we were gay and you couldn't cut all that off from him and just leave his life full of worry. So the first one I thought of having, it was when Lee was over. I thought that would be an excuse to have one. And I thought of all these people from New York or—everywhere, the people he wasn't seeing—that's why so few people from Washington—sort of came

---

64. Joseph Kennedy was one of the owners of the New York restaurant Le Pavillon.

GLEN ORA, MIDDLEBURG, VIRGINIA

to them, in a way. And it turned out—well, he loved it. So then he'd say, well, let's have—every now and then— I think we only had about five in all. But after, maybe after three or four months or when there'd been sort of a ghastly month and I had such a stiff neck from being tense, or he'd been having a bad time, he'd say, "Let's have another one of those parties." And, well, he just loved them because then he was—it's sort of a way to renew yourself. He'd always tell me to go visit Lee or go to New York or something, when he could see the tension of there was getting to me. Because you see, when we came in there, I was very weak and plus all the thing of the campaign, plus the baby, plus—and to hit that place running and start to do all the work of running the house, getting a chef, doing the food, the flowers, the reconstruction, restoration, whatever it is. Sometimes at the end of the day you'd just feel one jump away from tears, but you wanted to be so cheerful for Jack when he came home, which I nearly always was, but he could see when it was getting to be a bit too much. And that first winter—I couldn't sleep very well. He'd always send you away and—when he knew you were tired. And then you'd come back so happy again. I always think our whole married life was renewals of love after, you know, brief separations.

JACQUELINE KENNEDY RIDING AT GLEN ORA WITH CAROLINE AND JOHN

Where would you go on the weekends in that first—

Glen Ora.

Glen Ora.

We didn't use—it's funny, he never thought of using Camp David, either. I'd sort of had this thing about having to get a house in the country, and he'd hated Camp David when he went there with Eisenhower. He said, "It's the most depressing-looking place"—which it is, from the outside. Then Taz Shepard, his naval aide, kept pestering and pestering him to go there. And Tish used to say to me, "The navy's so hurt and demoralized he won't go there." So finally, one weekend, he said, "All right, let's go to Camp David." Then he got to rather love it because it is comfortable, so then we'd go there a bit, but go to Glen Ora[65] mostly on weekends, which he didn't like really, at all.

---

65. An estate in Middleburg, Virginia, which the Kennedys rented in 1961 and 1962. Writing to a friend

RIDING AND FOX HUNTING

Why didn't he like Glen Ora?

Well, you know, there's nothing for him to do. Camp David, I suppose, you could have a movie at night. And it's just a rather small, dark house. He liked to see me ride—you know, be happy being out in the air all day, because he always said Daddy[66] told him, "Keep her riding and she'll always be in a good mood." Well, in a way, the thing that that means is exercise and fresh air, which is true. You make an extra effort every day to go out and play tennis, though I couldn't play it. Or just get in the air, walk ten times around the South Lawn. Because if you just stay indoors and smoke cigarettes and work at your desk and talk on the telephone until you know your throat is all tight, you can't be gay for anyone. Then we started to go to Camp David that spring. And he'd always come down. I think rarely he came Friday evening, he'd always come Saturday, sort of at lunchtime. And then he'd sleep all Saturday afternoon and then he'd watch, all the afternoon, television or something from his bed. It was just a letdown for him. And we'd always have a friend for the weekend, have dinner, go to bed early, church the next day, papers, another nap. Because he said, "I don't really care about Glen Ora because all I use it for is to sleep."

He preserved his weekends very faithfully. Almost every weekend he went off.

Practically every weekend, except the—which was the—'62? There'd be some weekend, election things he'd have to do, or a couple of fund-raising things in New York or something? And then this fall, we did have two or three weekends at our new house in Virginia—and—[67]

He was off on trips a couple of times.

---

in July 1962, she called it "the most private place I can think of to balance our life in the White House." Campaigns, travels, and pregnancy had kept Jacqueline from riding regularly since her marriage in 1953.

66. JOHN VERNOU BOUVIER III (1891–1957) was the debonair father whom Jacqueline adored.

67. In 1963, the Kennedys built a seven-bedroom yellow ochre stucco and fieldstone house, with a breathtaking view of the Blue Ridge Mountains, on thirty-nine acres in Atoka, Virginia. They named it Wexford, for the Kennedy ancestral home in Ireland.

Tampa, Dallas.[68] You know, because it was a campaign year, you didn't expect to have many.

Had you always known Tish? Is she an old friend?

I'd known Tish when I was at school in Paris. She was with Mrs. Bruce at the embassy there and then when I was in Rome, she was with Mrs. Luce.[69] And she was just such a mountain of energy. But I remember just thinking, "I can't go in there unless I have Tish," and calling her up right after Jack was nominated. Nominated or elected? I guess it was elected. And, well, Tish is great and I love her but, so much of her energy was rather extra that I—now that I think of it, she really made me tireder than I'd had to be. Because she'd send you so many extra things that you really didn't have to answer. And on weekends, she'd keep sending folders down until I stopped it. Or as I'd be sitting with Jack in the evening, some messenger would come flying in and throw a folder in my lap. You know, it began to drive me crazy, and then Jack told me that I must stop using my desk in the East Hall—the West Hall, where we sat. He said, "You can't have your desk in the room where we sit, where we live." So then he made me move it down to the Treaty Room. And it was so good because often, when we'd be alone in the evening, he'd be looking at a book or doing some of his papers, and I'd go grab a folder off my desk and try to check off all the little things I had to do. But it would just put you in not the right atmosphere that you should be in when your husband

---

68. JFK spent the long weekend before Texas in Tampa and Miami, where he made speeches, and Palm Beach, where he stayed at his father's house with his Harvard friend Torbert Macdonald and watched televised football. Having lost substantial support in most of the Deep South states he had won in 1960 over his stand for civil rights, he considered it essential to his reelection to carry Florida in 1964.

69. EVANGELINE BELL BRUCE (1918–1995) was the second wife of David Bruce (1898–1977), who was JFK's ambassador in London after occupying the same job in Paris and Bonn. Clare Boothe Luce (1903–1987) was the second wife of Henry Luce (1898–1967), founder of what was probably the most powerful single print influence on American public opinion of those years, the Time-Life organization. Partly influenced by their longtime friend Joseph Kennedy, who had persuaded Luce in 1940 to write the foreword to Jack's first book, *Why England Slept*, and who went to the length of watching his son's Democratic acceptance speech on television with Luce after they dined together, the conservative publisher had been surprisingly benign toward JFK during the 1960 campaign. But when Kennedy became President, his more doctrinaire wife, a former Connecticut congresswoman and ambassador to Italy, tended to lecture him as if he were still the student he was when they had first met.

JACQUELINE KENNEDY AND HER CHILDREN AT
LETITIA BALDRIGE'S FAREWELL PARTY, 1963

comes home. And, you know, so he arranged that part of my life. And once it was in the Treaty Room you could let Tish's things pile up for days, and then go do it all in one big session.[70]

Nancy was a much closer friend?[71]

---

70. Jacqueline had taken a room in the family quarters that recent presidential families had called the "Monroe Room" and renamed it the "Treaty Room." Used by presidents from Andrew Johnson to Theodore Roosevelt as a Cabinet Room, it was restyled by Mrs. Kennedy as a dark green Victorian chamber featuring Ulysses Grant's ornate cabinet table, other late-nineteenth-century furniture and fixtures, and framed facsimiles of agreements signed in the room, such as William McKinley's peace treaty ending the Spanish-American War.

71. **NANCY TUCKERMAN** (1928–), Jacqueline's close friend (whom the First Lady called "Tucky") and White House social secretary from June until November 1963, had known her since the age of nine, when they both attended the Chapin School in New York, and later roomed with her at Farmington,

Nancy was my roommate and ever since she came, the difference that life was. How much more time there was to be able to enjoy—to make yourself so that Jack would enjoy you more. I tried to get her sooner, but she wouldn't come.

Nancy is the nicest girl. She's also a very funny girl and a very sharp one.

Yeah.

Underneath the surface, shy—different than the exterior.

And she's feminine. I mean, Tish is sort of a feminist, really. She used to tell me she loved to have lunch in the White House Mess so she could argue with men. She's great, but she was so different from me and just exhausted me so.

How about Pam?[72]

Pam was fantastic because in the beginning I didn't think I'd need a press secretary and other people, the one person had done them both. But when I saw what Tish was like about the press, Jack got so mad. Tish had her own press conference before inauguration at the Sulgrave Club. She was coming there to speak. She got television and everything there. She was laughing and saying, "Yes, we're going to hang pictures on all the walls upside down"— modern, this, that. And, you know, it really caused trouble. It was the first set of bad, sensational headlines, and Jack said, "Not one of my cabinet officers has had an interview. Would you mind telling me what the hell Tish Baldrige is doing?" She just loved the press so that I saw that if I was to keep any privacy of our life—and she was always saying, "We got to have Betty Beale[73] to the first state dinner"—I must get someone who had the same reactions I did.

---

where, as Tuckerman recalled, Jackie had her walk under her horse's belly "twenty times a day to get over my fear of horses." Expecting a baby, Mrs. Kennedy planned to be "taking the veil" and winding down her public commitments from the brisk regimen pressed on her by Tish Baldrige.

72. PAMELA TURNURE (1937–) was Mrs. Kennedy's press secretary. Jacqueline asked her to give reporters "minimum information with maximum politeness."

73. ELIZABETH VIRGINIA BEALE (1911–2006) was an extroverted and widely read Washington social columnist.

THE FIRST LADY THANKS SENATE MINORITY LEADER EVERETT DIRKSEN, VICE PRESIDENT
JOHNSON, AND MAJORITY LEADER MIKE MANSFIELD FOR THEIR HELP IN SECURING A
CHANDELIER FROM THE U.S. CAPITOL FOR THE TREATY ROOM, JUNE 28, 1962

NANCY TUCKERMAN, CHIEF USHER J. B. WEST
(DRESSED AS JBK'S BOARDING SCHOOL HOUSEMOTHER), AND MRS. KENNEDY

And little Pam had been a friend of my sister's. Jack had gotten three of them—Lizzie Condon,[74] who's now in my office, Pam, and Nini[75]—jobs in the Senate one summer, and Pam had been in his office. Pam had stayed, the others had gone away and gotten married. And I just knew that she'd have all the same reactions I did. She was going over to work somewhere in the White House anyway, but I asked her if she'd be my press secretary and she was terrified and she didn't want to. And I told her if she did a good job—if I thought she was doing a good job, the press would always think she was no good, and if they thought she was good, she wouldn't be helping me the way I wanted, so it was very difficult for her because she's very sensitive. But she's just been ideal and it's been hard for her.

She's a great girl. West was—you inherited.

Yes, J. B. West, the chief usher at the White House. He came there under Franklin Roosevelt as an usher. I guess he got to be head usher under Truman. And, well, he runs that whole place, you know. He was one of the people who contributed most to being happy in that place. Just did everything. I'm running out of superlatives now, or energy.

Mrs. Pearce?[76]

Oh, Mrs. Pearce. Well, she couldn't have had better credentials as a curator—everything from Winterthur, and this bright, bright little girl. And Mr. West explained to me what happened to her. Because here, this young

---

74. ELIZABETH GUEST CONDON (1937–) was later married to the film director George Stevens, Jr.

75. NINA GORE AUCHINCLOSS STEERS (1937–) was Jacqueline's stepsister.

76. LORRAINE WAXMAN PEARCE (1934–), the first White House curator, was an alumna of the Winterthur graduate program and a specialist in the French impact on decorative arts in America. Although she found Pearce "as excited as a hunting dog," Mrs. Kennedy was displeased by what she saw as Pearce's desire for the limelight. For her part, with no political experience, the young Pearce felt baffled by the complex interplay among the First Lady, her Fine Arts Committee, the White House Historical Association, du Pont, and Boudin. After a year, Jacqueline had her reassigned to oversee the new White House guidebook. In September 1962, the First Lady wrote du Pont, "Why are some people so avid for publicity—when it poisons everything. I hate & mistrust it & no one who has ever worked for me who liked it has been trustworthy."

little girl came, and so excited about what she was doing, and suddenly she'd stop working and letters wouldn't be answered. Someone would have given a fifty thousand dollars something, or someone would have written six months ago, or six weeks ago, not gotten an answer, and she was always having tea with other curators. And Mr. West said to me, "There's something I think I ought to tell you, Mrs. Kennedy. There's a disease around this place which we call White House–itis, and it hits more people—some of them, the ones you least expect." And it really hit Lorraine Pearce. One day, I found her in Jack's bedroom with Mr. Ginsburg and Levy—who run a very good furniture—American furniture store in New York. But there, in Jack's bedroom, in our private floor, on the floor, looking under his table or his bed. And I said, "Lorraine, what are you doing bringing these men up here?" Well, she'd get outraged and she'd say, unless she could have them inspect the marquetry or something, she was going to write to the President herself. And she just got so grand that, after a while, she stopped being useful and you had to get rid of her. She told me it would take ten years to write the guidebook and I said, "I'm sorry, we don't have ten years"—and "if the President can do all he's doing." So then the little timid-mouse registrar, Bill Elder,[77] came as curator and he was very good as curator. He never wanted any publicity, but he was also so in love with looking at the bottom of furniture and stuff that he never answered a letter or the telephone either. But he was much better. But finally Lorraine, with me pressuring her, got things together and, I suppose, she and I wrote the guidebook. She'd send a batch of illustrations and do part of the text and I'd pick all the ones I wanted in. You know, it was like drawing teeth and Jack used to say, "What is wrong with that girl? She had the chance of a lifetime, the best job in America for someone of her field—to have that now, with all this interest." And White House–itis just went to her head. And then Tish got it. Pam never got it. I think very few of the people on Jack's side got it. I don't know, you'd know more about that. Tish loved to pick up the phone and have "White House calling" or "Send all the White House china on the plane to Costa Rica" or tell them that they had to fly string beans in to a state dinner. And oh, she sort of arranged Ireland, when they said, "Well, we grow wonderful peas here." You know, just anything that was sort of this

---

77. WILLIAM VOSS ELDER III (1933–) succeeded Mrs. Pearce as curator.

power thing. And White House–itis—it's fascinating. You can see which of your friends it affects that suddenly start to treat you differently. I used to think if I ever wrote a book, it would be called "The Poison of the Presidency" because it poisoned so many relationships with people outside.

How would that happen?

Well, some people who don't see you as much as they'd like would say terrible things about you. Or, some that were your old friends would always be the same, but others would be so excited about being known but then they'd go tell just little tidbits like, I don't know, "Caroline said this or that." They'd make up something, just to show that they'd been there. Or the other people who suddenly never spoke to you before, but start calling you up or trying to send you some marvelous present. And one person, André Meyer, who was the first person to give to Jack's library, who's this very crusty man, he's head of Lazard Frères in New York, who didn't want to give to the White House—he's sick of being dunned and touched, and when I told him I didn't want him to,[78] then, I think he got to like me and he was the biggest help of all. When Jack died, he came ten days later with a check for $250,000 for the library before we'd almost even said anything about it. I used to see him when I'd go to New York because he had the apartment under ours at the Carlyle, and I'd be tired up there. I'd just like to go down and have dinner with him and he said, "You will see, when you leave the White House many people who you think were your friends will no longer be. But I will always be your friend because"—and I see it now so well, I mean, I always—

Oh, really?

I mean, I always knew which ones. Everybody's still a friend, but you see the ones who get so excited about power and go over to the new, which is fine. You see it in what some people write, well, you always know—

---

78. ANDRÉ MEYER (1898–1979) was a French Jewish refugee who headed American operations for the Paris investment bank Lazard Frères. He first met the First Lady when he contributed the Aubusson rug for the French Empire–inspired Red Room. After President Kennedy's death, Meyer became one of Jacqueline's closest friends.

Mr. Kennedy always said you can always—if you can count your friends on five fingers of one hand, you're lucky. And I have the friends I always knew I'd have, which I—

I met André Meyer the other day in New York. I was having dinner with Mendès France,[79] who was also staying at the Carlyle. They ran into each other in the elevator. A very nice man, he spoke with affection of you.

I sort of think he's rather a misanthrope—

He is crusty.

Until he loves you and then—and he loved and admired Jack so, without hardly ever knowing him. He always said he was the only Dem—he said, "I am so ashamed of my colleagues in Wall Street. They do not see what this man is doing"—you know.

I think that's enough for the day.

Yeah.

---

79. PIERRE MENDÈS FRANCE (1907–1982) was French president from 1954 to 1955.

The
FIFTH
Conversation

TUESDAY, MARCH 24

1964

*D*uring the campaign, Cuba emerged as an issue. Had the President been much concerned about Castro? Do you remember in '59 when Castro first came in, what he felt?[1]

I remember how awful he thought it was that he was let in. We knew Earl Smith then, who'd been Eisenhower's ambassador at the time. When we were in Florida—that's all Earl could talk about.[2] Yeah, then Jack was really sort of sick that the Eisenhower administration had let him come and then the *New York Times*—what was his name, Herbert Matthews?[3]

That's right.

I can remember a lot of talk about it and wasn't—didn't even Norman Mailer write something?

---

1. FIDEL CASTRO RUZ (1926–) and his guerrilla army entered Havana in triumph in January 1959, having overthrown the Cuban dictator Fulgencio Batista. That April, he visited Washington, D.C., at the invitation of the National Press Club and was refused an audience by President Eisenhower. The following year, Castro began importing Soviet oil and expropriating American firms.

2. EARL E. T. SMITH (1903–1991), a Newport-born sportsman and financier, of New York and Palm Beach, was ambassador to Havana from 1957 to 1959. His wife, Florence Pritchett Smith (1920–1965), had been a friend of President Kennedy's since school days.

3. HERBERT MATTHEWS (1900–1977) was a *New York Times* correspondent in Cuba whose reports were criticized for being too pro-Castro.

Norman Mailer was very pro-Castro, yeah.[4]

Yeah. I remember Jack being—

Did Earl Smith think it was—talk about Communists—Castro as a Communist, or working with the Communists at that time? He's written a book, as you know—[5]

Yeah—*The Fourth Floor?* Well, he was always saying his troubles with the State Department—I remember there was a man named Mr. Rubottom he kept talking about. And how hard it was—warning against Castro and how just it was like, I don't know, dropping pennies down an endless well. He just never could get through to the State Department. So, I suppose he thought he was a Communist, yeah.

And the President's view then was that, as you say, our policy was wrong in not letting it happen. But on the other hand, he wasn't—he had no sympathy with Batista.

No. No, I can just remember the talk about it, but you know. I'm not very good at—

Then came the campaign. And then after the campaign—remember when Allen Dulles came to—

Oh, Allen Dulles came to Hyannis after—yeah.[6] The first two people Jack

---

4. **NORMAN MAILER** (1923–2007) was a novelist and essayist best known for *The Naked and the Dead* (1948). Mailer wrote the laudatory "Superman Comes to the Supermarket" in *Esquire* about JFK's victory at the 1960 convention, but the following spring, after the Bay of Pigs, he denounced the President for sponsoring the invasion and declared Castro one of his "heroes."

5. Smith's 1962 book *The Fourth Floor* lambasted Assistant Secretary of State Roy Rubottom and other Eisenhower officials for being too relaxed about letting Castro seize power in Cuba.

6. **ALLEN DULLES** (1893–1969) was a Wall Street lawyer and brother of Eisenhower's secretary of state who served as director of Central Intelligence from 1953 to 1961. Along with J. Edgar Hoover, he was JFK's first reappointment as President-elect—and, like Hoover, in the name of continuity. On July 23, 1960, Dulles came to Hyannis Port to brief the newly minted Democratic nominee on national security.

thought he had to keep were J. Edgar Hoover and Allen Dulles, and nice as Allen—well, turned out to be not so—*[chuckles]*

Nixon in his book wrote that the President had been told during the campaign about this, which is wrong, since Dulles and the President both said he didn't know about it until November, about the fact that we'd been secretly training the Cuban—[7]

Well, he never said to me that he knew anything, so I believe that.

When did you first become aware of all this brewing?[8]

Well, you always knew the Cuba problem. Wasn't the weeks before it happened, every press conference or every week there was something about Cuba?

The stories began to appear in March saying that an invasion was likely, or something like that.

And then all the time at his press conferences, Jack would keep having to say United States troops won't be committed, sort of dodging everything that way. Then I knew about all those people being trained. But I just remember, well, it was like the second time, when Keating was going on every week

---

7. In his 1962 memoir *Six Crises*, former Vice President Nixon insisted that during the July briefing, Dulles told Kennedy that for months, the CIA had "not only been supporting and assisting, but actually training Cuban exiles for the purpose of supporting an invasion of Cuba itself." Nixon complained that JFK had abused this access to classified information in October 1960 to criticize Eisenhower's government for failing to help "fighters for freedom" eager to overthrow Castro. In Nixon's telling, in order to preserve the operation's secrecy, he felt compelled during the debates with Kennedy to argue the other side, although in secret he had actually been a champion of CIA plans to upend Castro.

8. Referring to the attempted invasion of Cuba at the Bay of Pigs in April 1961 by anti-Castro Cubans, backed by the CIA. The Agency had given Kennedy to believe that if the exiles, after landing, managed to establish a beachhead in Cuba, public dissatisfaction with Castro might generate a national uprising that would topple the dictator and put the exiles in power—and that if they failed, they could "melt into the mountains" of Cuba as guerrillas. None of these assurances proved accurate, which inflicted a severe blow to Kennedy's prestige. JFK's circle blamed the CIA for its faulty intelligence and planning. The CIA and its partisans blamed Kennedy for refusing to suspend his order that U.S. military forces stay out of the battle.

about something that the missiles weren't out or there were more missiles there.[9] I mean, it was just Cuba, Cuba, all the time in one way or another.

What did you—do you remember what the President's feeling was about the invasion before? Did he—for example, you mentioned the Fulbright meeting the last time.

Well, obviously leading up to it, he was always uneasy. But the time I really remember well was the weekend before, which would be April 13 and 14. We were down in Glen Ora with Jean and Steve Smith, and it was one afternoon—you'll know if it was Saturday or Sunday—about five o'clock in his bedroom, he got a call and he—I was in there and he was sitting in the edge of the bed, and he asked—it was from Dean Rusk—and it went on and on, and he looked so depressed when it was over. And I said, "What was it?" and everything. And I guess Dean Rusk must have told him—or just been very much for it, or something—or did Jack say, "Go ahead," then? I guess that was a decisive phone call.[10]

I think this was the phone call about the air strike.

Oh, that Dean Rusk wanted to take it away, I guess. That's right. So anyway—and then Jack just sat there on his bed and then he shook his head and just wandered around that room, really looking—in pain almost, and went downstairs, and you just knew he knew what had happened was wrong. But I suppose he was in—you know, it was just such an awful thing. He was just in—well, anyway. Usually, as I said, he made his decisions easily and

---

9. In September 1962, Senator Kenneth Keating, New York Republican, charged that the Soviets had placed offensive missiles in Cuba and that the Kennedy administration was trying to conceal their presence. This was weeks before the CIA provided President Kennedy with the first hard evidence, gathered from U-2 photographs, of the missiles on the island.

10. By that Sunday afternoon, April 16, 1961, six American B-26s painted with Cuban insignia had already destroyed almost half of Castro's air force. CIA officials had presumed that, once the invasion was under way, JFK would be willing to discard his public pledge not to invade Cuba and authorize U.S. military forces to openly support the freedom-fighters then landing on Cuban beaches. Rusk's call warned the President of the importance of concealing any American role in the invasion. Kennedy thus witheld U.S. air power until the exiles were established on Cuba, at which time such a strike might be plausibly explained as coming from Cuban soil. At that moment, a ban on American air strikes was likely to doom the invasion, and Kennedy knew it.

would think about them before or once he'd made them, he was happy with them. And that's the one time I just saw him, you know, terribly, really low. So it was an awful weekend.

Do you think his being low related to that particular decision to—about the— cancel the air strike or to the general decision to have gone ahead with the invasion, or was that—

I think it was probably a combination of all of them, don't you?

Yeah.

I mean, the invasion in the beginning and then no air strike—half doing it and not doing it all the way, or should—I don't know. Just some awful thing that had been landed in his lap that there wasn't time to get out of. And then all the things that he told me about Cuba—I can't remember if he told me at the time or later—but you know, the meetings and how he'd say, "Oh, my God, the bunch of advisers that we inherited!" And then later on, when Taylor was made chief of staff, he'd say, "You know, at least I leave that to the next President"—or "If Eisenhower had left me someone like that. Can you imagine leaving someone like Lyman Lemnitzer?" and you know, all those people in there.[11] I mean, just a hopeless bunch of men. And I can remember one day—would it be after it had failed, I guess, or before?—at the White House? Him especially, I was on the lawn with the children and he especially came out with Dr. Cardona[12]—

---

11. LYMAN LEMNITZER (1899–1988) had been appointed by Eisenhower in 1960 as chairman of the Joint Chiefs of Staff. In March 1962, Lemnitzer approved a highly classified plan, called Operation Northwoods, for the U.S. government to commit acts of terrorism in Miami and other American cities and blame them on Castro as a pretext for a full American invasion of Cuba. The plan even had suggested that if a U.S. astronaut perished during a mission, the finger should be pointed at Castro. Appalled by Lemnitzer's proposal and still fuming over the general's ham-handed advice during the Bay of Pigs, JFK denied him a second term that fall as chairman of the Joint Chiefs.

12. JOSE MIRO CARDONA (1902–1974) was a Havana lawyer, professor, and prominent Batista critic who, after the revolution, was briefly Castro's prime minister before he broke with him and fled to Florida. Before the Bay of Pigs, Cardona was leader of the committee of anti-Castro Cubans who were quietly cooperating with the CIA and the tiny group of Kennedy officials involved in the forthcoming invasion. Had the Cuban exiles managed to seize a substantial portion of their island, they would have declared Cardona provisional president of Cuba.

Oh, yes. That was after.

And, you know, well, he thought he'd been wonderful afterwards then. And he just—

I think that was a Wednesday afternoon—

Oh.

Because I was sent down to Florida on Tuesday night and brought—Adolf Berle[13] and I—and brought Dr. Cardona back and took him in late Wednesday afternoon, and I think he brought him out and introduced him to you.

And then he'd keep shaking his head, and said Cardona had been wonderful. But, if you want to go back over the chronology of Cuba, there was that awf— that weekend. Then we went back to Washington Monday. Then Tuesday we had the congressional reception, and Jack was called away in the middle of it, and went over to his office and didn't come back until I was in bed.[14] You know, it was funny, because the next year at a Congressional reception, he was called away for something else of a crisis. But last year it just seemed those receptions were always nights something awful happened. So then you say Wednesday was the day everything happened. And I think it was Wednesday we had to have our pictures taken—or maybe it was Thursday. But Jack was as restless as a cat. It was with Mark Shaw and he just came up and sat down for about ten minutes—we didn't have any picture of the two of us together that you could mail out.[15] Oh, it was an awful time, and you know, he really looked awful.

---

13. **ADOLF BERLE** (1895–1971) was a law professor, economic theorist, and FDR-era diplomat who was assisting the State Department on Latin America.

14. On Tuesday evening, April 18, JFK was summoned from the annual White House reception for Congress to the Cabinet Room, where a Caribbean map with tiny magnetic ships had been set up. Kennedy told Admiral Arleigh Burke, chief of the U.S. Navy, "I don't want the United States involved in this." Burke replied, "Hell, Mr. President, we *are* involved!" As a compromise, the President allowed six jets from the U.S.S. *Essex* to fly over the invasion beachhead for an hour.

15. **MARK SHAW** (1921–1969) was one of the most well-known fashion and celebrity photographers of the time.

PORTRAIT OF JACQUELINE KENNEDY TAKEN DURING THE BAY OF PIGS DEBACLE

It must have been unbearable to go to the Greek dinner in the midst of all this.[16]

Yeah, then we had to go to the Greek dinner that night. We'd had a lunch for them one of those days, either the day before or the day after. And you know, they were so nice, the Greeks. They were almost our first visitors. But I remember so well when it happened, whatever day it was, it was in the morning—and he came back over to the White House to his bedroom and he started to cry, just with me. You know, just for one—just put his head in his hands and sort of wept. And I've only seen him cry about three times. About twice, the winter he was sick in the hospital, you know, just out of sheer discouragement, he wouldn't weep but some tears would fill his eyes and roll down his cheek. And then that time, and then when Patrick, this summer when he came back from Boston to me in the hospital

---

16. **CONSTANTINE KARAMANLIS** (1907–1998) was prime minister of Greece. By Wednesday evening, when the Kennedys attended a Greek embassy dinner hosted by Karamanlis, the President knew that the invasion was an inescapable failure.

and he walked in the morning about eight, in my room, and just sobbed and put his arms around me. And it was so sad, because all his first hundred days and all his dreams, and then this awful thing to happen. And he cared so much. He didn't care about his hundred days, but all those poor men who you'd sent off with all their hopes high and promises that we'd back them and there they were, shot down like dogs or going to die in jail. He cared so much about them. And then Bobby came to see me. You know, obviously there were meetings all the time—probably that afternoon or something in the White House—and Bobby came over to see me and said to, you know, "Please stay very close to Jack, I mean, just be around all afternoon." If I was going to take the children out—you know, in other words, don't leave anywhere. Just to sort of comfort him. I mean, just because he was so sad.

He said something to me that day or the next day about Bobby and wondering about making Bobby head of the CIA. Do you remember that?

Oh, I remember him saying that a couple of times, if only he could have had Bobby as head of the CIA. Well, then I suppose he just thought politically that would be too—

Too risky.

Yeah. But you know, he so wished he could have Bobby there. Then I don't know when it was he got John McCone.[17]

About—not for another six months or so. He got him in the fall. One of the great things, of course, was the fact that the President, having really been led into this by very bad advice, nonetheless never blamed anyone publicly and had that wonderful Chinese proverb, so-called, do you remember? "Victory has a hundred fathers—"

---

17. JOHN MCCONE (1902–1991) was a California businessman, chairman of Eisenhower's Atomic Energy Commission, and Nixon supporter in 1960, whom JFK appointed to succeed Allen Dulles, after firing the latter in the wake of the Bay of Pigs disaster.

"Fathers. Disaster is an orphan."[18]

"Is an orphan." Where did he get that? Did you ever know?

I don't know. We could see if it's in Mao Tse-tung, because I told you he had an awful lot of Chinese proverbs. *[chuckles]* But he was always collecting things like that.

How did he feel about—it was Lemnitzer, it was, I think, and the Joint Chiefs he held more responsible privately than anyone else, my impression.

Yes, you know, he never really spoke unkindly about them, but with sort of hopeless, wry laughter, he'd talk about Curtis LeMay. I remember the time of the second Cuba, he got a picture of all our airplanes in Florida, or all over the country just standing on all the runways.[19] And he called up LeMay. But, you know, there that man was shouting to go and bomb everything and have a little war and had left all our planes out. You know, LeMay was hard to work with. But, it was the whole thing—the Joint Chiefs, and then, I guess, poor Allen Dulles. And then again, there's Dean Rusk. I don't know if you should have— It seems to me if you're going to do it, you should have had air cover. You know, Dean Rusk, being timid, but all of that—Jack coming in so late to something and everybody—I just wished if he had to do it, they'd let him alone. That was before the hundred days.[20] I mean, it was silly. He never liked that hundred-day business in the papers but it was obviously some little press thing—Roosevelt.

---

18. At an April 21, 1961, press conference, the President said, "There's an old saying that victory has a hundred fathers and defeat is an orphan." JFK accepted full responsibility for the failure as "the responsible officer of the government." Americans rallied to him and gave him the highest Gallup Poll approval ratings of his presidency—81 percent.

19. CURTIS LEMAY (1906–1990) was the truculent Air Force chief of staff, known for his leadership of World War II strategic bombing and the postwar Strategic Air Command. During the Cuban Missile Crisis of 1962, LeMay became the fiercest of those demanding that JFK start bombing Cuba immediately.

20. Since the sunburst of recovery programs created by FDR to fight the Great Depression during the first hundred days of his presidency, this metric has been used by the press ever since to issue wildly premature assessments of new presidents.

But you know, before they were even over—so you can see how early that was in the White House.

How did you feel about Dulles after this?

Well, he always liked Allen Dulles and, you know, he thought he was an honorable man, and Allen Dulles always had liked Jack. And I think Allen Dulles sort of cracked up. Oh, because a while later he went out of his way to have him to dinner—or to make someone—I know what it was. Or was it Charlie Wrightsman?[21] Yes, Charlie Wrightsman and Jayne were in Washington, and they were coming to the White House. This was just a couple of weeks after Cuba, or a month—and always Allen Dulles had been their little lion. They'd have him down, and trot him out in Florida and everything. And Charlie Wrightsman was there, and he said he wasn't going to see Allen Dulles—usually when he was—when in Washington, he did—because of the way Allen had bungled the Bay of Pigs. Well, that just disgusted Jack so. He was so loyal always to people in, you know, trouble. And so he took me aside and said, "Have Dulles over here for tea or for a drink this afternoon." And he made the special effort to come back from his office and sit around with Jayne and Charlie Wrightsman, just to show Charlie what he thought of Allen Dulles. And, I mean, it made all the difference to Allen Dulles. I was with him about five minutes to ten before Jack got there. He just looked like, I don't know, Cardinal Mindszenty on trial. You know, just a shell of what he was.[22] And Jack came and talked—put his arm around him. What's that thing about Morgan? "If you just walk with—through the bank with your arm around me, you don't have to give me a loan?"—or anything?[23] Well, wasn't that nice? It was just to show Charlie Wrightsman.

---

21. **CHARLES WRIGHTSMAN** (1895–1986) was an Oklahoma oil tycoon and social friend of the Kennedys, along with his wife, Jayne Larkin Wrightsman (1919–), who was a close friend to Jacqueline and who served on her Fine Arts Committee to supervise and raise funds for the White House restoration.

22. **JÓZSEF CARDINAL MINDSZENTY** (1892–1975) of Budapest was sentenced, after a 1949 show trial, to life imprisonment for "treason" against the Soviet-dominated government of Hungary.

23. As legend had it, when asked by a friend for a loan, one of the banking Rothschilds replied that he would do better: he would escort the friend through the Paris bourse and thereby elevate the friend's standing among financiers. JFK had long enjoyed this concept. After the 1960 election, for example,

But it shows something about Jack. But I mean, he knew he—Dulles had obviously botched everything up. You know, he had a tenderness for the man. And then I guess right after that or Cuba, whenever, he got General Taylor.

Yes. First, he got General Taylor to head an investigation. Remember General Taylor and Bobby made a kind of inquiry into what happened. And then, then he brought General Taylor into the White House.

That's right.

As a kind of military adviser.

General Taylor always used to be in his gray suit then, and sometimes Jack would say, when there'd be a meeting of the Joint Chiefs, you know, that you could just feel these waves going out from them wondering about what Taylor would be like and what a difficult situation it was for Taylor.[24] And it was to his amazement; it worked very well.

Had he known General Taylor before this?

I suppose he'd met him a couple of times because he was always talking about his book. And you know, and then he'd say, "Imagine, can you imagine Eisenhower doing that?"—whatever all the things were that made General Taylor leave. General Taylor and General Gavin both wrote books, didn't they?[25]

Yes.

---

the President-elect told his campaign adviser Hyman Raskin of Chicago that he would give him a better thank-you gift than a federal job: he would call Raskin to his Georgetown house for counsel.

24. As a retired general, Taylor wore civilian attire.

25. JAMES GAVIN (1907–1990), fabled commander of the 505th Parachute Infantry Regiment on D-day, was JFK's first ambassador to Paris. Like Maxwell Taylor, General Gavin had quit Eisenhower's Pentagon over defense strategy and published a book (*War and Peace in the Space Age*) explaining why.

But—and so he always thought so highly of him. He knew just where to turn the minute he needed his military adviser.

We in the White House staff felt very badly, quite apart from the general horror of the thing, but we felt that we'd served the President badly, and some had thought—some had been for the project and others had been against it. But all of us felt that we hadn't done the job that the White House staff ought to be doing in the way—that we'd been too intimidated by all these great figures and hadn't subjected the project to the kind of critical examination it was our job to do. Did he ever comment on that?

No, he never did—but, I mean, I don't think all of you should feel that way because look at what you did at the second Cuba. The thing was you were all cutting your teeth in there and nobody had warned you about this thing. And you—all these supposed experts when you come in fresh yourself, what can you do but sort of take their advice? That's why Lyndon Johnson's so lucky. At least he has a team of people who've been tried. And you hope to God that if the country's been run these past eight years and there'd been crises that those men would know something what they were talking about. So he used to talk later, never about his staff, but, you know, about who he was left, who he inherited to turn to for advice. And that's what he was rather bitter about.

And when the chips were really down, it was Bobby whom he turned to, wasn't it, more than anyone else to talk to and have counsel with?[26]

That's right. And I remember—and setting Bobby up with that committee[27] and I think that's where Bobby and General Taylor's friendship started because I would say after Jack, General Taylor was the man in Washington that Bobby is the closest to, I think—I mean, besides his friends or people in the

---

26. It was after the Bay of Pigs that JFK convinced his brother to expand his portfolio and become his confidential adviser and troubleshooter on foreign, defense, and intelligence policy—especially toward Cuba and the Soviet Union.

27. President Kennedy asked Taylor to head a committee to conduct a postmortem on the Bay of Pigs failure. Other panel members were Robert Kennedy, Allen Dulles, and Admiral Arleigh Burke.

PRESIDENT AND MRS. KENNEDY SPEAKING WITH RETURNED
MEMBERS OF THE CUBAN INVASION BRIGADE, MIAMI, 1962

Justice Department. But there's this really mutual respect they both have for each other. And it's very touching—a very young man and a man who's at the end of his career.

You said, in an earlier tape, that the times that you remembered the President being most depressed and under pressure really—the state committeeman fight in 1956 and the Cuban thing.

Yes, well, not depressed at the state committeeman thing. That was more nervous, apprehensive, he couldn't stop talking about it. You know, then he had to do something to win. This one was sort of blundering along. He wasn't running his own show as he was doing in the Massachusetts fight. And then the awful depression when it ended and caring so about those people.[28] And

28. JFK felt responsible for the almost 1,200 invaders captured by Castro. The evidence was his willingness to brave domestic political criticism by encouraging a public campaign, including a "Tractors for Freedom" committee, headed by eminent Americans, to meet Castro's ransom demands for about

I think the compassion that shows, well, the way he used to talk to me about Cardona afterwards, and the way—then he really felt obligated to get those prisoners out. That was—was that the Christmas later or two Christmases later?

Two Christmases later.

First there were the tractors and Bobby felt so committed to do that. And just at that time, there came an article about Bobby—remember those other boring ones, where they say he was ruthless? And I just thought, "If they could have known the compassion of that boy." You know, you just couldn't let those people molder away in jail. Probably it would be better if you could have, than people see that poor brigade staggering back and remind you all over—the whole country, all over again, of the big failure. But just this urgency to get them out. And then Jack would get so belted for the tractor thing. But he had to do whatever thing he could to get them back. *[tape machine turned off, then]* Should I tell about that?

Yes.

I have another—I just thought of something else about Bobby's compassion. It must have—last winter—you can find out when it was—that best spy we had in Russia was caught. Was it Penkovsky or Penovsky?[29]

Yes, Penkovsky.

Well, Bobby was coming out of a meeting in the White House, and he saw me in the garden, and he came over and sat down on a bench, just looking so sad. And he said he'd been out to see John McCone and he said, "It's just

---

$60 million worth of tractors, drugs, baby food, and medical equipment in exchange for their freedom. In December 1962, the Kennedys welcomed the liberated Cubans at a raucous rally in Miami's Orange Bowl, where Jacqueline told the ex-prisoners in Spanish that she hoped John would grow up to be as brave as they were.

29. OLEG PENKOVSKY (1919–1963) was a valuable secret agent for Western intelligence in Moscow when he was exposed, arrested, tried, and executed.

awful, they don't have any heart at CIA. They just think of everyone there as a number. He's Spy X-15." And he said that he'd said to them, you know, "Why? This man was just feeding you too many hot things. He was just bound to get caught. And they'd keep asking him for more. Why didn't someone warn him? Why didn't someone tell him to get out? He has a family. A wife or children or something." Bobby was just so wounded by them—just treating that man like a cipher. I guess he even thought John McCone was rather—

Well, people get into a kind of professional sense about all this and they no longer see people as human beings. And one of the most outrageous things was the attack on the tractor deal. I mean, if there was anything that was something which this nation should have seen as its duty, it was to do everything possible to get those people out, and the attack on it was always a very bad thing to me.

I know.

Remember, Mrs. Roosevelt and Walter Reuther and Milton Eisenhower formed a committee to do that.[30]

And then everybody blasted it. And oh, the heartlessness of them. Well, anyway—

I think one reason the President felt so strongly about Miro Cardona and the members of that committee is that three or four of them had sons.

That's right. I know Cardona had a son, didn't he? Then when the Cuban brigade came in 1962—I guess it was Christmas—to— Well, first they all came up in the afternoon to the Paul house in Florida.[31] Just the five of them, or six. You know, Oliva[32] and they all had these—they all showed us

---

30. Tractors for Freedom Committee.

31. To avoid disrupting the Joseph Kennedy household in Palm Beach, the President and First Lady leased the neighboring home of Mr. and Mrs. C. Michael Paul.

32. ERNEIDO OLIVA GONZALEZ (1932–) was deputy commander of invasion Brigade 2506 and had just been released from Castro's prison. The following year, he and some of his comrades received U.S. Army commissions.

pictures of what they looked like before—they had in their wallets. They all had these wonderful, sort of El Greco faces. Really thin. When they pulled pictures out of what they looked like before, they really looked sort of like fat members of Xavier Cugat's band.[33] I mean, they didn't have any pathos in their faces. And how they were with us—you know, there they were sitting with Jack—nothing bitter, just looking on him as their hero. You know, they were nice men too. Then they came—since November—they must have—when I was in this house—they came in February especially up to Jack's grave to lay a wreath, and Bobby brought them—one of them around to see me. And they all said that they were getting out of the army or everything—that now that Jack was dead, they had no more hope or idealism or anything. They'd just all go out and try to get some jobs because it was he they were all looking to with hope.[34] They're the men that had got them into it. It's rather touching.

The President was deeply moved, wasn't he, at that Miami business?[35]

Oh, yes. That was one of the most moving things I've ever seen. All those people there, you know, crying and waving, and all the poor brigade sitting around with their bandages and everything.

I think he was carried away and said some things that weren't in the text of his speech.

[chuckles] I remember his speaking, and then I had to speak in Spanish. You know, a wonderful man that you should speak to sometimes is Donald Barnes.[36] Of all the interpreters Jack ever had, he was always the one with

---

33. **XAVIER CUGAT** (1900–1990) was a popular Spanish-born bandleader who had spent his childhood in Cuba.

34. A large reason that Oliva and his comrades were so disillusioned was that President Johnson had just shut down the considerable program of covert action against Cuba that had been quietly supervised by the Kennedy brothers.

35. In the Orange Bowl, with the freed Cubans shouting "Guerra! Guerra! Guerra!," JFK, much affected by the scene, accepted Brigade 2506's flag and pledged to return it "in a free Havana."

36. **DONALD BARNES** (1930–2003) was the government's senior Spanish interpreter, and was duly interviewed for the Kennedy Library's oral history program.

Spanish. He was so head and shoulders above any other. And he made you have a good relationship with the person. That man was in so many—I don't know, someone should interview him.

Is he, what, State Department?

State Department interpreter. Some of them weren't very good. The one we had in Paris was just hopeless. Poor Sedgwick,[37] trying to say his sort of flowery eighteenth-century French, which no more sounded like a translation of Jack. Jack said the two best interpreters he'd ever seen were Barnes and Adenauer's interpreter, who he used in Germany instead of our own. He asked Adenauer if he could borrow his.

Did he ever talk about the future of Castro and Cuba? Did he think that—what did he think, do you think?

Gosh, I don't know what he thought. I remember asking him this fall—oh, yes, that day that I told you about—it was one day in October, when he woke up from his nap and he looked very worried. I said something and he said, "This has been one of the worst days of my life. Ten things have gone wrong and it's only two-thirty." And he named some of them, which I should have written down. Anyway, one I can remember was that some little raid on Cuba had failed.[38] And I sort of said, "Well, what is the point of all these little raids?" But he didn't—he sort of talked—he didn't really answer that question. He obviously didn't want to sit down with me and talk about Cuba because it was a worry to him. So I don't know what he had in his head or what his thoughts were.

Jean—did you see the interview that Jean Daniel—[39]

---

37. CHARLES SEDGWICK (1912–1983).

38. Raids from the sea were part of the U.S. covert action waged against Castro's Cuba.

39. JEAN DANIEL (1920–) was editor of the French socialist journal *L'Observateur*. In October 1963, he was scheduled to interview Castro. Before his departure for Havana, his friend Ben Bradlee arranged for him to see President Kennedy in the Oval Office. Daniel lunched with Castro on November 22, 1963, and they learned together of the President's assassination, which Castro pronounced "bad

Yes.

Did that sound—what did you make of that?

Well, I thought it no more sounded like Jack. And I can remember being in Mrs. Lincoln's office when Jean Daniel was brought in and being introduced to him first.[40] Then that came out after Jack was dead, didn't it?

That's right.

Well, it didn't sound like Jack. I can't remember what it said now, but it didn't sound—didn't ring true.

The language didn't sound like him. Some of the things that were said did sound like him and some didn't.

I don't even know if Daniel spoke English.

I think Ben Bradlee brought him in, as I recall.

Well, when I saw him, he was alone. But maybe Ben sent him.

Ben sent him, I guess. The—you know, eventually Miro Cardona got mad at the United States government and issued a blast, and so on.[41]

Yes, I can remember later on, Cardona became rather a nuisance.

I always felt the President understood—had a certain sympathy with the frustrations—

---

news." In the December 14, 1963, *New Republic,* Daniel wrote that during his conversation with JFK, the President had been surprisingly outspoken in accepting American responsibility for the seizure of Cuba by Castro and the excesses that followed, telling Daniel that "to some extent," Batista had been the "incarnation" of American "sins" against Cuba, and that "now we shall have to pay for those sins."

40. EVELYN NORTON LINCOLN (1909–1995) was JFK's personal secretary from 1953 until his death.

41. Miro Cardona had been angry that after the Cuban Missile Crisis, the Kennedy administration seemed less aggressive about trying to overthrow Castro.

Yes, you know, and he never said anything awful about him. Just, you know, that was one more worrying thing in a day when there'd be a blast from Miro Cardona.

The President had been interested in Latin America, particularly, because it became such a major interest in the administration. Of course he had gone to Argentina, hadn't he, in 1939 or something like that?

Yes, he'd been there. I think he'd been to Brazil and a lot of places—had he been? But—but he was really quite young then and I don't think— I never remember him talking especially about Latin America before. It was really when he got into the White House—well, we were there a very short time when he made his Alliance speech.[42] So he obviously must have been thinking about it during the campaign, in the interregnum, you know. And—oh, did I tell you about him, the trip to Mexico? No, the trip to Venezuela?[43] I went to an orphanage and there was a picture in the paper that evening. All the children were kissing me goodbye. And the headline was—you know, it was very complimentary, it said, "We love Mrs. Kennedy. Look, she permits herself to be kissed by gringo children." Or by, you know, Indian children. Whatever they were. And that just hurt Jack so for them and he said, you know, "Look at those people. You just don't know of the inferiority complex they have, that the United States has given them." And isn't it trag—sad that they should be writing something like that? And you could see on the visit to Mexico, as it went along, how López Mateos really began to see that Jack believed all those things he was saying about "our revolution was like yours."[44] At last, they had someone they could trust who felt about them.

That must have been an exciting visit—the Mexican visit.

---

42. Kennedy's Alliance for Progress was designed to increase economic cooperation with Latin American countries and position the United States as the friend and champion of reform, not dictatorship.

43. In December 1961, the Kennedys went to Venezuela and Colombia.

44. In June 1962, they visited Mexico City, riding through ebullient crowds, as guests of President Adolfo López Mateos (1909–1969), president of Mexico from 1958 to 1964, whom both Kennedys liked and admired for his social reforms.

To me that was the most exciting of all.

More than even Berlin?

Well, I didn't go to Berlin, you see, because I was having John—Patrick. I guess Berlin was to him the most unbelievable. But—so what did I have? Paris and Vienna, and Colombia and Venezuela. Well, Vienna[45] was incredible in that it was miles in from the airport and back, and it was a dark, gray day. And just to see those crowds going on for twenty-five miles mostly weeping and waving handkerchiefs. That was one of the most impressive crowds I've seen. But, my gosh, the movie of Mexico—I saw it the other day.

It was fantastic.

You know, it looked like a pink snowstorm—that paper coming down, and the cheers, and the "vivas." And they'd keep thinking of new things to yell "vivas" about. *"Viva Kennedy!" "Viva Los Kennedys Católicos!" Viva* everything!

He had an extraordinary sympathy for Latin America, the problems of Latin America which was, which they had, which they got and it—

And he liked the Latins, too. And I remember I was so surprised because I thought, and I said this to him, and he agreed—of all the great men that I met while we were in the White House or before—you think, there's de Gaulle, Macmillan, Nehru, Khrushchev—the one that impressed me the most was Lleras Camargo of Colombia.[46] You know, he wasn't at all—and Betan-

---

45. She refers to their arrival for JFK's meeting with Khrushchev in June 1961.

46. HAROLD MACMILLAN (1894–1986), the Conservative British prime minister from 1957 to 1963, made his visit to Kennedy in April 1961. Soon he was JFK's closest friend among foreign leaders. They were related through the marriage of Kennedy's late sister Kathleen (1920–1948), known as "Kick," to William Cavendish, Marquess of Hartington, nephew of Macmillan's wife, Lady Dorothy. Hartington had died in World War II. Alberto Lleras Camargo (1906–1990) was a former journalist and the Colombian president from 1958 to 1962. During the Kennedys' visit to Bogotá in 1961, Camargo had given Mrs. Kennedy a tour of his presidential palace, a glittering museum of Colombian history, which she later considered to be an inspiration for her restoration of the White House.

JACQUELINE KENNEDY VISITS MEXICO

court[47] enormously, but Lleras Camargo more. He was this thoughtful—he almost seemed—not German, but Nordic in his sadness. And just this dedication—that man getting thinner and thinner. When he came here to the hospital and I went to see him, nothing was ever in the papers about it. And he came in so thin to Jack's office. I said, "He looks so awful since we saw him in Colombia." And he said yes, he's done all that, working for the Alliance, and he said he'd help

47. RÓMULO BETANCOURT (1908–1981), Venezuelan president from 1945 to 1948 and 1959 to 1964, known as the "father of Venezuelan democracy."

again. And then I said to Jack—I'd always had this mania before about making my children learn French because I saw how that other language absolutely doubled my life, and made you be able to meet all those people that you—but I said, "I'm going to make my children learn Spanish as their second language." We should just—if de Gaulle and everyone want to have their own little thing—but really, we should turn to this hemisphere. And I'm going to do that, anyway.

I think one of the greatest things he did was to restore a sense of this being a common hemisphere, which had gone out of the United States entirely since Roosevelt and the Good Neighbor policy.

And it's so shocking—he noticed it in Mexico, and I noticed it again—I remembered it before. When we say America there, meaning our country, but America to them means both continents. They say North America and South America. And, you know, you have to bite your lip a couple of times when you're talking about America. And, well—

The Kennedy name means more—it's the best asset we have in Latin America at the moment. I wish, you know, I wish the new administration, for example, would ask Bobby to go down to Venezuela—

They want—Venezuela asked especially for Bobby, and Lyndon Johnson wouldn't send him.

Did this just happen, or wait—to go to—for—because you know, to mark Betancourt, the first president of Venezuela who had served out his term. It would have been great.

Yeah, I suppose.

I hope you'll go there sometime.

I'll go but that won't have anything to do with policy.

No, but it will remind them what America—what North America is capable of, which would mean a lot. At the same time that all the Cuban things were going, there was this problem of Laos.[48] Do you remember anything about that? There was some talk of American intervention there which—

Oh, yeah. Well, it just seems always there was Laos, Cuba, South Vi—you know, I remember Laos so well—and Berlin, but I can't remember which month was which. And didn't he go on the television and speak about Laos?

Yeah, that was next year, I think, the year after the crisis was sort of simmering. No, no, that was, no you're right, it was that spring that he did.

And then twice he went on about Berlin, didn't he?

Yeah, um-hmm, spoke about Berlin in June.[49]

See, I don't remember. You know, there was always something like that about to blow up, and always Jack living with that and the pressure of being in the White House, and yet trying to live in an ordinary way and be what you should be for him when he came home. You know, hear what he had to say, but not ask too many questions about something painful. I remember once this year about South Vietnam. Well, usually, I was so good about not

---

48. In 1961, Kennedy resisted pressures to deploy the U.S. military against pro-Communist forces in Laos. Instead he authorized negotiation, which resulted, the following year, in the country's neutrality.

49. At the end of World War II, when the Allies drew up plans for postwar Germany, they left Berlin deep within the Soviet zone of occupation. The city itself was effectively divided into two sectors—East Berlin for the Soviets, West Berlin for the Americans, British, and French. By the late 1950s, Soviet-backed East Germany was an economic ruin, in contrast to the "miracle" of West Germany. Vast numbers of East Germans were escaping to the West through Berlin. To stop this refugee flow and score points against the Free World, Khrushchev demanded that the city be unified, which, because of its geographical position, would make it subject to Soviet whims and effectively force the West out of the German capital. The Western allies had committed themselves to preserve their rights in Berlin, if necessary, by going to war. When Kennedy left Khrushchev after their harsh Vienna encounter in June 1961, the Berlin Crisis was on, with the President calling up American reservists. Then suddenly in August, the Soviets and East Germans built a hideous wall around West Berlin to stop the "brain drain" to the West. Although Kennedy opposed the wall politically, he privately realized that the Soviet leader was providing himself a face-saving means to wind down the Berlin Crisis. The President told aides, "A wall is a hell of a lot better than a war."

asking questions, but then with all those flames and Diem and everything,[50] the only time I really did, I asked him something and it was at the end of the day. And he said, "Oh, my God, kid"—which was—it sounds funny but I got used to it—it was a sort of a term of endearment that I suppose his family used. He said, "I've had that, you know, on me all day and I just"—see, he'd just been swimming at the pool and sort of changed into his happy evening mood, and he said, "Don't remind me of that all over again." And I just felt so criminal. But he could make this conscious effort to turn from worry to relative insouciance.

That was a great source of strength, I think, to be able to do that.

So, I wasn't asking him about—and then, and then he said to me either that time or another, "Don't ask *me* about those things." He said, "You can ask Bundy to let you see all the cables." *[Schlesinger laughs]* Or "Go ask Bundy." And I said, "I don't want to see all the cables." I used to get all the India-Pakistan cables because I loved to read Ken Galbraith's cables.[51] And I used to get the weekly CIA summary. But finally, I just couldn't bear to read through those anymore. They put me into such a state of depression. There was never one good thing in them. Jack had to read those all the time. But he'd say, oh, "Go ask Bundy everything you want to know about that—he'll tell you." So I decided it was better to live—you get enough by osmosis and reading the papers, and not ask, and live in—I always thought there was one thing merciful about the White House which made up for the goldfish bowl and the Secret Service and all that was that it was kind of—you were hermetically sealed or there was something protective against the outside world. You didn't realize, you didn't hear mean things people were saying about you until a lot later. And you could sort of live in your strange little life in there. He couldn't but—I mean, as far as your private life went. And I decided that was the best thing to do. Everyone should be trying to help Jack in whatever way they could, and that was the way I could do it the best—you know, by

---

50. NGO DINH DIEM (1901–1963) was president of South Vietnam from the French withdrawal in 1955 until his death in a military coup. Jacqueline refers to protests like that of the Buddhist priest who burned himself to death in Saigon in the summer of 1963 to protest Diem's repressive policies.

51. Both Kennedys were engaged by the literary quality and humor of the cables from JFK's ambassador to India.

being not a distraction—by making it always a climate of affection and comfort and detente when he came home. And the people around that he—I would try to have people who'd divert him. I mean, there were always people from Washington or something, but who wouldn't be—right on the subject that he'd thrashed about all day, and good food, and the children in good moods, and if you ever knew of someone who was in town or could get someone interesting, you know, try to do that.[52]

Did you do all the inviting?

Yes.

He had absolute confidence in you.

Yeah, and a lot of times if I couldn't think of someone, or something, I'd call up Mrs. Lincoln and say, "If the President wants anyone, tell him to ask whoever he wants for this evening." A couple of times, you'd arrange a little dinner of six people and it might be a night where he wanted to go to bed. So, I must say our last year was just one or two people all the time and then he'd decide when with Mrs. Lincoln, or else—you know Walton, or anyone.[53]

---

52. During times of stress, Jacqueline would cheer the President up by leaving him hand-drawn cartoons and limericks, bringing the children to his office, and having him served some of his most preferred foods, such as from Joe's Stone Crab from Miami. In private, she also performed uncanny impersonations of some of the people with whom JFK had to deal. She could imitate the French ambassador doing his own impersonation of de Gaulle.

53. WILLIAM WALTON (1910–1994), journalist, novelist, painter, and soldier, had been dropped into France at the start of the D-day invasion. A close friend of both Kennedys (he hung paintings in JFK's Oval Office after the inauguration), Walton accepted Jackie's appeal to serve as chair of the U.S. Commission of Fine Arts, which oversaw the aesthetic design of federal buildings and monuments. "It is all going to be involved with all the things we care about," she wrote him in June 1962. "Lovely buildings will be torn down—and cheesy skyscrapers go up. Perhaps saving old buildings and having the new ones be right isn't the most important thing in the world—if you are waiting for the bomb—but I think we are always going to be waiting for the bomb and it won't ever come and so to save the old—and to make the new beautiful is terribly important."

Do you remember when President Nkrumah came?[54]

Oh, yes. He was—I think he was the very first visitor we had. He came up and sat with us in the West Hall, you know, in our private part—private—sitting—

Apartments?

Apartments *[chuckles]* and Stas was there, and Lee. And Stas had just told us before that Nkrumah had bought the biggest yacht in the Mediterranean that belonged to some shifty Greek friend of Stas's—the *Radiant*. So Stas asked him about it, and his eyes sort of rolled and he said, "Yes, it's being used to train the Ghanaian navy!" And Jack had a good laugh about that later with Stas. But he was very—you know, he was nice, he was gay, he had this laugh. You didn't realize what a bandit he was going to turn out to be.

Of course, he behaved in the most terrible way recently, but that was quite a—agreeable visit, wasn't it?

Terribly agreeable, and he was so—you could see he was so delighted to be in the family apartments and I think he saw the children. He was so happy. And then I guess he'd given me some present, so I wrote him a thank-you letter in my own handwriting and said, trying to be polite, because Jack made you feel how important it was that you make the Africans—how awfully everybody had always treated the Africans—how Eisenhower had kept Haile Selassie[55] waiting something like forty-five minutes, and this chip on their shoulder they had anyway. So, I wrote him in my own hand and to be nice I said, "Would you send me a picture of yourself because you were our first visitor"—foreign visitor. So about two weeks later, the Ghana Ambassador in all his robes came wading in and gave me the picture, but you know, in the beginning, I liked

---

54. KWAME NKRUMAH (1909–1972) became the first president of an independent Ghana in 1960. Soon Nkrumah was busy amassing a corrupt fortune, placing restrictions on his people's freedoms, and flirting with the Soviet Union.

55. HAILE SELASSIE (1892–1975) was the Ethiopian emperor, known as the "Lion of Judah," and by tradition descended from King Solomon.

Nkrumah. The only person I met who you knew was a bandit before he came and turned out to be all you expected was Sukarno.[56]

Sukarno was as bad as—

Again, those were sort of working visits, whatever you call them—but Jack brought him up to the West sitting room just before lunch. I think he sort of had all these little ways of doing something a little bit extra for people. So one thing was to come up and either have a drink before lunch or tea, whatever it was, with me, up there. He saw that coming into the house would mean something to them. And so I'd gotten these State Department briefing papers on Sukarno and it said that Mao Tse-tung had published his art collection, which meant an enormous amount to him. He was so flattered. So that morning I called the State Department or someone and said, "Could I please get those volumes over?" because I thought it would impress Sukarno so, if he saw them on our table. Well, they got there about twenty minutes before he did, and I hardly had time to flip through them. So I said you know, "Mr.—whatever you call him, President or Prime Minister"—I forget, but I knew—"we have your art collection here," and we started to look at the volume together, it was enormous. Sukarno was in the middle—all three of us on the sofa, and Jack and I on each side. And he thumbed through the pages and it was just a collection of like Varga girls![57]

Oh, really?

You know, every single—Petty girls![58] Every single one was naked to the waist with a hibiscus in her hair. *[Schlesinger laughs]* And, you know, you just couldn't believe it, and I caught Jack's eye and we were trying not to laugh at each other. I mean, you know, trying—it was so awful, but Sukarno was

---

56. SUKARNO (1901–1970), after leading Indonesia to independence from the Dutch, was its first president from 1945 to 1967 and widely known for both lust and corruption. He also, after a fashion, collected art.

57. ALBERTO VARGAS (1896–1982) was a Peruvian-born painter who created pinups of beautiful women, both nude and clothed, which appeared in *Esquire* and *Playboy*.

58. GEORGE PETTY (1894–1975) painted female subjects in poses similar to those of Vargas.

terribly happy and he'd say, "This is my second wife, and this was"—But he was sort of—I don't know, he had sort of a lecherous look. And he was—he left a bad taste in your mouth.

Anyone else you didn't like among the—

I didn't like Adzhubei and—I didn't like him.[59] He came up to the Cape. Oh, all right, it was very good what Jack did with him and Pierre arranged that, and the interview and everything. But he came up there for that interview and he's a big, brash guy. Maybe he's very sensitive underneath, but he came in the room, and John came in the living room—at the Cape—came running out of the dining room or something, having escaped from Miss Shaw as usual, and Adzhubei said, "Ah, here is your son. In a few years he and my son will be shooting each other in a war," or something. Just—

Very funny.

You know, the most—with a big laugh. I mean, he had that same heavy-handed humor Khrushchev had, but I thought much worse. Yet I liked enormously his wife. I didn't really like Madame Khrushchev too much, and I hated the daughter that Khrushchev had in Vienna.[60] She looked like some *Wehrmacht* blonde who ran a concentration camp! But Adzhubei's wife[61] was the only Russian woman—see, Mrs. Khrushchev and Mrs. Dobrynin— Dobrynin asked Jack specially if I'd have his wife to lunch alone, and I did— but both of them have this really gamesmanship thing.[62] If you'd smoke, they'd say, "You shouldn't smoke so much. Russian women don't smoke." Or "Did you go to engineering school?" You know, always trying to make themselves seem better. I suppose it was a chip on their shoulder. But I'm trying to be

---

59. ALEKSEI ADZHUBEI (1924–1993) was Khrushchev's son-in-law and editor of *Izvestia*. JFK received him in November 1961 at Hyannis Port for an interview that was published in both of their countries.

60. Mrs. Kennedy presumably refers to the daughter-in-law who accompanied the Khrushchevs to Vienna.

61. RADA KHRUSHCHEVA ADZHUBEI (1929–).

62. ANATOLY DOBRYNIN (1919–2010), a lifelong professional diplomat, came to Washington as Soviet ambassador in 1962.

polite and it didn't make it very comfortable. And Adzhubei's wife, Khrushchev's daughter, was the only one who was sort of funny who'd say, "Oh, don't you get tired of your children at the end of the day?" or "If only I could get a decent cook." You know, she'd make little jokes which—she was very shy, but she seemed sensitive. And I always wondered how she ended up with such a brash man. But maybe he's nicer underneath. Because if you notice in Bill Walton's report that he wrote about Russia when he went there after Jack was dead, Adzhubei was really impressed that a doll Khrushchev had given Caroline was in her bedroom.[63] It was one of those things she loved to take apart on a little table by her bed, also with the Virgin Mary and things. You know, so obviously they're sensitive as they can be underneath.

Madame Khrushchev—

Well, de Gaulle said to me in Paris—we were there before Vienna—"*Méfiez vous, c'est elle la plus maline*"—"Watch out, it's she who is the craftiest of the two." I loved her when she was in America with the Eisenhower visit. Then I just knew her through the newspapers. I thought she had such a nice face.

She seemed like Bess Truman—sort of a nice, comfortable—

Yeah. She was a bit *maline*, I thought. I mean, I got sick of all that, those little digs all the time, though she was very shy at the palace in Vienna where we had lunch. There was this protocol thing. For some reason, I outranked her because Jack was President and Khrushchev was just chairman of the whatever it is—so she wouldn't leave the room before I did. And I didn't like to go before an older woman, and you know, she was just so hanging back, and nobody could seem to help so finally, I said—in desperation I took her by the hand and said, "Well, I'm very shy so you have to come with me." And Tish[64] and some interpreter told me that she darted over to a Russian in her party on the wall and said, "Did you hear what she said to me?" You know, and she

---

63. Walton called on Soviet officials in Moscow on a trip arranged before the President's death to meet Soviet artists.

64. Social secretary Letitia Baldrige.

NIKITA KHRUSHCHEV AND JACQUELINE KENNEDY IN VIENNA

was sort of beaming. So obviously, they're all shy underneath—I mean, have their little chips. But Khrushchev with his heavy humor was—I mean, he'd say nice—he was—

Does he have any charm, Khrushchev?

Yeah, it's just one gag after another. It's like sitting next to Abbott and Costello, or something, to get through that dinner.[65] But—this is at—

Sort of a professional jolliness?

Yes, but it's better than, I don't know, sitting next to Kekkonen of Finland and asking him how long he walks every morning before breakfast. But then, you know, they had this ballet and all these swooping ballerinas in Schönbrunn would come swooping towards Jack and Khrushchev and me and Madame Khrushchev, and I said, "They're all dancing. They're all paying most attention to you, Mr. Chairman President. They're all throwing their flowers"— and he said, "No, no, it is your husband they are paying attention to. You must never let him go on a state visit alone, he is such a wonderful-looking young man." I mean, he'd say something sort of nice every now and then. And then like a fool—I told Jack this later—he couldn't believe it! I was running out of things to talk to that man about. And all—and Jack always said, "You mustn't talk to these great men"—I mean, Mrs. Kennedy[66] would read up about Russia or the wheat crop, or something. "That's the last thing they want to hear about. Talk to them about something different." Well, I'd just read *The Sabres of Paradise* by Lesley Blanch, which is all about the Ukraine in the nineteenth century, and the wars and things, and the dance. It sounded to me so rather romantic, the Ukraine, so I was telling him how I loved all that and the dance, the *lezginka* and the Kabarda stallion, and he said something about, "Oh yes, the Ukraine has—now we have more teachers there per something, or more wheat." And I said, "Oh, Mr. Chairman President,

---

65. After the two leaders' first day of talks, the Kennedys and Khrushchevs were feted with a dinner and performance at Schönbrunn Palace.

66. Rose Kennedy, who came to Vienna.

don't bore me with that, I think the romantic side is so much"—and then he'd laugh. [67] And then all I can remember—you know, at last he could let down, too. So, God knows what we were probably talking about—the czar, I don't know. Oh, and then I knew that one of those dogs that had puppies— one of those space dogs—I knew all the names of those dogs—Strelka and Belka and Laika. So I said, "I see where—I see one of your space dogs has just had puppies. Why don't you send me one?" And he just sort of laughed. And by God, we were back in Washington about two months later, and two absolutely sweating, ashen-faced Russians come staggering into the Oval Room with the ambassador carrying this poor terrified puppy who'd obviously never been out of a laboratory, with needles in every vein. And Jack said to me—I had forgotten to tell him that—he said, "How did this dog get here?" And I said, "Well, I'm afraid I asked Khrushchev for it in Vienna. I was just running out of things to say." And he said, "You played right into his hands, reminding him of the space effort."[68] But he laughed.

How did he like Khrushchev?

Oh, well, that time in Vienna there was no—remember what he said at the end of that—their conversation. He showed me all the transcript— "It's going to be a cold winter." And he said that in really scared—then I think you'd seen just naked, brutal, ruthless power and—you know, then Khrushchev thought that—saw that perhaps he could—thought he could do what he wanted with Jack. Khrushchev could be jolly, but underneath there's a—

He was very tough there. The President came back very concerned, I remember.

Oh, he really was. I think he was quite dep— really depressed after that visit.

Had he gone there with any particular expectations about Khrushchev or this was really sort of a testing out, wasn't it?

---

67. In his memoirs, Khrushchev recalled, "Obviously she was quick of tongue or, as the Ukrainians say, she had a sharp tongue in her head. . . . Don't mix it up with her; she'll cut you down to size."

68. As Khrushchev loved to boast, the Soviet Union's space program in 1961 was ahead of America's.

I think he'd gone there expecting to be depressed, but I think it was so much worse than he thought. I mean, he hadn't gone there with any lovely illusions they could all work together. But then I used to tell him, for some strange reason, I liked Gromyko's face.[69] But this was before the second Cuba. Because one day—it was the funniest thing—I came out for a walk and there were he and Gromyko sitting in the Rose Garden. Before we'd done it over, there was a tiny, little bench that—you know, two lovers could barely squish on to it. And he and Gromyko were sitting there on that little love seat, talking. And Jack told me later he wanted to get him out of the office and talk alone, and I walked by, so Jack called me over. And I said to them, "The two of you look so absurd just sitting in each other's laps like that." And then Gromyko smiled. People say he looked like Nixon, but he had a nice smile when he smiled.

Oh, really? He always looked awfully wooden to me.

Well, if he did smile, or something, I don't know. But then, you know, all the things he said to Jack before the second Cuba. That was really clever of Jack, the way he did that. And then the other time they met in the Oval Room and Jack said to him, "We don't trade an apple for an orchard in this country."[70] See, I can't remember what year, why they were seeing each other then, but I know—I think Gromyko must have come three times.

The third one was in '63.

Maybe four.

But the—on the whole, were state visits fun or were they a nuisance?

---

69. ANDREI GROMYKO (1909–1989), the severe Soviet foreign minister, fouled his relationship with JFK in October 1962 by denying to his face in the Oval Office that the Soviets had placed missiles in Cuba.

70. This was in October 1961, during a conversation in the White House family quarters, in which JFK deflected Gromyko's bargaining attempts on West Berlin by saying, "You're offering to trade us an apple for an orchard. We don't do that in this country."

Well, they were—

Or would it vary, I suppose.

They weren't a nuisance. I'd say they were really quite a strain. You know, the week that there was one, you'd really be tired. And you'd have to think—later on they got much better—but in the early days, you'd have to do so many things, I mean, just like you would for a dinner in your house now if you didn't have any help. You had to see about the table and the flowers—I mean, sometimes Bunny Mellon and I would be there before—just before it was time to get dressed for dinner, doing the flowers.[71] You know, before you got in the people who could do them. And the food, and then we had to work out a way that it wouldn't come always cold from the kitchen. You know, there's no pantry in the White House, the kitchen is below, and there used to be these endless waits. And then the entertainment you'd have to work on and get a stage but—it was a lot of strain anticipating them and—I'd say the only one that really was hard going was the Japanese—Ikeda, who was, you know, a very nice man but neither he nor hardly anyone in his party spoke a word of English. So, that was a bit heavy going for lots of meetings. But I liked them—I liked Abboud of the Sudan, I did like Karamanlis, Madame Karamanlis especially. So many. Each one was—and what it meant to them. That was what was so touching.

Macmillan came in April, remember?[72] You'd known him before, had you, or the President had?

The—yes—Jack had met him, what, right after in Key West and then in—he met him in London after Vienna. It was just before Vienna that he came?

---

71. RACHEL "BUNNY" MELLON (1910–), a pharmaceuticals heiress and second wife of the philanthropist and arts patron Paul Mellon (1907–1999), was Jacqueline's close friend. Mellon served on her Fine Arts Committee and advised her on the restoration, the remaking of the White House gardens—she and JFK collaborated on the transformation of the Rose Garden into a tree-edged setting for outdoor ceremonies—and, ultimately, President Kennedy's Arlington gravesite.

72. The British prime minister made his first White House visit to Kennedy in April 1961.

He came in April, before Vienna.

Well, I forget if that was the time.

He must have known him before through the Devonshires though.

I don't know.

Maybe not.

But I know they'd corresponded ever since Jack was first in the White House. But, yes, then we had lunch, just Sissy and David[73] and Macmillan and Jack and I, which was so nice, and they—but it was such a happy atmosphere and they would stay in and talk. That was a very rare and touching relationship between those two men. They really loved each other. And, oh, well, if you could see their letters, and—I'll show them to you someday because I can't do them all on the tape. But the one he wrote Jack by hand the summer after Patrick, when he just was through the Profumo thing.[74] And how Jack went out of his way to send him some telegram when he resigned and tell David that it could be in all the papers—of all that he'd done for the West. He loved Macmillan. You know, Macmillan had a way of looking like sort of a joke. Just his face had that sort of suppressed mirth and his funny clothes and things, but, oh no, he was a—

---

73. DAVID ORMSBY-GORE (1918–1985) was British ambassador to Washington during the Kennedy years. A descendant of the Tory hero and British prime minister Lord Salisbury (1830–1903), he had known JFK since before World War II, when Joseph Kennedy served in prewar London. Ormsby-Gore was related by marriage to both Kennedy and Macmillan. As a Conservative member of Parliament, Ormsby-Gore had sporadically discussed disarmament with JFK throughout the 1950s. Both he and Macmillan pushed the President to fight hard for a comprehensive test ban treaty that would reduce the harshness of the Cold War arms race. (After his father's death in 1964, Ormsby-Gore became Lord Harlech.)

74. In October 1963, suffering from a prostate ailment, Macmillan resigned. His defense minister, John Profumo, had recently been embroiled in a sex and espionage scandal that tarnished the Macmillan government's reputation. Friends speculated that the ordeal might have led to Macmillan's malady, or that he was grateful to use the excuse of ill health to resign a job that had abruptly became unpleasant for him.

He was a sharp old customer—

Yeah.

And I think—I had the impression the President was particularly impressed by his strong feeling about nuclear—about getting the nuclear thing under control.

Yeah, I know, I know.

I know he used to write eloquent letters about the horror of nuclear war.

Yes, and what did Jack say? That was one of the things he said—what Macmillan had done for the—Jack said, he really cared about the Western Alliance.

What did—did the President like Gaitskell?

Yes, he did. Didn't he?

Yes, he did. Do you remember his reaction to Harold Wilson?[75]

Oh, he couldn't stand him.

There was a special relationship. But why—the President and Macmillan, what would they talk about besides politics, because obviously they had a great fund of other things? Macmillan is a publisher and loved history.

Well, they would be so irreverent and funny. Jack would tell me some of the things they said with the men at dinner—you know, after lunch, that I don't think I should say on a tape, even. What is it? One thing was, oh, people say that the younger generation have lost all hope living with this nuclear something. Look at them, they're perfectly fine, they're twisting and—but, I don't

---

75. **HUGH GAITSKELL** (1906–1963) and Harold Wilson (1916–1995) were leaders of the Labour party opposition to Macmillan.

know, just funny things. They'd amuse each other so. So then, we may—the one time I was ever together with them was that time at lunch in the White House. And when they came out, somebody said something about Nehru, and I said how Nehru put his—had given Lee a miniature of two Indians on a couch together and given me one of just a lady sniffing a rose and how he'd had his hand on Lee's thigh at the airport, or—something rather irreverent.[76] He just looked shocked, but you know, it was so funny. That isn't—that doesn't describe what I mean. Jack had this high sense of mischief and so did Macmillan, so I've never seen two people enjoy each other so. Obviously all of the important things they were talking about alone, but when it ended up with Sissy and David and us and him—you know, or going down to Adele Astaire Douglass's—who'd been married to a Cavendish. Talk about a lot of family things, I guess, but always this wonderful humor underneath it all.

The President's year—when he went to London in '38–'39—he wasn't there very much, but it obviously struck a responsive chord, didn't it?

I always thought it was really British history that he patterned himself on more than ours. I mean, that he read, he was always—well, I told you all the speeches—Burke's "To the Electors of Bristol" and Warren Hastings and you know, Charles James Fox.[77] He really gave himself a classical education through his own reading. I don't think you get that in this country anymore. Mostly through being sick and having read the classics and then the English people—and then that made him pick out what he thought was best in American thought and oratory. So he had such an admiration for all—the last time we were in London together, I guess was '58, maybe—and had a dinner of all his old friends. Well, when you look at them all, it was rather discouraging. David Gore was the only one who ever amounted to anything and he was—Jack always used to say he was one of the brightest men he'd ever met in his life—he and Bundy, he used to say. But you know, the others were,

---

76. During Mrs. Kennedy's official visit to India, accompanied by her sister, in March 1962.

77. WARREN HASTINGS (1732–1818) was Britain's first governor-general of India. Charles James Fox (1749–1806) was a Whig political leader and the scourge of King George III, whom he considered a tyrant, which led Fox to support the American Revolution against him.

well, kind of defeatist or turned into nothing or—he wasn't like Joe Alsop, who dearly loves the lord and just gets so excited at the mention of anyone English. Seeing them now really depressed Jack. Of all those young men who'd been his friends in '38 and '39—Hugh Fraser, Tony Rosslyn—[78]

Well, he was in the government, but it's a disappointed life.

Yeah.

Did he ever know Churchill?

William Home, that was a great friend of his.[79]

Alec's brother.

Yes. He'd liked Kick and he'd written—you know, he'd gone to prison because he wouldn't fire on civilians in a town and that's where he wrote *Now Barabbas*. Then he wrote *The Chiltern Hundreds* about Kathleen. Kathleen—she was the model for the American girl. She used to go see him in prison. And well, William was wicked and outrageous and fun. Jack always enjoyed him. But his plays got worse and worse and worse.

You played the reluctant prime minister—[80]

Prime minister. Oh, dear. Well, Poor William he has about four children to support and he has to write too quickly.

Did he know Alec in that—Home—in that period?

---

78. HUGH FRASER (1918–1984) and Anthony St. Clair-Erskine, 6th Earl of Rosslyn (1917–1977), both served as postwar members of Parliament.

79. WILLIAM DOUGLAS-HOME (1912–1992) was a playwright who ran unsuccessfully for Parliament during World War II, stating his opposition to Winston Churchill's insistence that the struggle be fought until Germany surrendered unconditionally. His brother Alec (1903–1995), who was Macmillan's foreign secretary, succeeded him as prime minister in October 1963.

80. Douglas-Home had written the plays *The Reluctant Debutante* and *The Reluctant Peer*.

JOE, KATHLEEN, AND JACK, LONDON, 1939

WATCHING THE BLACK WATCH REGIMENT PERFORM ON
THE SOUTH LAWN OF THE WHITE HOUSE, NOVEMBER 13, 1963

I don't think so.

He's quite different from William, I gather.

Yeah, well, William's sort of mad. Jack said something at the Black Watch,[81] you know, this little speech before, about all of us I suppose are drawn to lost causes and Scotland's history captured him at an early age—it really was a long series of lost causes but it triumphed in some ways more than ever now. And as we were walking off the lawn up to the balcony, where we'd watched the whole show, Jack said, "I wonder if David Gore knew what I meant." Well, he'd meant that Alec Douglas-Home, a Scotsman, was now prime minister.

---

81. Nine days before his death, the President and his family witnessed a performance on the White House South Grounds by pipers of the Scottish Black Watch (Royal Highland Regiment). The Scotsmen were later asked by Mrs. Kennedy to perform in her husband's funeral ceremonies.

Did he like Alec Douglas-Home?

Well, had he met him?

Yes.

Had Alec Home come over?

Yes, he—not as prime minister, but he'd been over as foreign secretary—they met—

I think he did like him—I mean, I know he didn't dislike him. But, the first time I ever saw Alec Home was at Jack's funeral, and I liked him.

He's a nice man. Had he ever known Churchill?

The time we met Churchill was in Monte Carlo and some people—we were staying in—we had a house in Cannes with William Douglas-Home and his wife and—

This was when?

It was either—1958, I guess. And the Agnellis[82] had asked—we were going over to have dinner with them and then they took us before dinner to Onassis's yacht to meet Churchill.[83] Jack had always wanted to meet Churchill. Well, the poor man was really quite ga-ga then and a lot—you know, we all came on the boat together and he didn't quite know which one Jack was. He started to talk to one of the other men there, thinking he was Jack, and saying, "I knew your father so well," and this and that, and that was cleared up. Then Jack sat down with him and talked. But it was hard going. I don't think he'd met him before. But of course, you know, he'd read everything he—

---

82. GIOVANNI AGNELLI (1921–2003) was chief of his family's automobile firm, Fiat.

83. ARISTOTLE ONASSIS (1906–1975) based his family, business, and yacht *Christina* in Monaco in the late 1950s and was frequently host to the aged Churchill and his wife Clementine. The Kennedys actually met Churchill aboard Onassis's yacht during both the summers of 1955 and 1959.

He really had read practically everything of Churchill's.

I felt so sorry for Jack that evening because he was meeting his hero, only he met him too late. All—think of all he could have—he was so hungry to talk to Churchill at last, or meet him and he just met Churchill when Churchill couldn't really say anything.

Adenauer also came over that first spring.[84]

Yes. Jack used to say sort of what a bitter old man Adenauer was, or how he had to be pried— He used to say, "Eighty-nine? Wouldn't you think he'd give up then, but they had to haul him off screaming." He got awfully fed up with Adenauer and all that Berlin. He'd take one private home because his mother's had an appendix or something and they'd start another weeping round. And he hated that ambassador here. The only two ambassadors he really disliked were that one, Grewe, and the Pakistan ambassador—Ahmed. Well, the new one's named Ahmed, so, this was the Ahmed before this one.[85]

Well, the Germans wanted reassurance all the time and it got to be a pain in the neck.

And you know, how much more of it can you do than reassure them? Well, he really did it, obviously, when he went to Berlin.

Do you remember much about the trip to Canada?[86]

---

84. KONRAD ADENAUER (1876–1967) was the first chancellor of postwar West Germany, retiring in 1963. JFK's admiration for Adenauer's role in building German democracy was tempered by his annoyance at Adenauer's ceaseless demands that the United States demonstrate its commitment to defend West Berlin from Communist threat.

85. WILHELM GREWE (1911–2000) was Adenauer's Washington envoy. The Pakistani diplomat was Aziz Ahmed (1906–1982).

86. JOHN DIEFENBAKER (1895–1979) was the Conservative prime minister of Canada when the Kennedys made their first official foreign visit there in May 1961. During their talks, the prime minister could not disguise his low opinion of the informal, young new President. Allegedly one of the Americans accidentally left behind a document, written by Kennedy's aide Walt Rostow, on which the President had casually scribbled his view that the fusty Diefenbaker was an "S.O.B.," and which urged an effort to "push" the Canadians on various subjects. (During the trip, Kennedy also badly reinjured his back

Oh, yes, that was our first—

It was your first trip.

I remember everything about it, you know, getting off—and Vanier, the Governor General, is the most marvelous looking old man—and Madame— you know, white mustache, sort of like C. Aubrey Smith.[87] And Madame Vanier, very mother—everyone curtsies to them. And I rode in from the airport with her—that must be about fifty miles from the airport to Ottawa. And she would be telling me how to wave and always calling me "dear." She was very protective. I was still very tired then and so I had to leave the receiving line that night and halfway through, and Jack was so sweet, rather protective, getting me out of there. I just had so little strength then. So before we went to Europe, I took a whole week off in the country so that I'd sleep and build up my strength and it was all right. But everyone was saying that Ottawa was so cold and never gave receptions to—nice ones to anyone, and I guess, especially to America, or something. And they really were—well, they seemed like terribly enthusiastic crowds and everyone was flabbergasted. You know, you could tell they meant it. Here you often say to state visitors—you're riding in from the airport—"Washington is blasé and I've never seen them go so mad for any visitors as they do for you." Because they are hopeless here, they just stand. But he didn't like Diefenbaker.

But Diefenbaker already was sort of erratic and crazy, was he?

---

while planting a ceremonial tree.) The following year, JFK further antagonized Diefenbaker by inviting the leader of his opposition, the Liberal party's Lester Pearson, whom Kennedy had known during his tenure as ambassador in Washington, to a White House dinner and seeing Pearson privately for a half hour. While campaigning for reelection, Diefenbaker tried to shake the Americans' obvious preference for Pearson's party by threatening to release the offending memorandum of 1961, warning that "all Canadians" would resent the evidence of American lordliness. JFK ordered his envoy in Ottawa to stand up to Diefenbaker. He later denied to Ben Bradlee that he had written "S.O.B." on any paper and wondered aloud why Diefenbaker hadn't done "what any normal, friendly government would do . . . make a photostatic copy, and return the original." (To the President's delight, Diefenbaker's party lost.)

87. CHARLES AUBREY SMITH (1863–1948) was a British actor and stereotypical Englishman, who looked like Georges Vanier.

Oh, yes. And, you know, Mrs. Diefenbaker is such a nice woman. But—oh, we had lunch at Diefenbaker's house and he insisted on telling all these Churchill stories in accent and calling him "old Winston" or "the old boy," or something. You know, it was just painful. He didn't like Diefenbaker. And then you know the story of that—what, there was a paper that was left behind?

The Rostow memorandum.

Yeah, well, Diefenbaker really tried to blackmail Jack with that. And whatever Jack said back to him was rather clever—something of—"How did you get this paper?" You know, he never liked that man, and he always liked Lester Pearson.

You had met de Gaulle before—when he came over here.[88]

I had just met de Gaulle. Jack was campaigning in the Oregon—out in Oregon and I just met him at a reception at the French embassy and I guess I talked to him for about ten minutes.

Was he easy to talk to?

I suppose he wasn't—I just—I told him how much Jack admired him and made up some completely— But I thought he was easy to talk to when we were in France.[89]

That was a nice visit, wasn't it? To Paris.

Yeah. Because I'd ask him things of history—or all the things I wanted to know, like who did Louis XVI's daughter marry, the Duke of Angoulême, did she have any children, and this or that. Then he leaned across the table to Jack at lunch and said in French, "Mrs. Kennedy knows more French history

---

88. This was in May 1960, when de Gaulle came to Washington as Eisenhower's guest.

89. Referring to the Kennedys' triumphal reception in France when they were received by de Gaulle for a state visit in May 1961, before the Vienna summit with Khrushchev.

LEFT: MRS. KENNEDY IS GREETED AT THE ÉLYSÉE PALACE BY PRESIDENT DE GAULLE, 1961
RIGHT: DE GAULLE ESCORTS MRS. KENNEDY TO DINNER AT VERSAILLES

than most Frenchwomen." So Jack said, "My God, that would be like me sitting next to Madame de Gaulle and her asking me all about Henry Clay!" So,
you know, he was very pleased. But then you could ask de Gaulle so many
things, again, not talking about the obvious. De Gaulle has a very—a sort of
courtly, rather nice way with women. I mean, I know he was interested in me
and everything and impressed by Jack. Also, Bundy was sitting right across
from us at this first luncheon. You know, Bundy really looks very young, and
de Gaulle said to me rather imperiously, *"Et qui est ce jeune homme?"* because
he was also staring at Kenny O'Donnell. I don't know if Dave Powers was at
the lunch too. And I said, "Head of the National Security Council"—I don't
know if he knew what that meant—and I said he was the most brilliant young
head of Harvard, so he leaned across and said something about Harvard in

very halting French—you know, slow French, that you would say to someone who might not speak it. And Bundy answered in this brilliant French. I was just so proud. You know, it was strike one for our side or—yeah—or first run for our side.

What was Madame de Gaulle like?

Well, she just looked so long-suffering, poor woman, so tired. You know, they have more state visits than anyone. So sweetly going through—very nice, but just limping through it all. At Versailles, well, the table was fantastic. You know, he'd had all the gold, there was Napoleon's inkwell or something was in front of us and the tablecloth was—it had a lot of gold embroidery on it. So Jack turned to Madame de Gaulle and said—his one attempt of talking to her because she just sits there staring ahead, she's so tired, and said, "This is the most beautiful tablecloth." And her answer was, "The one at lunch was better." And he said, "Oh," and they fell into silence again. You know, in all the foreign state visits, it's different than here, the two men sit next to each other. I always asked Jack if he'd like to do that at the White House.

Oh, really? In other words, the head of state sits next to the other head of state.

Yeah, so it would go, from right to left, Madame de Gaulle, Jack, de Gaulle, and me. And whenever you'd go to their dinners here, it would be done that way most of the time. Jack said, no, he didn't want to do it that way. He said he saw enough of them all day in his conferences.

He and de Gaulle got along well, then, didn't they? I mean it was—

Oh, I think de Gaulle was very impressed by Jack.

There weren't any premonitions then of the mischief that de Gaulle was to make later?[90]

---

90. De Gaulle's efforts to distance France from NATO and the United States in order to demonstrate French singularity and grandeur.

THE FIRST LADY AND ANDRÉ MALRAUX, MAY 11, 1962

Well, I know Jack always knew that because he said it—I know he said it before the trip or—and he'd read everything that Roosevelt said. He knew de Gaulle had this thing about the West, so I guess there wasn't anything then—problem, but I think Jack knew it would come. Oh, he asked de Gaulle about his relations with Churchill and Roosevelt. And de Gaulle said—oh, gosh, will I get it?—"With Churchill we were—I was always in disagreement but we always reached an accord. With Roosevelt I was never in disagreement and we never reached an accord." Or that's the gist of it—he said it so much better—and again, I didn't write that down.

Had you known Malraux before the trip?

No, I'd always—Nicole Alphand asked me what would I like to do in the French visit and you could see that anything you said, they'd turn the place upside down. So I said, "Please, Nicole, I don't want anything. Whatever you plan is wonderful. The only thing I'd like to do, somehow—could I meet

André Malraux?[91] Do you think I could even sit next to him at some thing?" And you see how really protocol and ruthless the French are because, of course, about four days before we got there, both his sons were killed in an automobile crash. And at the first reception that first night—at the Elysée—suddenly the doors open and these two black crows come in, their faces just all white and puffy from crying through the receiving—and all Malraux's tics going at once. And the whole place just fell into a hush. But obviously, it was the one thing I'd asked and so it was— So the next day, Malraux took me to the Jeu de Paume and then after, Malmaison, and then he was fine.[92] And I think it gave him, in a way—I don't know, I suppose it's good to have some-

---

91. ANDRÉ MALRAUX (1901–1976), art historian, novelist, and brave hero of the French Resistance during World War II, was de Gaulle's minister of culture. His 1938 novel *L'Espoir* (*Man's Hope*) was based on his experience fighting alongside anti-fascist forces during the Spanish Civil War. "For the most part," Malraux once wrote, "man is what he hides." Jacqueline had read Malraux's books closely and was drawn to his life story, humanist sympathies, mastery of cultural history, and his belief that the arts and architecture could elevate a society ("the sum," he had written, "of all the forms of art, of love, and of thought, which, in the course of centuries, have enabled man to be less enslaved"). She asked to meet Malraux during the state visit to Paris and hear him speak about some of the paintings she most admired.

92. Jacqueline had sent word that in his grief, Malraux need not bother with her, but he insisted on keeping his commitment to be her host, which touched her deeply. At the Galerie Nationale du Jeu de Paume, the great French museum, Malraux stood before canvases by Manet, Renoir, and Cézanne and reacted to them. He had also had Bouguereau's *The Birth of Venus* moved beside Manet's *Olympia* so that Mrs. Kennedy could view the two nudes in juxtaposition. During their visit to the Château de Malmaison, which had been restored by Napoleon's Empress Josephine and served as the seat of French government from 1800 to 1802, he lectured her about the turbulent Bonaparte marriage. "What a destiny!" said Jacqueline. After touring the house and its famous rose garden, she felt newly inspired in her efforts to improve the White House and its grounds, which benefited from her knowledge of French literature, history, and art. Her instant intellectual communion with Malraux led to a correspondence by diplomatic pouch. In April 1962, she happily showed him through the National Gallery in Washington and, along with the President, honored him at a dinner for the Western Hemisphere's Nobel laureates, which JFK, in his toast, pronounced the most extraordinary White House gathering of talent since Jefferson had dined there alone. During the gallery tour, Jacqueline suggested an American visit by the *Mona Lisa*, which rarely left the Louvre. With the assent of de Gaulle, who was willing to make a friendly gesture toward Kennedy if it required no relinquishment of French political power, Malraux defied the Paris arts bureaucracy and arranged "a personal loan" of the *Mona Lisa* (which he considered "the subtlest homage genius has paid to a living face") to the President and Jacqueline. In January 1963, the Kennedys welcomed Malraux and his wife to the National Gallery for the unveiling. A million and a half people viewed the painting in Washington and the Metropolitan Museum in New York. That November, on hearing of the President's assassination, Malraux cabled the First Lady, "Nous pensons a vous et nous sommes si tristes" ("We think of you and we are so sad"). When Malraux published his autobiography, *Anti-Memoirs*, in 1968, he dedicated it to Jacqueline.

thing to do after something like that happens. But that's when our friendship started, and just listening to him.

Did he and the President connect?

Well, not so much then. They couldn't have that much time to see each other, but when Malraux came over here, they really did, and then they came out to the country, you know, for lunch.[93] And then Malraux came back for the *Mona Lisa* and again we had another evening of just us and then the Alphands. But you know, it's funny, as we were walking from the dinner at Versailles to the theater I was first with de Gaulle, and Jack was behind with Madame de Gaulle and Malraux. And there are all these statues down the long hall and Jack said to Malraux, "Who's that?" And Malraux said to the interpreter, "Tell the President he has picked the only one that isn't a fake." Which was true. And I thought again—that's what I said about Jack's eye. You know, that really impressed Malraux.

Had the President ever read Malraux? Any of the novels or—

I think he'd read *Man's Hope*, but you know, he knew—

Could you—an attractive man, but can you understand his French easily?

Well, he talks so fast, but I can. Or else he repeats—it's like being taken over this incredible obstacle course at ninety miles an hour. You know, what he makes your mind jump to, back, forth. He is the most fascinating man I've ever talked to. But again, he's rather disillusioning because he sort of admires the simplest things. I mean, that dinner at the White House, he—well, his most impressive moment was when they took the color—you know the color flags—the Honor Guard—downstairs. And then, who was it? Oh, Irwin Shaw told me his greatest moment in life was when he was head of a brigade or something, in the Maquis.[94]

---

93. Referring to Glen Ora, where the Kennedys gave Malraux and his wife a Sunday champagne brunch.

94. IRWIN SHAW (1913–1984) was an American novelist, whose first book was *The Young Lions*. The Maquis were guerrillas of the French Resistance, mainly in the countryside.

And he worships de Gaulle like, I don't know, some cocker spaniel adores its master. I mean, he seems to have this incredible intellect and then certain sort of blind spots. And very old-fashioned France and *la gloire* and flags, and—but anyway—

How were he and de Gaulle together? Did you see them?

No, I didn't see them together very much, but you know, he was de Gaulle's lieutenant all through those years. Oh, de Gaulle—well, de Gaulle was rather grand with him, especially as I wanted to talk to him—he was always sort of leading you away. You know, in public he's very—he treats him like some servant, like Nehru treats the man who sleeps outside his door, or something.

Jim Gavin was our ambassador.

Yes.

His was always a rather puzzling appointment. I know the President wanted to do something for Jim, who certainly is a fine man. Do you know why he was—did you ever—did the President ever say why?

Why he was appointed? I think he asked him to do something else, didn't he? Which he wouldn't do. I don't know why. Oh, he thought they'd like Gavin because of—

Ah, yes. General.

Yeah, he thought they'd like him because of the war, but then I know he was rather disappointed when Gavin's cables would come back. Jack used to quote Winston Churchill—"Never trust the man on the spot." And you know, that he'd gone so—I remember Malraux saying about him, "Oh, yes, Gavin, *il est Gaullist.*" And you know something else nice that Jack did? This is the same sort of thing that he did about Allen Dulles and the Wrightsmans. When the *Mona Lisa* came over here, Gavin was no longer ambassador. He'd had to resign for money reasons. The Alphands[95] came to dinner one night, we were discussing who they would have at the French Embassy and the *Mona Lisa* dinner. She could only have a hundred and two and I think she was up to ninety-nine or something—Jack put Dick Goodwin on the list because he wanted to show how much he thought of him.[96] But also he said, "But you don't have the Gavins here." And Nicole said, "No, no, why should we have the Gavins?" And Jack said, "Well, I think you better ask them." And when they'd gone home, Jack said, "Can you believe it?" He said, "But there was Gavin, who was the most pro–de Gaulle ambassador they ever had. And they're probably one of our ambassadors that they liked the best. And then he's out and they weren't even going to ask him to the dinner." He was disgusted.

As you say, ruthless.

[whisper] I'm sort of running out.

How did he like Hervé?

Oh, old Hervé? You know, he'd get amused by him sometimes. And then—amused and sort of irritated the way, you know, Hervé has that phobia about protocol. But then, as he always said, de Gaulle never spoke to Hervé. You know, it was very hard for Hervé. And every time we'd see David Gore or Caroline would go to play with Alice Ormsby-Gore, or something, you'd hear Hervé moaning all around Washington. But he enjoyed—Hervé could be funny sometimes.

Very good mimic.

---

95. HERVÉ ALPHAND (1907–1994) was French ambassador to Washington, much aided by his wife Nicole (1917–1979).

96. RICHARD GOODWIN (1931–), a former law clerk under Justice Felix Frankfurter, had worked for JFK since 1959 as campaign speechwriter, assistant special counsel, and diplomat, and was slated in November 1963 to replace August Heckscher (1913–1997) as the President's chief adviser on the arts. While in Paris, Jacqueline had consulted Malraux about the possibility of creating an American counterpart to Malraux's culture ministry and "what was realistic" to expect.

Yeah, do you remember the toast he made at that party for Ken Galbraith about a Gemini? That he was a Gemini and Jack—it was just after Jack's birthday—and Jack was a Gemini. And he wished a toast—all Gemini men were virile, brilliant, kind—it was terribly funny—and he wished to congratulate his government on having chosen him, as a Gemini, to be ambassador to a Gemini President, and then he ended, *"Vive Lafayette!"* You know, just the whole parody. I always used to tease him so about Lafayette. So he can—he was all right.

The
SIXTH
Conversation

TUESDAY, JUNE 2

1964

*W*e left off last time at the—after the meeting at Vienna, when Khrushchev brought up the whole Berlin thing in a very tough way.[1] You remember the President said to him, "It looks as if it's going to be a long, cold winter." The whole Berlin business, of course, involved constant relations with the Germans. What was the President's feeling about these dealings with West Germany?

As I said before, he tried so hard not to bring problems that irritated him all day home. For himself really more than me, but that was one thing that he—that just irritated him so and he'd say, "What do you have to do to show the Germans that you care?"—that we would defend Berlin. And then it would always—it just seemed the least tiny thing could happen—some colonel drop his hat on the Autobahn and it would give—Adenauer would start flaming up all over again, and saying that we were going to pull out, and the ambassador here, Grewe, would come running in. And Jack really got irritated with the Germans. And, I remember after the missile crisis, which is much later, he got so irritated with de Gaulle because—what did de Gaulle say? That because we jumped in to take care of Cuba, it showed we only were interested in the things nearer our shores and not over there. Well, when you think of it, it wasn't until after his visit to Berlin in June '63 that he finally did convince them. And then he was really happy after that. And then all these

---

1. Since 1958, Khrushchev had been issuing deadlines and using other tactics in an effort to force the United States and other Western powers out of West Berlin.

leaks to the—to the press. The Germans were always doing that, leaking to the press both in Germany and in Washington, little things of lack of confidence. Adenauer, something he'd say about him—I guess he sort of admired Adenauer, but he said, "Look at that man, eighty-nine, just hanging on so hard." I forget when Adenauer left.[2] But he said, "Can you imagine it, and trying desperately to get back in again?" And, you know, Adenauer really gave him a pain. But I can remember the Berlin crisis, just sort of coming all through that—I guess was it the—

It was constant really from the middle of—summer of 1962 until the Cuban crisis.

So, it was then a year after Vienna that it finally came and he made a speech?[3]

Yeah, no, I mean from the summer of 1961. It began the summer of Vienna and it went from there until the Cuban crisis, really, in November '62.

Well, when did he make his Berlin speech?

He made his speech in June 1961, after he got back from Vienna. He made the speech calling for an enlargement of the military, of the defense budget.

But is that when he said, "We do not like to fight but we have fought before."

Um-hmm.

And "They said that Stalingrad was untenable and free men have always fought"—yeah, and "They said Stalingrad was untenable," and this and that, and "We do not like to fight, but we have fought before."[4] Anyway, I could just remember one of the few times—I always thought with Jack that anything,

---

2. Adenauer stepped down as chancellor in October 1963.

3. JFK's television speech from the Oval Office on the Berlin crisis of July 25, 1961, in which he announced a defense budget increase and call-ups of American reservists.

4. The President's exact words were these: "I hear it said that West Berlin is militarily untenable. And so was Bastogne. And so, in fact, was Stalingrad. Any dangerous spot is tenable if men—brave men—will make it so."

he could make—once he was in control, anything, all the best things would happen. In this childish way, I thought, "I won't have to be afraid when I go to sleep at night or wake up." But you could see after that Khrushchev meeting, I mean, he was really in a gloom, which he wouldn't talk about, but you could just tell by a sort of—a certain quietness and lowness. So, I thought—I remember a couple of times, just a little shooting pain of fright going through me, thinking is—"Cannot even Jack make this turn out for the best?" And so this mounting thing—and then, when he was going to go on television to speak of Berlin, all the tension and everything around the White House. And I can remember again him march—and scribbling on the pages and, you know, for a few days before. And maybe he'd read me a line or something. But, and then I can remember that day, looking out—my dressing room window looked on the Rose Garden—and his office and all the television cables, and I remember thinking, "Shall I go over in his office and watch it?" But then I thought, "No, that might make him more nervous," or "People would start taking pictures, or something. I'd better just watch it up here." And, well, that was one of the grimmest speeches I've ever seen him make.

It was probably the grimmest speech he gave.

Yeah. And you just couldn't believe that you were sitting there thinking that, well, you really might have to go to war. And then—

Grimmest speech except, of course, for the Cuban Missile speech.

That was sort of the first one, so it almost frightened me more because by the time of the missile crisis—of course, you were scared all through it, but, you know, Berlin was the first one and then it did turn out all right. So, well, that's what I remember about that.

Yes, Berlin was the—really the big thing in the summer and fall of '61, and then as a result of our reaction, you remember, Khrushchev then extended the deadline and so—

That's right.

In, I believe, November.

And then, I remember thinking a couple of times how true it was—something rather interesting about Jack that he had by nature, and in politics I used to see it, this conciliatory nature, which never meant that you sort of sucked around people or tried to curry favor, but—what did he say? Pol—"In politics you don't have friends," or something, "you have colleagues," or—

Interests—was it?

No, it's—is it "You don't have friends or allies, you have colleagues"—well, you can look it up. But I often used to say to him, some man would come to dinner, a newspaperman or a politician, and I'd say, "But you were so nice to him," or "You're speaking nicely about him, and I was so mad about him for what he wrote two weeks ago or said two weeks ago that I've been cutting that man dead all day, and now I'm meant to be nice to him?" And Jack would say, "Of course, you know, that's all over, and then he did this and that." So, you know, his relationships always changed and he never made it hard for anyone to come back and be forgiven or, you know, go on in a new relationship with him. Which was so true in marriage too. It just carried him to every phase. And I remember thinking, "Thank God he has that side and not that old funny Dulles side where nobody, you know, where you'd have to make people grovel so!"[5] And I remember thinking of the Inaugural Address—"Let's never negotiate out of fear"[6]—because I thought how humiliating really for Khrushchev to have to back down. And yet, somehow Jack let him do it with grace and didn't rub his nose in it.[7] And somehow, that was the quality which we should all be the most grateful for. It's how we got through all these crises.

---

5. Referring to Eisenhower's often intractable secretary of state, John Foster Dulles (1888–1959).

6. "Let us never negotiate out of fear, but let us never fear to negotiate"—an admonition contributed to the speech by Galbraith.

7. Notably after the missile crisis, when Kennedy ordered his aides not to crow about the apparent American victory, explaining that if Khrushchev felt embarrassed, the Russian might feel compelled to launch some other gambit that might take the world to the edge of destruction. The President also knew that his private settlement with Khrushchev was less clear-cut than the public impression that he had managed to win the Soviet leader's unconditional surrender. In fact, Khrushchev had made a tacit deal with Kennedy to remove the missiles if the President would force the withdrawal of (outmoded) NATO missiles from Turkey and (on condition that Castro would permit on-site inspections of his military installations, which he never did) pledge never to authorize a U.S. invasion of Cuba.

Yes, it was a marvelous thing this—to leave a way for your opponent to retreat and preserve his dignity.

Yeah. And if you wanted lots of popularity in the newspapers or something, you'd go around shouting things about "No one's going to tell him to say this to America," and then you'd just be, everybody'd be shooting before you knew it. So, it's that side of him which—it was always so easy when you were married. I mean, a little tiny thing might come up that would cloud—but you never really had a fight, but I might say something that would sort of hurt his feelings and there'd be a certain quietness that day. And then suddenly, I'd come running and say, "Oh, I'm so sorry!" and throw my arms around him, and he'd just laugh and everything was over. He never would hold, or make you really—that just ran all through his personality. And you know, Bobby's getting it—and it was a side of Bobby that's lacking a bit which he's developing much more now and which since November he's spoken to me so much about Jack, the side that he admired in him so much. It was really easier for Jack to be that way when he had Bobby doing a lot of the things. But it was also much more part of his personality. Bobby will get that way.

As the Berlin thing was dying down in November, Nehru came and made his visit—

Yes, and—that was a rather nerve-wracking visit.[8] Lots of consultations with Galbraith, and everything. And Galbraith kept saying Nehru wanted no fuss, and everything private. And I remember Jack had shown me a memorandum the winter before about—was it Sihanouk of Cambodia?

Prince—yeah, Prince Sihanouk.

Well, anyway, who—from the State Department—it was saying, "This man will say that he wants nothing special, no treatment, but yet he'll be furious if

---

8. JAWAHARLAL NEHRU (1889–1964), the Indian prime minister and Gandhi lieutenant who had been imprisoned during his country's independence struggle, came to the United States in November 1961. Kennedy found Nehru grimly unaffected by his charm. He later called it "the worst head-of-state visit I have had." (Actually Nehru was merely a head of government.)

you don't lay the red carpet out and sort of have throngs." So Jack sort of was wondering whether Galbraith's advice was quite right because he thought Nehru would like a lot more pomp. But no, Galbraith thought he just wanted to be received in our home. Well, Hyannis just seemed a little too depressing, so we went to Newport and we met him at—whatever that air force base is there.[9] He came over with his daughter and Galbraith and the Indian ambassador, B. K. Nehru. And Jack had had a most unsatisfactory time with Nehru when he'd been a congressman in India. He said they'd warned him, "Whenever Nehru gets bored with you, he taps his fingertips together and looks up at the ceiling." And Jack said he'd been there about ten minutes when Nehru started to look up at the ceiling.

When had they met?—I hadn't realized they'd met before.

Well, Jack had toured the Far East with Bobby and Pat.[10]

Was it '51?

It was before we were married.

Yeah, '50 or '51.[11]

It was when he met General de Lattre, whom he was so impressed with.[12] That's when he nearly died in Okinawa. If Bobby hadn't come in, he would have died then. He got a fever of 105 or -6. And he met Nehru on that trip, I think. So, anyway, they came and it was decided the men would eat in the dining room.

---

9. From the Newport naval station, the Kennedys took Nehru to the Auchincloss estate, Hammersmith Farm.

10. His sister Patricia.

11. In fact, it was 1951.

12. During his visit to Southeast Asia, Kennedy greatly annoyed the commander of French forces in Indochina, Jean de Lattre de Tassigny, by asking why the Vietnamese should want to give their lives merely so that their country would remain a French possession.

Angie Duke was there too.[13] And Mrs. Gandhi[14] and I would have a little ladies'
lunch in the living room—and Lem Billings was with us.[15] Well, of course, she
hated that. She liked to be in with the men. And she is a real prune—bitter,
kind of pushy, horrible woman. You know, I just don't like her a bit. It always
looks like she's been sucking a lemon. And Jack brought Nehru back on the
Honey Fitz and Caroline and I were waiting for him at the front door, which
she'd picked a little flower for him and made a curtsey. That's the first time he
sort of smiled. And then we went and had a drink before lunch and Nehru never
said one word. It was just such heavy going. You could ask him something,
anything. Just that real Hindu thing—you learn it in India, that they don't look
on social gatherings as a time to speak. I don't know if they're contemplating—
but I also say it's just damned spoiled brattishness because you should make an
effort when other people are trying. So anyway, they had their lunch, and I
don't know what they talked about. And then we all went back in the helicopter,
Nehru in the best seat, Caroline on Jack's lap next to him, back to Washington.
And that night they came for dinner. And I think it was when—anyway, it
was the first dinner of that fall in the White House. And we lit the fire in the
Oval Room[16] and then went downstairs to meet them at the front door. And
of course, somebody hadn't opened the flue of the fireplace, so when we came
back in that room the smoke was just so thick and everyone's eyes were pour-
ing. That wasn't a very good start. And it was meant to be, as you remember, a
rather small dinner, but yet it wasn't quite small enough or big enough because
we were in the State Dining Room, and just enough of us so that it was rather
like sitting in a church with not enough people there. And I remember Jack told
me later that Mrs. Gandhi, all through dinner, really lit out at Jack on our policy
somewhere and this and that and she said lots of nice things about Krishna

---

13. ANGIER BIDDLE DUKE (1915–1995) was a tobacco heir and diplomat who served as JFK's chief of
protocol.

14. INDIRA GANDHI (1917–1984) later succeeded her father as Indian prime minister.

15. LEMOYNE BILLINGS (1916–1981), a New York advertising executive, had been Kennedy's friend
since their time at Choate School. Mrs. Kennedy told the chief of the Executive Mansion's household
staff that Billings had been their houseguest "every weekend since I've been married."

16. Meaning the Yellow Oval Room in the family quarters, which Jacqueline was transforming into
an elegant parlor.

Menon[17] and everything. And you know, Jack really didn't like her. My sister was there and I so badly wanted her to sit next to Nehru, who should have sat next to Lady Bird. And so I said, "What shall I do?" And Jack said, "Call up Lady Bird before because she might expect to go and ask her if it's all right." Which I did, and she was sweet, and understood. Which just shows one more thoughtfulness that Jack always had for his vice president. Well, Nehru does sort of like pretty women in the most unlecherous way. But it's just the only—he sort of talked between Lee and I, and you could get him to say something about something and make a little joke. So, he was rather nice then. And I think he asked us to come to India. I think that's when he did it. That's when the whole idea started. And that's the part I remember. Oh, he always took—there's a picture of him taking my arm.

Yes, yes.

Well, we got sort of, to be a little bit friends in Newport, and then the helicopter and the plane. And you know, he always takes your arm. He was sort of sweet to me and they did bring the most touching, thoughtful presents for the children and—little boxes, little costumes, nothing very fabulous. So they'd obviously cared about the trip and had this chip on their shoulder, I don't know. We tried to be so nice to them. And then the next night there was a big dinner at the Indian embassy and again I sat next to Nehru. I found him very easy and charming, you know, and he seemed to so like to have someone make a—you know, I always felt that he liked me. But I just think it was really sticky going in the conferences.

What did the President—did the President say anything afterwards? Was he disappointed in Nehru?

I think he was. I think the meetings got absolutely nowhere and there was an awful lot of tapping the fingers and looking up at the ceiling. And you know, "Nehru's like trying"—did Jack say that about Nehru or someone else? "It's like trying to grab in your hand something and it turns out to just be fog."

---

17. VENGALIL KRISHNAN KRISHNA MENON (1896–1974) was Nehru's defense minister and an impassioned critic of U.S. foreign policy.

THE KENNEDYS AND PRIME MINISTER JAWAHARLAL NEHRU
AT THE INDIAN EMBASSY, NOVEMBER 9, 1961

And that's what it was like. And I think Nehru—in a way he was—would you say jealous of Jack, or something? Well, it was just someone so different than—

I think the generational thing played its part here. I think he must—I'm sure he—infinitely—was infinitely pleased that a man like Jack Kennedy was President of the United States, but on the other hand, a young, brilliant man half his age was bound to make him feel uncomfortable.

And then Mrs. Gandhi, his daughter, who's one of those women who when marriage and love and all those things don't turn out right, it's as if something—It all goes back inside you and the poison works inside like an ulcer, so she's a truly bitter woman. And she's the kind of woman who's always hated Jack. You can name so many violently liberal women in politics who were always suspicious of Jack. And they always loved Adlai. And I thought one reason—this is just my own sort of psychology—but that Jack so obviously demanded from a woman—a relationship between a man and a woman where a man would be the leader and a woman would be his wife and look up to him as a man. With Adlai you could have another relationship where—you know, he'd sort of be sweet and you could talk, but you wouldn't ever—wouldn't ever come down to a definite thing. I always thought women who were scared of sex loved Adlai—because there would never be the—

The challenge wasn't there at all.

Yeah. Not that there'd be the challenge with Jack but it was a different kind of man. So, you know, all these sort of twisted, poor little women whose lives hadn't worked out could find a balm in Adlai. And Jack made them nervous, which I used to tell Jack would say, "Why doesn't so and so . . . " and I'd say, "Jack, it's the greatest compliment to you." Which is, I know, is true. He didn't quite see it. He said that about your wife, as a matter of fact.

Oh, really?

He was very upset—when you came out for him, then a day or so later Marian came out for Adlai Stevenson—and he couldn't understand why because he'd—I think he'd just been down to lunch the day or so before, or a week before, and had a very nice time. You know, and he liked Marian and everything.[18] Well, I said, "That's because Arthur's so mean to her, *[Schlesinger laughs]* and Adlai was so nice." "I saw them together later, you know." I said, "That's different, that's her own personal problem, you know. That's got nothing to do with you. You mustn't hold it against Marian." And then later on when we were all in the White House together, then he—loved her and saw that she didn't really dislike him.

Oh, no, Marian, I may say, lived to regret that. I got such a—I remember a funny letter from Bobby after that. Something—he was writing about something else and he had a postscript to the effect, "I see you can't control your wife any better than I can control mine."[19] You know, that was an act of old loyalty on Marian's part.

---

18. MARIAN CANNON SCHLESINGER (1912–) was the painter daughter of a Harvard physiology teacher, who indeed endorsed Stevenson in 1960.

19. "Can't you control your wife? Or are you like me?"

Yeah.

She thought I was—shouldn't, you know—[20]

But I mean, in my marriage, I could never conceive—and I remember I said it in an interview once, and all these women—we got all these irate letters— someone said, "Where do you get your opinions?" And I said, "I get all my opinions from my husband." Which is true. How could I have any political opinions, you know? His were going to be the best. And I could never conceive of not voting for whoever my husband was for. Anyone who I'd be married to. I suppose if I was married to—well, you know. So that was just so strange because that was—I mean, it was really a rather terribly Victorian or Asiatic relationship which we had, which I had—

Yeah, a Japanese wife.

Yeah, which I think's the best. But anyway, that was Mrs. Gandhi.

She was a rancorous woman, and spiteful. I mean, she exuded spite. Was Nehru different on his home ground?[21]

Well, he was terribly sweet again to Lee and I, and he would come home every afternoon and take us for walks in the garden and we'd feed the pandas, and I think what he liked—one of his sisters, Mrs. Hutheesing—I guess she's the rather right-wing one who lives in Bombay, but she's great fun.[22] And she said to me—she'd come into Lee and my room and talk. And she said, "It's so good for my brother to have you two girls here. It's some relaxation." Because she says his daughter fills the poor man's life with politics. It's politics at lunch, politics at tea, politics at dinner. He never has any relaxation. So that visit—I

---

20. When Schlesinger announced his support of JFK before the 1960 convention, some old friends and Stevenson backers denounced him as a Benedict Arnold.

21. This refers to Mrs. Kennedy's official visit to India of March 1962, which she diplomatically balanced afterward with a stopover in the country's rival, Pakistan.

22. KRISHNA NEHRU HUTHEESING (1907–1967), a writer, was the prime minister's youngest sister.

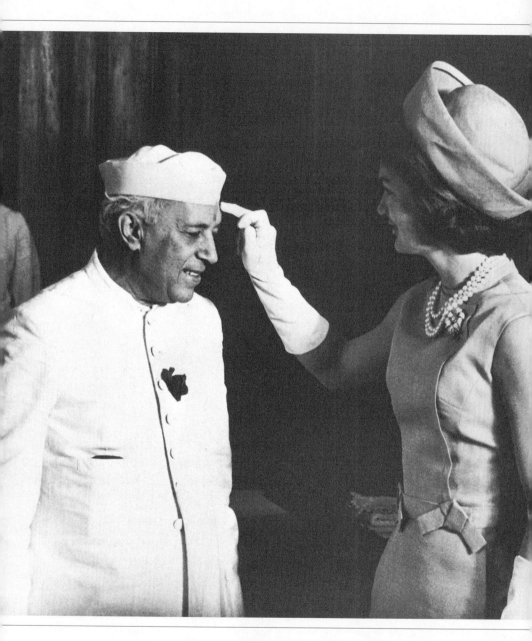

PRIME MINISTER NEHRU AND JACQUELINE KENNEDY IN INDIA

mean, nothing profound was talked about or even that we were going to Pakistan next, but, you know, it was a relaxation for him—the kind of thing I'd try to bring into Jack's life in our evenings at home. Someone who wasn't connected with what was worrying him all day. And so he just loved that trip and we got to be—well, he used to walk me back to my bedroom every night—two nights, I think, we were there, and sit in there for about an hour and talk to me.

And he'd be lively, would he? He wouldn't have this kind of vacant, passive—

Well, never lively, but sort of gentle and he would talk and he has those great brown eyes. I'd read all his autobiography and I'd ask him about some of those, you know, times—and he talked.

What would he talk about? About his own past and—

Well, I asked him about the times in prison, and everything—his life. And yeah, he'd talk about some of that. Or else he'd talk about people there, or make a little joke. He always was so—I've written it all down somewhere, everything we talked about, so maybe I can find it. It's the only thing I ever wrote down.

Oh, good. No, let's find that and the Library should have a copy.[23] The other big thing that happened in the fall of '61, or another one, was the resumption of nuclear testing by the Soviet Union and then—which confronted us with the problem of whether we should resume nuclear testing or not.[24] That was an old interest of the President's, was it?

Yes. I can remember him being so worried at the time about our resuming, and how long you should—you could possibly put it off and then everyone—I mean, that was a terrible time for him. There was nothing that wor-

---

23. Meaning the future Kennedy Library.

24. In the fall of 1961, after the Vienna summit, the Berlin Crisis, and the building of the Berlin Wall, Khrushchev tried to demonstrate Soviet might by ordering the largest nuclear test explosions ever. A furious JFK felt compelled to resume U.S. testing.

ried him more through—would it be '61 and '62?—than all this testing. But it started so long ago. Because I can remember when David Gore came to Hyannis the fall we were married—would be October or November 1953—and he was doing something at the UN on disarmament and he and Jack were talking. And you know, it was the first time I'd ever heard—it seemed so extraordinary—you never saw it in newspapers here. That you should sort of disarm or come to some agreement and then that would be possible without selling out or—you know, when you always thought all the Bertrand Russells[25] and "ban the bombers" and people were all sort of "pinks"—I mean, I just thought this from reading David Lawrence[26] in the newspapers. And I remember then—from then on, Jack started to say in his speeches that it was a disgrace that there were less than a hundred people working on disarmament in Washington—or less than ten, maybe.

Less than a hundred.

Less than a hundred. But he said that in all—and I think he said it all through his Senate campaign.[27] He certainly said it all through his campaign for the presidency, you know, but it started so long ago that he was thinking about that. And in a way, then David Gore came back again—in maybe '58 or—yes, or '57—I don't know what year he and Sissy came to the Cape. Again they'd be talking about that. And I remember when Harold Macmillan resigned last summer.[28] Well, Jack was so sad for that man—that he should have to go out in all the messy, sad way he did, you know, and he said, "People really don't realize what Macmillan has done," and he said he was the greatest friend of the Atlantic Alliance. But he said this nuclear disarmament thing—he just cared about that for so long. So that's what I tried—and then he sent him this

---

25. **BERTRAND RUSSELL** (1872–1970) was a British pacifist, philosopher, and Nobel laureate in literature.

26. **DAVID LAWRENCE** (1888–1973) was a conservative journalist and founder of *U.S. News & World Report*.

27. In 1958.

28. Actually in October 1963.

touching telegram and I remember poor Macmillan then.[29] Not many people were saying nice things to him. And David asked if the telegram could be made public, and Jack said, "Of course." And that's what I tried to put in when I talked to him on Telstar[30] just last week on Jack's—what would have been his forty-seventh birthday. You know, the things that I knew that Jack thought about him, and I found that telegram and read it and tried to say what Jack had said about him—and I kept thinking, "I just hope de Gaulle's listening." Not that anything matters now.

I have the impression that we would not have had a test ban treaty if both the President and the prime minister had not been so deeply committed and forced the issue so constantly on their advisers.[31]

---

29. Mrs. Kennedy did not know Macmillan remotely as well as the President had, but after Kennedy's death, she achieved a moving kind of intimacy with her husband's British friend by letter. At the end of January 1964, at midnight, she wrote Macmillan by hand in response to his condolence letter: "Sometimes I become so bitter, only alone—I don't tell anyone—but I do truly think that any poor school child looking at the record of the 1960s—could only decide that virtue is UNrewarded. The two greatest men of our time, you and Jack—all you fought for and cared about together. . . . And how does it all turn out? De Gaulle is there . . . and bitter old Adenauer—and the two people who have had to suffer are you and Jack. . . . You worked together for the finest things in the finest years—later on when a series of disastrous Presidents of the United States, and Prime Ministers who were not like you, will have botched up everything—people will say 'Do you remember those days—how perfect they were?' The days of you and Jack. . . . I always keep thinking of Camelot—which is overly sentimental—but I know I am right—for one brief shining moment there was Camelot—and it will never be that way again. . . . Please forgive this endless intrusion—but I just wanted to tell you how much Jack loved you—and I have not his gift of concision." Macmillan replied, "My dear Friend—this is how I used to write to Jack—so I am going to write it to you. . . . You have written from your heart to me, and I will do the same. . . . Of course one becomes bitter. How could you not be? . . . May God Bless you, my dear child. You have shown the most wonderful courage to the bitter outer world. The hard thing is really to feel it inside." On June 1, 1964, the day before this oral history interview, Jacqueline reported to Macmillan that she was feeling better now and the worst had passed. Later she wrote him that she was trying to raise her children as Jack would have wished—and that if she prevailed, then that would be her vengeance against the world. (This was one reason why, in later years, Jacqueline was particularly cheered when told by friends that she had succeeded as a mother.)

30. Launched in 1962, Telstar was the first communications satellite to allow television images to be beamed across the Atlantic. On the President's forty-seventh birthday, Jacqueline and Robert Kennedy appeared from Hyannis Port (using the same CBS crew that had produced her White House tour broadcast) in an international tribute that included Macmillan, Berlin mayor Willy Brandt, and other foreign leaders.

31. In August 1963, Kennedy, Khrushchev, and Macmillan consented to a treaty to ban nuclear tests in the atmosphere, outer space, and under water. De Gaulle, eager to build his own French nuclear deterrent,

I know. I know that's true, and I also think having David Gore here at the time made it—

Indispensable, yes.

Yeah. Sometimes—well, we can go into that relationship at another time, but so many things happened. He would come for dinner, and something awful would be going wrong in British Guiana or somewhere, and he would—all the time of Skybolt he was with us—and he would call and everything would be kept smooth. But what I just wanted to say about—I was thinking when I thought of Jack and Macmillan really making this test ban thing possible—of just how outrageous of de Gaulle. Of the one thing that really matters and that egomaniac not to be associated with that when that's going to be the one thing that matters in this whole century. And then Graham Sutherland, who's a painter, who I saw a couple of weeks ago about doing a picture of Jack—but he said something to me so interesting. He said, "The extraordinary thing about President Kennedy was that power made him a better man," and he said it made so many people worse men. He knew Winston Churchill. He painted him. He said Winston, you know, became less nice—and of course, it made Adenauer meaner. And of course, de Gaulle was the classic example. Well, it made—Jack a chance to work for good and I really think Harold Macmillan too.

Do you have any memory of the President's impression of people like Arthur Dean, or McCloy or Foster, in connection with the test ban?[32]

Not really.

---

refused to sign it. (JFK privately carped at the time that de Gaulle would be remembered for one thing—his failure to accept that treaty.) Despite Kennedy's large efforts, the document did not preclude underground testing, but it represented the first serious mutual effort by Americans and Soviets to control the Cold War nuclear arms competition that threatened the planet from 1949 until 1991. Especially after the almost-apocalypse of the missile crisis, Kennedy considered it his proudest achievement. He signed it on October 7, 1963, in the Victorian splendor of Jacqueline's new Treaty Room.

32. ARTHUR DEAN (1899–1980), William Foster (1897–1984), and John McCloy had all been asked by JFK to help to negotiate a test ban treaty with the Soviets.

PRIME MINISTER HAROLD MACMILLAN AND JACQUELINE KENNEDY
IN FRONT OF NUMBER TEN DOWNING STREET, LONDON, 1961

This again was one of those prolonged things that kept dragging on for a long time.

Yeah. And oh, the discouragement, and then you just think of Arthur Dean. I remember I used to feel sorry for him—just sitting in Geneva all his life—because I'd been in that depressing city. And now that's the kind of thing you wouldn't talk about at night. But I don't remember hearing him say he was disappointed with anyone or—I remember him saying wonderful things about Harriman—

Yes. When Harriman came in at the end it was a—I think the Russians feel that when Harriman is sent to negotiate that the United States means business, and that that was absolutely necessary to—[33]

And it was very touching, Jack's relationship with Harriman, because, of course there were all these young men around, and here was this man who went back so many administrations. But he just kept going up and up, didn't he?—and getting to do more and more important things, and then Jack was so happy, saying for Averell—well, he was so happy for Averell Harriman really after the test ban treaty, he thought—you know, that "That's really quite a crown." And there'd been something in Teddy White's book, a little footnote, about Averell Harriman, saying that he had done all these extraordinary things in foreign policy, but that domestically everything he'd done was disastrous.[34] And I remember Jack feeling sort of sorry for him when he read that part of the book and feeling so happy that this crowning thing came at the end for Averell Harriman.[35]

---

33. W. AVERELL HARRIMAN (1891–1986) was the son and heir of one of the late nineteenth century's most famous railroad barons. He served as Franklin Roosevelt's wartime ambassador to Moscow and governor of New York before he was a high official in JFK's State Department. The President sent Harriman to Moscow to demonstrate the seriousness of his commitment to achieving a treaty and was impressed by Harriman's brilliant success. In December 1963, he lent his Georgetown house to Mrs. Kennedy for her family to use as they waited to move into their new home.

34. THEODORE WHITE (1915–1986), a friend of JFK's who had overlapped with him at Harvard and wrote the landmark book on presidential politics, *The Making of the President, 1960*. In that volume, White wrote that "no man proved more capable of exercising the end form of American power around the globe" than Harriman, but that "no man proved more incapable of understanding American domestic politics" than Harriman.

35. In fact, it was not the political end for Harriman. He soldiered on as a senior diplomat for the two Democratic presidents who followed John Kennedy.

In—

I gave him a copy of the test ban treaty which the Archives[36] did especially for me—you can't tell it from the original—when we left his house after he lent it to us after November.

That's wonderful. It was in that winter that—in that fall and winter—that Hickory Hill began and in the winter of '62, there was a meeting at the White House which David Donald, who is a professor at Princeton, spoke about the Civil War.[37] I wasn't there, but the President mentioned it to me later. He apparently found it stimulating.

Yes, those seminars that Bobby did—well, Jack always wanted to go to them but he just wanted to go to hear you. I mean he'd heard that you'd finished Jackson and everything and it was an effort to go out, so finally when he heard there was going to be an interesting one, which was this Civil War-Reconstruction thing, he said, "Let's have it at the White House." It was the first one—it was meant to have been at the Gilpatrics. And it was so strange because I remember when the question period started, everyone was very quiet and rather nervous in the White House and the President there, and Jack asked Donald, "Do you think"—it's the one thing that was on his mind—"Would Lincoln have been as great a President if he'd lived?" I mean, would he be judged as great—because he would have had this almost insoluble problem of the Reconstruction, which, you know, either way you did it would have dissatisfied so many people. That was his question. And Donald, really by going round and round, had agreed with him that Lincoln, you know, it was better—was better for Lincoln that he died when he did. And then I remember Jack saying after the Cuban Missile Crisis, when it all turned so fantastically, he said, "Well, if anyone's ever going to shoot me, this would be the day they should do it."[38]

---

36. National Archives of the United States.

37. Eminent officials of the Kennedy government attended what came to be called "Hickory Hill seminars" (named for the venue of the first), which were held in various of their homes. Organized by Schlesinger, an academic would lecture and take questions on his own expertise. The evening with the Lincoln historian David Herbert Donald (1920–2009) took place in the Yellow Oval Room.

38. After Khrushchev promised to withdraw his missiles from Cuba, JFK ruminated to Robert

Oh, really?

I mean, it's so strange, these things that come back, because he saw then that he would be—you know, he said, it will never top this. Strange those things come back now.

Had that Lincoln question that he asked Donald—one that he discussed before? Been on his mind?

Oh, yes, because all the time we discussed it. The first year I was married, I took a course in American history at the Georgetown School of Foreign Service from Professor Jules Davids, who was this brilliant man. And I'd never taken American history and I used to come home full of these things and I was so excited—Thaddeus Stevens and the radical Republicans, I can remember. And these awful poems they were writing about Lincoln. And Jack was excited that I was so interested. And then when he was doing *Profiles in Courage,* I told him how great Davids was, and he had him do some research on it. So at that time, we would talk a lot about Lincoln and the Reconstruction, and, you know, if he lived and that—and that was back when we were married was '53, '54, and then his book was '54–'55—so we talked about it years before.

There was another Hickory Hill meeting at the White House—Isaiah Berlin.

Where they talked about Russia.

Yes.

Yeah, well, Jack loved that and he loved to just listen to Isaiah Berlin.[39] I mean, that was the side—you should read this article in *Show* magazine now,

---

Kennedy that it might be the night to go to the theater, referring to Lincoln's assassination in Ford's Theatre at the zenith of his political reputation. Robert replied that if he did, he would want to go with him.

39. ISAIAH BERLIN (1909–1997) was a British diplomat and historian who had served in Moscow during World War II.

which I think is quite unfair in its judgment of Jack but it starts from the premise that *Melbourne* was his favorite book and says what he really was most like were these great Whig houses and Whig liberal families who, you know, had everything and lived a stimulating life, yet cared. Well, he loved all those brilliant English people. He used to tell me about going to Emerald Cunard's[40] when he was a boy in London with his father to listen. When we were in London together, we'd go to the old Duchess of Devonshire's for lunch and she'd have a couple of people around. I mean, he loved so to hear those people talk. Or hear David. You know, they knew so much, their educations were so incredible. That's when he was happiest. So he loved Isaiah Berlin.

Do you want to say something about the relationship of David? Because I think that was a very fundamental thing in all this. I have the impression he talked with greater—more intimately with David than with any member of the—

Yeah.

—of his own cabinet.

Well, I suppose—

Outside of Bobby.

Exactly. And if I could think of anyone now who could save the Western world, it would be David Gore. But—well, they started as friends obviously in London, and Kathleen, who was Jack's favorite sister, was Sissy's best friend. And, I guess, David was the closest of all those friends then. I mean, so many of them ended up with rather sad lives, or this or that.

This is back in '38–'39.

---

40. MAUD ALICE BURKE (1872–1948), known as Lady Emerald Cunard, born in America, was a famous pre–World War II London hostess.

Yeah. Hugh Fraser was sort of a friend, but not very bright, and you'd always wonder if Hugh would get a job in some government and he never did, or it was a pathetic one. But whenever David was here, we'd see him and Jack used to say that David Gore was the brightest man he'd ever met. He used to say that he and Bundy were. But he'd say that David more so than Bundy because Bundy's intelligence is almost so—it's so highly tuned that he couldn't often see the larger thing around him. I mean, David was more rooted, more compassionate. I can't describe it.

David has more wisdom, I think, than—Mac is a brilliantly intelligent man but David's judgment is more—

And David has also the conciliatory sort of side that Jack did. You know, Bundy can get mad and then sort of arrogant and then make conciliation impossible. And Bundy in the missile crisis, when you think of that great mind, in the beginning he wanted to go in and bomb Cuba. And at the end, he wanted to do nothing. So, if you'd been relying on that great intelligence, look where we'd be? But—

How often would he see David?

Well, we'd see them a lot. We'd always see them. They would stay with us, usually on vacations, or they'd come for a weekend to Camp David, or the country, or the Cape. Or they'd come for dinner maybe once a month or so. You stopped asking them too much. We used to do it rather spontaneously, and of course they'd be involved in something official and then they'd get out of it, so I thought I just can't do that to them. So we didn't see them as much as we would have. We would have seen them every week if they hadn't been ambassador.

It killed the Alphands, as it was.[41]

---

41. The French ambassador was intensely jealous of Ormsby-Gore's extraordinary relationship with the Kennedys. The President and First Lady placed some distance between themselves and the Alphands also because of de Gaulle's growing resistance to JFK's overtures and efforts to keep France firmly in the Western Alliance.

And they'd always be talking on the phone. So many times, "Get me the British ambassador." And David would tell you sometimes of the extraordinary places he'd been when he was ferreted out to talk to Jack. And as I said, with David—well, there was this one thing about British Guiana which one night David really was worried about and Jack said, "Well, what shall I do?" and it was against rather our position, but David said, "You should call U Thant"[42] and tell him whatever it was. So anyway, Jack did that and everything, you know, worked out well. And then this Skybolt thing—after Nassau,[43] David came back to Florida with us and, of course, the next day the whole thing blew up. Godfrey McHugh came tearing in, saying, "Have you heard the wonderful news, Mr. President? They've just shot off Skybolt and it worked," or something. And Jack said, "What? Goddamn you, Godfrey, get out of here!" And he—so, anyway, he and David sat there and everything was so awful. And they called Gilpatric, and McNamara was away and then David went into another room and called Harold Macmillan. But you know, that closeness kept—well, I mean, everything could have blown apart between England and America then. And of all Jack's friends now, David Gore's the one, I'd say next to Bobby and me, he's the one who's been the most wounded.[44] Perhaps that's not fair, but he's the friend that I'll always see for the rest of my life. So many of the others I can't bear to see because I miss—Jack's lacking. I mean, the Bartletts, the Bradlees, the people you saw like that. Anyway—

---

42. U THANT (1909–1974) was a Burmese diplomat who served as secretary-general of the UN from 1961 to 1971.

43. Kennedy met with Macmillan for three days at the Lyford Cay Club in the Bahamas in December 1962. Before the meeting, the United States, citing technical problems, had cancelled its program to build Skybolt missiles, which had been promised to the U.K. for its nuclear deterrent force. When this was announced by the British defense minister, Peter Thorneycroft, Macmillan suffered political embarrassment—especially with Parliament critics who complained that he was too close and subservient to Kennedy. At Nassau, the President tried to bolster Macmillan by offering him Polaris missiles in return for lease of a submarine base near Glasgow. After the meeting, Ormsby-Gore accompanied the Kennedys to Palm Beach. There General Godfrey McHugh (1911–1997), the President's air force aide, made his inopportune report that whatever technical difficulties Skybolt had suffered, they had evidently vanished. Mortified to have injured Macmillan, JFK asked the Columbia political scientist Richard Neustadt to investigate the gaffe. Studying Neustadt's report with fascination in November 1963, Kennedy urged Jackie to read it.

44. By JFK's death.

Well, David is one of the—sort of intellectually and emotionally he's a rich person, and a generous one, and—

And he's not—ambitious. I always kept hoping he'd give up his title and be prime minister one day, but I think he'll be foreign secretary. He's not—he doesn't have this drive that Jack did, but he still cares. I suppose he can do as much that way.

Well, I've been after him too to try to get him to give up his title, but it's clear that he's probably not—not going to do it.

It isn't because he cares that much about his title. It's just that he's never been pushy.

That's right. He thinks if he does this it will signal the fact that he wants to be prime minister, which he thinks is an absurd thing for him to want to be. Well, of course, it isn't. In the winter of or in early spring of '63, one big thing, of course, was the steel crisis and—were you—you were around then?[45]

And I remember how really outraged Jack was. You know, it's one of the few times—he really controlled his temper. I mean, you never saw him lose it, but just sometimes that flash. I mean, he was really—what Roger Blough did to him—

He felt that Roger Blough had double-crossed him.

---

45. **ROGER BLOUGH (1904–1985)** was board chairman of U.S. Steel from 1955 to 1969. In March 1962, the Kennedy Administration brokered an agreement with the Steelworkers Union and industry chieftains to hold down wage and price increases that were potentially inflationary. But in April 1962 Blough told JFK that U.S. Steel was raising prices by 3.5 percent, thereby violating the deal. Most other large steel firms did the same. Furious, the President felt betrayed. He publicly denounced the steel men as enemies of the public interest. Robert Kennedy opted for what he called "hardball." He had a grand jury consider antitrust indictments, and ordered the FBI to "interview them all—march into their offices the next day" and, with the benefit of subpoena, to examine the moguls' expense accounts and other personal records for evidence of unlawful collusion. (In this effort, the FBI called a reporter at 2:00 or 3:00 a.m., which brought public complaints about brutal tactics.) Clark Clifford and other administration officials badgered the steel men to rescind their price increases. Within seventy-two hours, Blough and his colleagues backed down.

Yes. I just remember the expression. His mouth was really tight. And you just didn't do that, you just didn't behave that way. Bobby said to me later that if we'd known the people like André Meyer or something, or had more friends in that community, perhaps it could have all been arranged with less bitterness. But then I can remember that it was back and forth between his office and the White House and calling everyone and getting—Clark Clifford was the one person they found who they thought the others would trust—and sending him up to negotiate and which person would back out. It was the man—I met him the other day.

From Chicago.

Was it Laughlin?[46] Or whichever company first broke, and he was at the Library dinner for Jack. Oh, and then I remember Bobby saying to me later, November, that—Remember how it said in the press that the FBI got sent into everybody's home at night or something—the reporters—

Woke up reporters at two in the morning.

Bobby was talking about how awful J. Edgar Hoover's been since Jack died and the way he curries favor with Lyndon Johnson by sending him all these awful reports about everyone. Bobby said that he'd always, you know, tried to deal so nicely with Hoover and whenever anything—anything the FBI ever did well, it was fine with him if Hoover took credit for it and anything the FBI ever did badly, you know, Bobby would take credit for it. And that was all the FBI, not Bobby, who sent those people in—which was what really caused an awful lot of the bitterness against Jack, wasn't it?

Yes. Yeah. Sort of sounds like—

I mean, I can't remember who they wrote up, or what reporter they would be waking up right now. But I remember Jack being upset at that.

---

46. Jones and Laughlin Steel Company.

Arthur Goldberg played an active role in this steel thing and Ted Sorensen, I suppose, I imagine. But the President was really—

It seems to me mostly Jack on the phone and Clark Clifford. But I suppose all the rest went on in the office—I don't know.

Would you say that this—he was madder over this than anything else, on any other occasion in the administration?

I think just after Roger Blough came in his office and told him that—you know, a flare. And as I say, the second closest thing I've seen to it is sometimes after the Germans have done one more damn irritating but relatively minor thing. Yes, I would say the steel thing. And then it changed from madness—I mean, all the time he was acting in the crisis, he wasn't acting out of madness and temper. Then it was just trying to see how you could—then he was working it like a chess board. Well, I guess you just don't do that.

How about Governor Barnett in Mississippi? Was he mad then or was he more—I suppose he was less—he felt betrayed by Blough. He had no reason, I guess, to expect Barnett to act differently from the way he did.[47]

Well, you see, Barnett—it was just so hopeless. And you knew the man was an inferior, welshing person to begin with. There was never rage there, it was—oh, I don't know, just hopeless. And you know what I can remember? I was in Newport in bed and he called me—it was that night—and at five o'clock in the morning, the phone rang and I guess he'd just gone back to the White House after staying up all night and, you know, I was so touched that he called me because he just wanted to talk, and he'd said, "Oh, my God!" You wouldn't realize what it had been like and I guess when, you know, the tear gas started to run out and the troops that were meant to get there in an

---

47. ROSS BARNETT (1898–1987) was governor of Mississippi from 1960 to 1964. In September 1962, the President and attorney general bargained by telephone with the mercurial Barnett for the peaceful entrance into the University of Mississippi at Oxford of its first African-American student, James Meredith. It failed. Kennedy had to send the army to put down the resulting riots, which left two people dead.

hour were still four hours away. And I guess that was just one of the worst nights of his whole life.

Was the civil rights thing something he talked much about?

You know, it was over such a long period of time, and there were always—all the Barnetts and then the Wallaces,[48] and I mean one sort of awful problem after another, and first thinking that Little Rock had been so badly handled, I guess he thought, and then you see him presented with an almost worse Little Rock[49]—Oxford and—oh, yeah, and then with—

What did he think of the Negro leaders? Martin Luther King, for example? Did he ever mention—

Well, I don't think—I don't know what he—well, I do know what he thought of him later. Well, he said what an incredible speaker he was during that freedom march thing and—and he acknowledged that having made that call during the campaign got them—Then he told me of a tape that the FBI had of Martin Luther King when he was here for the freedom march. And he said this with no bitterness or anything, how he was calling up all these girls and arranging for a party of men and women, I mean, sort of an orgy in the hotel, and everything.[50]

---

48. GEORGE WALLACE (1919–1998) served the first of his four terms as governor of Alabama from 1963 until 1967. In June 1963, a month after angry dogs were set upon black teenagers demonstrating for civil rights in Birmingham, the governor announced his intention to block a judicial order to enroll two African-American students at the University of Alabama at Tuscaloosa. In a ritual choreographed by the Kennedy brothers, who wished to avoid violence, Wallace stood in the schoolhouse door, denouncing "this illegal, unwarranted and force-induced intrusion by the federal government." Deputy Attorney General Katzenbach, backed by a federalized Alabama National Guard, asked the governor to step aside, which he did. That evening, on television, JFK announced that he was sending a comprehensive civil rights bill to Congress, citing "a moral issue . . . as old as the Scriptures and as clear as the American Constitution."

49. She refers to the storm surrounding President Eisenhower's use of the U.S. Army's 101st Airborne Division to compel the integration of Little Rock Central High School in Arkansas in 1957.

50. MARTIN LUTHER KING, JR. (1929–1968) was the best-known leader of the American civil rights movement when he delivered his "I Have a Dream" address at the March on Washington (which Jacqueline calls the "freedom march") of August 1963. When the event was over, JFK welcomed King

Martin Luther King?

Oh, yeah. At first he said, oh, well, you know—and I said, "Oh, but Jack, that's so terrible. I mean, that man is, you know, such a phony then." No, this wasn't—this was when it was just one girl, they had the conversation. And Jack said, "Oh, well"—you know, he would never judge anyone in any sort of way—oh, well, you know—he never really said anything against Martin Luther King. Since then, Bobby's told me of the tapes of these orgies they have and how Martin Luther King made fun of Jack's funeral.

Oh no.

He made fun of Cardinal Cushing and said that he was drunk at it. And things about they almost dropped the coffin and—well, I mean Martin Luther King is really a tricky person. But I wouldn't know—he never said anything against Martin Luther King to me, so I don't know. Bobby would be the one to find out what he ever really thought of him in that way. But Bobby told me later. I just can't see a picture of Martin Luther King without thinking, you know, that man's terrible. I know at the time of the freedom march when they all came in his office, well, he was always—I think he was touched by Philip Randolph.[51]

Philip Randolph's very impressive. He's an older man and has great dignity.

Yeah, and all that and he was very worried about that freedom march. It turned out all right, I guess.

---

and other leaders to the White House and said, "I have a dream." The FBI tape to which Mrs. Kennedy refers was of King and his colleagues relaxing at the Willard Hotel after the march. Hectored by J. Edgar Hoover with charges that the civil rights leader was influenced by Communists in his entourage, Robert Kennedy grudgingly authorized Hoover to tap King's telephone calls and bug his rooms, which in time produced transcripts of derogatory private comments made by King while watching President Kennedy's Capitol Rotunda and funeral ceremonies. Hoover was only too eager to share them with the attorney general, and the shocked brother of the late President conveyed their essence to Jacqueline. Thus she was bristling at King (although in 1968, despite the disturbing emotions in her that it was bound to evoke, she accompanied RFK to King's funeral in Atlanta and consoled King's widow).

51. A. PHILIP RANDOLPH (1889–1979) was chief of the Brotherhood of Sleeping Car Porters and one of the organizers of the March on Washington.

Worried that it might lead to violence?

Well, yes, everyone was worried, weren't they? And—but you know, civil rights just—well, that was just something that was always there, wasn't it? And then I remember he got mad at—When we were in Texas in November, he was mad to me about Lyndon because he said, "Lyndon's trying so hard to show everyone that he's a real liberal." That he'd done something down there and made some speech which had just caused infinitely more trouble, and then got all the South mad or something and then Lyndon was trying to make the—I don't know who—like him. The northern liberals, I guess. And he said, "If he'd just, you know, not tried so hard to do what was best for Lyndon Johnson, I mean, this whole problem would have been made so much easier." But I forget exactly which speech that was. You could find that out.[52]

The—one of the other things in the autumn of 1962, of course, there was a political campaign and there was also—the biggest thing was the Cuban Missile Crisis. How early were you—did you—were you told about the missiles?

I can't remember if people knew about missiles when Jack went away on that speaking trip. Did they?

They did, yeah.

Everybody knew?

No.

Just a few special people.

---

52. In May 1963, on the hundredth anniversary of Gettysburg, LBJ had delivered a civil rights speech at the battlefield that went beyond anything the President had theretofore said about the issue in public. (This was before Kennedy's television speech the following month declaring civil rights "a moral issue.") Johnson declared, "The Negro today asks justice. We do not answer him—we do not answer those who lie beneath this soil—when we reply to the Negro by asking, 'Patience.'" In private, the vice president stridently complained to Sorensen that the President wasn't doing enough about civil rights, either in Congress or in his efforts to change public opinion.

Yeah.

Was it ever in the papers then?

It had not—it was not in the papers. He went over the—the news arrived on a Tuesday and then the small—very small group knew. And he went away, remember, on the Thursday or Friday—on the Friday—and then came back on the Saturday, and then gave his speech on the Monday following.[53]

Well, I can't remember if I knew before, or if I—I'm sure I would have known if he was worried or something. But I can remember so well, I'd just gotten down to Glen Ora with the children and it was either—was it a Friday afternoon or Saturday afternoon?

Saturday afternoon.

Whenever he made up his mind to come back.

Saturday afternoon.

And you'd just sort of gotten there, and I was lying in the sun and it was so nice to be there, and this call came through from Jack and he said, "I'm coming back to Washington this afternoon. Why don't you come back there?" And there—you know, usually he would be coming down or I thought he'd be away for the weekend, or he would be coming down on a Saturday or I would have said, "Well, why don't you come down here?" or something. But there was just something funny in his voice and he never

---

53. On Tuesday morning, October 16, 1962, Bundy told the President in his White House bedroom that U-2 photography by the CIA had revealed the Soviets installing offensive missiles in Cuba—an eventuality that JFK had assured the public the previous month that he would never accept. Midterm congressional elections were three weeks ahead. Anxious to keep the missile problem secret from Americans until he and his advisers agreed on a strategy, Kennedy tried to maintain his normal schedule, flying to Chicago for a campaign address, before returning to Washington on the pretext that he was suffering from a cold. On Monday evening, October 22, JFK gave his television speech announcing that his "initial step" would be to throw a naval blockade (euphemized as a "quarantine") around Cuba and demand the missiles' removal.

asked me to do—I mean, he knew that those weekends—and away from the tension of the White House—were so good for me, and he'd encourage you to do it. It was just so unlike him, having known you'd just gotten down there with two rather whiny children, who you'd have to wake up from their naps and get back. But I could tell from his voice something was wrong, so I didn't even ask. I said, sort of, "Why?" And he said, "Well, never mind. Why don't you just come back to Washington?" So you woke them up from their naps and we got back there, I suppose, around six or something. And then I guess he told me. I think that must have been when. But I just knew, whenever he asks, or I thought whenever you're married to someone and they ask something—yeah, that's the whole point of being married— you just must sense trouble in their voice and mustn't ask why. And so we came right back. And then, those days were—well, I forget how many there were—were they eleven, ten something? But from then on, it seemed there was no waking or sleeping, and I just don't know which day was which. But I know that Jack—oh, he'd said something—I know he told me right away and some people had said for their wives to go away and Mrs. Phyllis Dillon told me later that Douglas had taken her for a walk and told her what was happening, and suggested she go to Hobe Sound or somewhere. I don't know if she did or not. And I remember saying—well, I knew if anything happened, we'd all be evacuated to Camp David or something. And I don't know if he said anything about that to me. I don't think he—but I said, "Please don't send me away to Camp David"—you know, me and the chil- dren. "Please don't send me anywhere. If anything happens, we're all going to stay right here with you." And, you know—and I said, "Even if there's not room in the bomb shelter in the White House"—which I'd seen. I said, "Please, then I just want to be on the lawn when it happens—you know— but I just want to be with you, and I want to die with you, and the children do too—than live without you." So he said he—he wouldn't send me away. And he didn't really want to send me away, either.[54]

What was his mood when he told you?

---

54. This has echoes of the British royal family's determination in 1940 to remain in London through the dangers of the German Blitz.

Well, it wasn't—you know, it wasn't exactly sort of "sit down, I have something to tell you." It was so much going on and then the thing—and then as the time went on, it turned out—well, you know—oh, the awful fluke of a couple of days. Like one day, they took pictures and there was nothing there. Then the next day was foggy. And then McCone, when—McCone had just gotten married again and had gone off on a honeymoon. Well, now that was one of the real problems. Then he'd stopped—all—there was something rather tricky there that, him being out of town on his honeymoon, didn't order another flight or didn't something, so you would have known a couple of days sooner.[55] There's something there where McCone, who was—I don't know whether to blame McCone—I mean, he could have postponed his honeymoon a bit, or whether it was just a hapless accident, but that was responsible for a delay. And then when those pictures came through and they knew then. Well then, as I say, there was no day or night because I can remember one night, Jack was lying on his bed in his room, and it was really late, and I came in in my nightgown. I thought he was talking on the phone. I'd been in and out of there all evening. And suddenly, I saw him waving me away— Get out, get out!—I'd already run over to his bed, and it was because Bundy was in the room. And poor Puritan Bundy, to see a woman running in in her nightgown! He threw both hands over his eyes. And he was talking on another phone to someone. Well, then I got out of the room and waited for Jack in my room, and whether he came to bed at two, three, four, I don't know. And then another night, I remember Bundy at the foot of both of our beds, you know, waking Jack up for something. And Jack would go into his own room and then talk on the phone maybe until, say, from five to six to seven. And then he might come back and sleep for two hours and go to his office, or—as I say, there was no day or night. And, well, that's the time I've been the closest to him, and I never left the house or saw the children, and when he came home, if it was for sleep or for a nap, I would sleep with him. And I'd walk by his office all the time, and sometimes he would take me out—it was funny—for a walk around the lawn, a couple of times. You know, he didn't very often do that. We just sort of walked quietly, then go back in. It was

---

55. Unbenownst to Mrs. Kennedy, even had the U-2 photographed Cuba a few days earlier, it would probably have given the Americans little advantage in trying to have the missiles withdrawn.

just this vigil. And then I remember another morning—it must have been a weekend morning—when all—there was a meeting in the Oval Room and everybody had come in one car so that the press wouldn't get suspicious. And Bobby came in in a convertible and riding clothes. And so, you know, and I was there—so—and then I went in the Treaty Room, where I—well, just to fiddle through some mail or something, but I could hear them talking through the door. And I went up and listened and eavesdropped. And I guess that was at a rather vital time, because I could hear McNamara saying something, "I think we should do this, that, this, that." No—McNamara summing up something and then Gilpatric giving some summary and then a lot of ques—and then I thought, well, I mustn't listen, and I went away.

Did the President comment at all on the question of whether there should be a raid to knock the bases out or blockade or what? I mean, you mentioned Mac Bundy's—

Well, that I all knew later and that was never told to me until much, much later. And the thing was—no, at the time, you know, at the time he—well, it was just so—he really wasn't sort of asking me. But then I remember he did tell me about this crazy telegram that came through from Khrushchev one night. Very warlike. I guess he'd sent the nice one first where he looked like he would—Khrushchev had—where he might dismantle, and then this crazy one came through in the middle of the night. Well, I remember Jack being really upset about that and telling me and then deciding that they would just answer the first, and being in on that.[56] I also remember him telling me about Gromyko, which was very early in it.

Oh, yes.

How he'd seen Gromyko and he talked to him and everything they'd said and that he really wanted to put Gromyko on the line of just lying to him and

---

56. On the final weekend of the crisis came two messages from Khrushchev—the first conciliatory, the second fire and brimstone. In what scholars later called the "Trollope ploy" (in Anthony Trollope's fiction, a woman hastens to interpret a friendly gesture as a marriage proposal) the Kennedy brothers opted to treat the first one as the definitive Soviet message, which helped save the situation.

never giving anything away. And I said, "How could you keep a straight face?" or "How could you not say, 'You rat!' sitting there?" And he said, "What, and tip our whole hand?" So he described that to me. And then I remember another thing which—the man that Roger Hilsman wrote me a letter about just this winter—but how one of the worst days of it all, the last day, suddenly some U-2 plane got loose over Alaska or something?[57]

Violated Soviet airspace.

Yeah, but some awful thing. Oh, my God, you know, then the Russians might have thought we were sending it in, and that could have just been awful. I remember him telling me about that. And then I remember when the blockade—oh, and then I remember hearing how Anderson at the Pentagon was mad at McNamara, wouldn't let—I don't know if that was afterwards or before—but all that thing.[58] And then I remember just waiting with that blockade. The only thing I can think of what it was like, it was like an election night waiting, but much worse. But one ship was coming and some big fat freighter had turned back, but it didn't have anything but oil on it anyway— and all these ships cruising forward. And I remember being—hearing that the *Joseph P. Kennedy*[59] was there and saying to Jack, "Did you send it?" or something. And he said, "No, isn't that strange?"—you know, and just remembering, and then finally, some ship turned back or was boarded or something, and then that was when you heaved the first relief, wasn't it? And I can't remember—the day finally when it was over and saying to me—and Bundy saying to me either then or later, that if it had just gone on maybe two more days, everybody really would have cracked, because all those men had

---

57. ROGER HILSMAN (1919–) was the State Department's intelligence chief. At the height of the crisis, an American U-2 accidentally flew into Soviet airspace—legally an act of war that might have inspired retaliation that could have spiraled into nuclear conflict. A furious Kennedy said, "There's always some son-of-a-bitch who doesn't get the word!"

58. When Kennedy made his initial public response to the missiles in Cuba (he used the more peace-like euphemism "quarantine"), some of the Joint Chiefs, such as the navy's George Anderson (1906–1992) and the air force's Curtis LeMay, thought the President was being too weak—even on Sunday, October 28, when Radio Moscow announced that the missiles were coming out to "prevent a fatal turn of events and protect world peace."

59. By coincidence, the U.S. destroyer *Joseph P. Kennedy, Jr.* was one of the ships blockading Cuba.

been awake night and day. Taz Shepard[60] in the Situation Room or something. I remember I had something to ask him once and they said, "You can't." He's been—day and night, you know, everyone. And you just thought—and then I wrote a letter to McNamara afterwards, which I showed to Jack. But I remember everyone had worked to the peak of human endurance.

Did the President show fatigue?

Well, as the days went on, yes. But he always—you didn't worry about him and fatigue because you'd seen him driving himself so much all his life—I mean, through some awful campaign and the day that you're bone tired, getting up at five to be at a factory gate and still—So you knew he always would have some hidden reserve to draw on. But, oh, boy, toward the end—you always think—I always think that if you're told how much longer you have to go on, you can always make it. But the awful thing with then was you didn't know. And finally, when it was over, I mean, I don't know how many days or weeks later it was, but he thought of giving that calendar to everyone. And he worked it out so carefully himself.[61]

What about—

And then it was a surprise. I didn't—I was so surprised when I got one because he told me he wanted to do it so he said, you know, "Ask Tish or Tiffany," or something. So I told her and then when they came, I was so surprised that I had one and I burst out crying.

Well, what about Stevenson and the UN side of it?

I don't remember any of that at the time. I just remember when the article by

---

60. TAZEWELL SHEPARD, JR. (1921–) was the President's naval aide.

61. JFK presented a gift of remembrance to Jacqueline and those around him who had been most involved in deliberations on the Cuban Missile Crisis. Each was a little silver Tiffany calendar for October 1962, with the fateful thirteen days highlighted in bold, and engraved with "J.F.K." and the recipient's initials.

AFTER THE CUBAN MISSILE CRISIS, PRESIDENT KENNEDY
GAVE CALENDARS TO MEMBERS OF HIS INNER CIRCLE.
HE PRESENTED HIS WIFE WITH THIS CALENDAR, SEEN HERE
ON HER DESK IN THE WHITE HOUSE FAMILY QUARTERS

Charlie Bartlett or something came out later. And—I don't know how much later that was.

Was it in—about six weeks later was it? In early December—Charlie Bartlett and Stewart Alsop.

So then I remember the discussion then. I don't think Jack ever said anything at the time or—Oh, didn't Lyndon just come to one of those meetings? And then to none of the others? I think he came either to the one at the end or the one at the beginning. If he came at the one at the beginning, he didn't want to get involved with everything that was going on, or what I think is more like it, he came at the one at the end and didn't want to give any opinion. As usual, he just didn't want to get put on position anywhere.

Yeah.

And he could have come to all those meetings too, and he didn't come to *one*. I don't know what he was doing. Then there was something with Chester Bowles too, or was that earlier?

No, that was the first—that was the earlier Cuba.

That's right.

Chester was in India.[62]

And Bobby said—I remember the first one, Bobby said to him—

No, Chester wasn't in India but he wasn't involved in this. No, this is the first Cuba that he was involved in.

That's right. And where he was going to say that he didn't disagree—that he

---

62. **CHESTER BOWLES** (1901–1986) was an advertising executive, governor of Connecticut, and Dean Rusk's number two before succeeding Galbraith as ambassador to India.

didn't agree, and Bobby said, "Everyone who leaves this room agrees," or something.[63] But I don't know.

Did the President have any particular reactions to Charlie's piece?[64]

Oh, yes. That was awful, wasn't it? It was awful with Adlai and this and that, and I think—it's all so involved now, but I think, wasn't Charlie's piece right?

Not really, no. I mean, everybody had taken a whole series of positions on this and various people at various times had taken various positions and various things had been suggested that, as you mention the case of Mac, who was both—you know, one time he was a hawk and another time he was a dove. And the thing was, there—two viewpoints existed, but I think, at one time or another, nearly everyone around that table had—took one or another of the viewpoints. It much oversimplified the—

Well, anyway, I mean, Jack was just upset over the flak of the article. And then I remember—was it later that winter or in February when I went to New York and went to the UN with Adlai? And Clayton[65] had told me that it would be so nice if we would ask Adlai to some of our private parties, that that could really make things up. Well, anyway, that really made an awful difference to Adlai when I went to lunch at the UN and I gave him a little watercolor that I'd done. I'd done it—Jack and I were just sitting there one night—of a Sphinx I have, and I just had it in my briefcase. And he framed it and everything, and then he did come down to a party. I mean, you had

---

63. After the Bay of Pigs, when Bowles let it be known around Washington that he had opposed the venture, an indignant RFK poked his finger at Bowles's chest and told him that his position had henceforth better be that he was for the invasion.

64. JFK's friend Charlie Bartlett collaborated with the columnist Stewart Alsop (1914–1974) on a *Saturday Evening Post* article claiming that during the crisis deliberations, Adlai Stevenson had "wanted a Munich." Because Bartlett was known to be close to the President, members of the Washington cognoscenti mistakenly took the piece as a signal that Kennedy wanted his UN envoy out. Stevenson himself was especially agitated.

65. CLAYTON FRITCHEY (1904–2001) was an ex-journalist and Stevenson aide who was a social friend of the Kennedys.

to do things to sort of soothe his feelings because he—but that did smooth over very nicely, finally. But you know what I was just thinking about the Cuban crisis? The difference between Jack and Lyndon Johnson, and where it's really going to make a difference in this country, is now there's a terrible crisis going on in Laos but nobody really knows it, except in the papers. And where's Lyndon?[66] And so these people go out to Hawaii and before they go, Lyndon hasn't met with them for three days. And where is he now? He's running all around Texas, getting high school and college degrees. And the poor man's terrified, in a way. Dave Powers[67] says he can't bear to go to Camp David or anyplace he's alone, that now he has beach chairs around the pool, and on weekends, he likes to sit in the pool and they have drinks there—and all his cronies. But he can't bear ever to be alone and face something awful, or discuss with these people. Maybe it's—maybe he wants to disassociate himself so if it goes wrong he can say, "I wasn't there," or "It's McNamara's war." Partly, I think, he's panic-struck and doesn't know what to do. And that man came in—there wasn't a problem for seven months, which Jack had made possible. And I guess it's very good for the country that he could go around and make this air of good feeling and lull so many people into this sense of security, which they wanted after all the tragedy of November. But you know, a president has to be—I mean, that's where the terrible things are going to happen, because every little group is off, you know, having their own different meetings on Laos and they're not think—on Vietnam— and they're not thinking of—I mean, Jack always said the political thing there was more important than the military and nobody's thinking of that.[68] And they don't call the people who were in it before in. And so that's the way chaos starts. If you read the story of the Bay of Pigs in the papers now, I mean, the CIA just operating so in the dark, saying, "Even if you get an

---

66. During the missile crisis, the vice president attended only one meeting of "Ex Comm," the ad hoc presidential panel quickly formed by JFK to fashion a solution to the problem by meeting around the clock. Other members were Rusk, McNamara, Dillon, RFK, Bundy, McCone, and Taylor. The reference to Laos is the covert efforts by both North Vietnam and America to undermine the 1962 agreement at Geneva to preserve the country's neutrality and independence.

67. Powers and O'Donnell had agreed to stay on with Johnson for a transitional period.

68. In mentioning her husband's warning, Mrs. Kennedy was eerily prescient about the problem that would doom America's involvement in Vietnam.

order from the President, go ahead with it."[69] Well, that's the kind of thing that's going to happen again. And, you know, I've seen it from the people I talk to in Washington now, sort of piecing things here and there together—and how Joe Kraft[70] told me Lyndon came to some—somebody's house in Georgetown the other night, got very drunk, stayed until three or four, and said, "I just don't know if I'm capable to be president, if my equipment is adequate." It was just in front of—this is off the track, talking about Lyndon, and people will think I'm bitter, but I'm not so bitter now. But I just wanted it to be put in context the kind of president Jack was and the kind Lyndon is. Stupid old Harold Stassen[71] said last weekend—and then if only someone else had said it, because it's rather a true thought—that Johnson would be like Harding, and it would be another era of good feeling, and business liked Harding and the senators liked Harding, and he didn't keep too much sort of tabs on the people who worked under him, so they could sort of be a bit corrupt here and there, which again—and then look what happened. You know. And that's what I just—you know that's going to happen. Lyndon can ride on some of the great things Jack did, and a lot of them will go forward because they can't be stopped—civil rights, the tax bill, the gold drain stuff.[72] And maybe you'll do something more about the Alliance and everything, but when something really crisis happens, that's when they're going to miss Jack. And I just want them to know it's because they don't have that kind of president and not because it was inevitable.[73]

---

69. In other words, even if the President orders the invasion halted, proceed anyway.

70. JOSEPH KRAFT (1924–1986) was a Washington columnist and denizen of Georgetown.

71. HAROLD E. STASSEN (1907–2001), the onetime Republican "boy governor" of Minnesota, had once been a serious presidential contender and later ran for the job so many times and so long after he had any remote chance of election that he became a minor national joke.

72. JFK had had to deal with a worrisome drain of gold reserves to Western Europe.

73. By now, Jacqueline's once-benign attitude toward Johnson as leader has hardened, along with Robert Kennedy's. Later in 1964, when Jacqueline studied a draft of Sorensen's soon-to-be-published book *Kennedy*, she insisted that the author change or delete almost every favorable mention of her husband's vice president, noting "several glowing references to LBJ, which I know do not reflect President Kennedy's thinking. . . . You must know—as well or better than I—his steadily diminishing opinion of him. . . . He grew more and more concerned about what would happen if LBJ ever became president. He was truly frightened at the prospect." Refuting a Sorensen claim in the draft that the President had "learned" about campaigning from Johnson, she wrote, "Lyndon's style always embarrassed him, espe-

What sort of a vice president was Lyndon?

It was so funny because Jack, thinking of being vice president and how awful it would be, gave Lyndon so many things to do. But he never did them. I mean, he could have made his council on human rights[74] or whatever it was into some—you know, gone ahead with it—equal opportunity, whatever it was. He could have done more with the space thing. He just never wanted to make any decision or do anything that would put him in any position. So, what he really liked to do was go on these trips.[75] And he never liked—Jack would say you could never get an opinion out of Lyndon at any cabinet or national security meeting. He'd just say, you know, that he agreed with them—with everyone—or just keep really quiet.[76] So what he'd do, he'd send him into Pakistan or something. Well, then he'd be really interested in the camel driver when he came back.[77] Or then he'd ask to go to Finland or something, and that would be fine. And

---

cially when he sent him around the world as Vice-President." In later years, however, time, distance, the end of Robert Kennedy's rivalry with Johnson, the death of LBJ, and her cordial relationship with Lady Bird softened Jacqueline's attitude toward her late husband's successor. She distinguished her objections to certain Johnson policies—especially the Vietnam War escalation, which she insisted Jack would never have countenanced—from her personal fondness for both Lyndon and Lady Bird, whom she made an effort to see during the 1980s and early 1990s when both former first ladies summered on Martha's Vineyard. In a 1974 oral history about Johnson for the Johnson Library, Jacqueline said that after the assassination, LBJ "was extraordinary. He did everything he could to be magnanimous. . . . I was really touched by that generosity of spirit. . . . I always felt that about him."

74. JFK had appointed Johnson to chair the President's Committee on Equal Employment Opportunities, as well as his space council.

75. In Johnson's defense, Kennedy was eager to give his vice president dignity, but—knowing his tendency to overreach if given the chance—not a great deal to do. He sent Johnson on so many trips in order to distract him from his boredom and powerlessness. As Johnson's aide and friend Jack Valenti later described LBJ as vice president, "this great, proud vessel was just simply unable to move. Stuck there in the Sargasso Sea—no wind and no tides."

76. On this Mrs. Kennedy was absolutely right. In the spring of 1963, during a meeting when JFK was debating whether to send a civil rights bill to Congress, he asked Johnson for his opinion, and the vice president acidly said he could not respond because no one had given him enough information to have a judgment. In a 1965 oral history interview, Robert Kennedy recalled that during the missile crisis, LBJ "never made any suggestions or recommendations as to what we should do. . . . He was displeased with what we were doing, although he never made it clear what he would do."

77. During a 1961 trip to Pakistan, LBJ invited a camel driver named Bashir Ahmed to see him in the United States. To his surprise, Ahmed took him up on his offer, and Johnson hosted him for a well-publicized visit to his Texas ranch.

VICE PRESIDENT LYNDON JOHNSON AND PRESIDENT KENNEDY AT THE WHITE HOUSE

he'd bring back a lot of little glass birds with "Lyndon" written all over that he'd give out. And he asked to go to Luxembourg. I mean, I think it's so pathetic when all you can find to do with a President who's dying to give you a lot to do, is take a state trip to Luxembourg and Belgium. And I know in Greece, they told us after his visit there that you just wouldn't believe the confusion and the frenzy and what was demanded of people and how there had to be masseurs, and the pandemonium, and it was so much more than any presidential visit those people had ever seen. That's what he liked. Oh, and Lyndon had tried so hard in the beginning. Godfrey McHugh had tried in the beginning to make Jack order four new *Air Force Ones*—707s—because we needed the one that could be the fastest. Moscow's was faster. And Jack wasn't going to spend that much money for four new planes, and Lyndon kept pushing him to do that. You know, Lyndon wanted a big—and then when Jack did get *Air Force One*, I think—I don't know if Lyndon had an *Air Force One* just like it or one of the older planes, but he always kept pushing for a bigger plane. And—or for more—all the kind of things like that he wanted, the panoply that goes with power, but none of the responsibility. And then every time he'd come home from one of these little trips, Jack would say to find out, very nicely, "Would he like to come and report to me?" Once we were in Florida in the middle of his rest and vacation, and if Lyndon would've come to report, it would have to be in the middle of the night, which wasn't great for Jack, and he thought it would be awful for Lyndon. But he'd say, "Find out if he'd like to or not," and Lyndon would always like to. So he'd always be flown down in a special jet and the press would all be alerted. And he'd come over, and of course, there'd be absolutely nothing to talk about, but it would look as if, you know— So that's the kind of vice president he was. But Jack always said he was never disloyal or spoke anywhere. Well, I mean, that's only smart, but it's true.

What about on political advice or dealing with Congress or so on? Did he seem to figure there?

No, Jack used to say— Then once he wasn't majority leader anymore, he'd either think—either Jack thought this or Lyndon thought this—but he wouldn't do anything with Congress. I don't think they'd have paid much attention to him. I mean, then they didn't like the vice—the Executive stepping in.[78] And Jack used to say more times, just amused—I told you, to Ben Bradlee—"My God, Mansfield gets more accomplished"—and you know, it was really Larry O'Brien and Mansfield. But I—and I think I might have said this on an earlier tape, but one of our last dinners at the White House, maybe two or three weeks before Dallas, Ben Bradlee was there, and Jack kept saying to him, "Now why don't you put Mansfield on the cover of *Newsweek*? Why doesn't someone write something nice about him?" Did I say that?

No.

And he said, "He's done more," and he said—The thing is, Lyndon snowed everyone so much. He wasn't cutting up Lyndon, because he never cut Lyndon up. But he was saying, he snowed everyone so with his personality. But he said, "After all, look, it was under Eisenhower, and after all, what was done?" And he named very negligible things. And he said, "The situation's so much worse now, more difficult"—and all these things and he named, I remember, sixty-eight percent of our program the first year, seventy-one or seventy-three, the second, and he said, "We're going to get this and this and that by." And then Ben was needling him, saying, "But you're not going to get the tax bill by and the civil rights bill by this year, as you've said. Anyway, the tax bill, as you said." And he said, "God, what does it matter, Ben? We're going to get the tax bill. It's going to come by in February. O.K., it's not this year but it's two months later." And the civil rights he predicted exactly—everything that would happen as the date. And Mansfield, he just thought, was extraordinary and that nobody recognized it because the man played quietly. So Lyndon, as vice president, didn't just do anything. But it was all right. It was fine.

The story has been printed to the effect that there was some consideration of dropping Johnson in '64.

---

78. Before the inauguration, Johnson had made a misguided attempt to persuade Democratic members of the Senate to allow him to continue to lead their caucus. When they slapped him down by formal vote, JFK noted that "the steam really went out of Lyndon."

Not in '64. But Bobby told me this later, and I know Jack said it to me some-times. He said, "Oh, God, can you ever imagine what would happen to the country if Lyndon was president?" So many times he'd say it—or if there was ever a problem. I mean, stories would come out about '64, but I don't see how you could drop him in '64.

Very hard.

But in '68, I know, he was thinking in some little way, what could you do? Well, first place, I thought Lyndon would be too old then to run for president. I mean, he didn't like that idea that Lyndon would go on and be president because he was worried for the country. And Bobby told me that he'd had some discussions with him. I forget exactly how they were planning or who they had in mind. It wasn't Bobby, but somebody. Do something to name someone else in '68.[79]

Do you remember anything in particular about the congressional campaign in '62? Of course, it was so dominated by the—overshadowed by the Cuban crisis. You didn't go out, I think.

No, I mean, he didn't ask me to go out. I don't know.

At the beginning, he planned a rather short campaign and then made a longer one. On the question of—would he ever talk about the legislative breakfasts?[80]

Oh, yes, because sometimes they used to be upstairs and, you know, the chil-dren would wander in. And sometimes, I'd wander out of my room in my dressing gown and all those men would come out in clouds of smoke. And—

The breakfast was on the second floor?

---

79. In the last year of his life, JFK asked his friend Charlie Bartlett whether he thought the 1968 Demo-cratic nominee would be "Bobby or Lyndon." Other sources have it that the President was vaguely pondering the liberal North Carolina governor Terry Sanford as a possible 1964 running mate, if neces-sary, or as the 1968 presidential nominee.

80. The President hosted a regular breakfast with congressional leaders.

Sometimes they'd be, and then later on they were in the Family Dining Room. The first one, all the antique chairs that Harry du Pont had, broke one by one. But he would talk about them and what was said if it was a good one.

Whom did he like particularly? Hubert? What did he say about—

Well, he loved Mansfield and Dirksen was always very nice with him. I don't know, I guess he was really, was very sad when Sam Rayburn died. And Mc-Cormack he'd always had trouble with. But, I guess McCormack was always alright at them. I don't know. It really wouldn't be fair for me to say. I don't know.[81]

One of the great mysteries around the White House was the—

I know one thing about the legislative breakfasts that Larry O'Brien told me. This is something interesting about Ted Sorensen. Larry couldn't stand Ted Sorensen, so one night he was telling me—well, they were obviously—the Irishmen would be jealous of the Sorensens—but he said so many times Larry would have prepared an agenda for the breakfasts and just before they were about to start Ted would ask to see it and take it. And he'd just change one or two sentences and then initial it "TCS" and pass it all around that way. And you'll see that heavy hand of Ted Sorensen in more places. I mean, he—you know, he wanted his imprint on so many things.

The self-assertion.

Yeah. I told you about the *Profiles in Courage* thing, and well, I mean, he was doing it to Larry O'Brien, everyone. That's just so sneaky.

---

81. EVERETT DIRKSEN (1896–1969) was senator from Illinois and leader of Senate Republicans from 1959 until his death. Although Dirksen's nineteenth-century style was so different from the President's, JFK had long had an excellent relationship with him. Not so with House Speaker McCormack, who still resented the meteoric political ascent that had enabled Kennedy to best him for control of Massachusetts Democrats. Increasing McCormack's ill humor toward the President was Edward Kennedy's victory over the Speaker's nephew Edward in 1962 for the state's Democratic Senate nomination.

He was a little better in the White House, though, wasn't he?

Oh, yes. But I mean, I just—

Well, that's such a petty thing. To—

Someone said he loved himself and finally he loved one other person, which was Jack.[82] And he also had such a crush on Jack. I can remember when he first started to try to speak like him or dare to call him Jack, and he'd sort of blush. And I think he wanted to be easy all the ways Jack was easy. The sort of civilized side of Jack, or be easy at dinners or if girls like you, and men. Because he knew he wasn't quite that way in the beginning, it almost went into a sort of a resentment. I mean, it was very mixed-up in his own inferior—he had a big inferiority complex, so you can see the thing sort of all working back and forth, but—and I never saw him very much in the White House.

He was very rarely invited—

Never.

Never.

I guess he came to a state dinner or so, but never a private one. Or maybe, maybe he came to one or two of the dances, I think. But that wouldn't have been—I mean, as he and Ted had the problems all day, that would be the last person you would invite at night.

One thing that mystified people over in the West Wing was the way George Smathers survived. The President would get very mad about Smathers, about Medicare, foreign aid, and say, "This will be the final test." Then Smathers would vote against it and then there he'd be again.

And I used to get so mad at that—and hurt. Then he'd say—well, he just

---

82. The "someone" was Robert Kennedy.

had such charity. His friendship with Smathers was before the Senate, really, and before he was—I mean, in the Senate and before he was married. And I guess they'd see each other a bit, off and on in the summer or in—you know, Stockdale was a friend of Smathers.[83] They weren't seeing each other so much lately. And it was really a friend of one side of Jack—a rather, I always thought, sort of a crude side. I mean, not that Jack had the crude side, but you could laugh or hear a story—you know, the kind of stories sort of Smathers tells—I don't know, but he didn't want to stick it to someone who'd once been a friend. And he knew when Smathers was hurting him, and he knew Smathers—

Kenny[84] hated Smathers.

Yeah, and I didn't like Smathers. But he wouldn't go back against someone who'd been his friend. And he was hurt by him and he wouldn't—he didn't see him as much and everything personally but he just wouldn't ever— finally say, "O.K.—you're out—now we're enemies," because he was just too kind. So he just let things go on.

Mansfield, he thought, was doing an excellent job in the Senate. And McCormack, all right. Boggs, did he ever mention?[85]

Well, I know he liked Hale Boggs very much, yes. Hale Boggs had been our friend before the White House. We used to see them. You asked me before who we saw. And Mansfield we saw. He always loved Hale Boggs.

He looked forward to the legislative breakfasts, did he?

Yeah.

---

83. EDWARD STOCKDALE (1915–1963) was a real estate speculator and Smathers aide who served as JFK's first ambassador to Ireland. Reportedly grief-stricken over the President's assassination, Stockdale fell to his death from a Miami office tower in December 1963.

84. Kenneth O'Donnell gauged senators in terms of their support for Kennedy measures.

85. HALE BOGGS (1914–1972) was Democratic congressman from Louisiana and House majority leader.

They were rather—they were fun. On—unreel this. Shall I send you this list— typed—with anything else that occurs to me?

Oh, just give me the little thing that—you don't have to type it. Just give me the scribbling.

Then I'll make a copy of it myself.

Do you want a piece of paper? Oh, here, I've got a whole pad.

Oh, really? Good. Thanks. [chatting after the formal interview] *What was this you said about Johnson doing a kind of, on tape, a confession on how inadequate he was?*

Oh, no, no. Joe Kraft said that someone who had been at that house got so frightened and was so, you know, rocked by seeing Johnson in his cups at four in the morning, saying he doubted if he had the equipment to be a president. But this person went home and put it on tape.

Oh, I see.

I don't know who that person was. *[ribbing Schlesinger]* Johnson putting it on tape! *[both laugh]*

I wondered exactly the—seems improbable. [long pause follows on tape, then] *Macmillan looked very well.*[86]

He did, didn't he? And the—he didn't have that funny, sort of droopy look he used to have.

No, exactly. He looked very—when I saw him—he looked very sort of spruce and chipper. And he looked like he'd just come in from the country and he looked—

---

86. When he appeared on the JFK 47th birthday broadcast.

Well, I hope things are looking up for him because he really—

Well, he intervened in a by-election at Devizes and gave a speech and the Tories held that—astonishing—and he felt, I think, very cheerful about that, as if, politically—

You know, in the Cuban crisis—I didn't say it in the tape, but I was so surprised that all these people that did go away whose husbands were working in it.

Really? Was there a—it seems to me that your reaction is sort of the reaction you'd have to have.

Yeah, and well, then, maybe a lot of them were friends and things later, you know, just not in government, or—but you know, the one thought there was, if anything was going to happen they wanted to get out with their wife and—I mean the mother and the children? My God, I don't think that shows you love your husband very much!

The
SEVENTH
Conversation

WEDNESDAY, JUNE 3

1964

*W*e ended up last time talking about the Cuban crisis, and the next event of great interest was the problem with the British over Skybolt. You remember, in December the President went to Bermuda and then afterwards, did Macmillan come back to Florida, I think, for a day?

I don't think so. Once they met at Key West. That was the very beginning.

That was the very beginning.

No, I don't think Macmillan did—

Oh, David Ormsby-Gore came back and Randolph Churchill, but not Macmillan.

Is this the Skybolt time?

Yeah.

That was at Nassau.[1]

---

1. Kennedy and Macmillan first met at Key West in March 1961. Randolph Churchill (1911–1968) was the journalist son of the ex–prime minister and a Kennedy family friend. As JFK was preparing to leave Nassau, Canadian prime minister John Diefenbaker, whom he so disliked, arrived for his own meeting with Macmillan, compelling the President to lunch with Diefenbaker as well as the British prime minister. During the meal, JFK and Macmillan diplomatically pretended that they liked Diefenbaker, and the Canadian pretended to believe it.

PRESIDENT KENNEDY AND PRIME MINISTER MACMILLAN IN NASSAU, DECEMBER 1962

The—the meeting was at Nassau.

Yeah.

After Nassau, I think David and Randolph came and spent a day, didn't they, at Palm Beach?

That's right. And is that what you want me to tell about?

Yeah.

First, they met in Nassau because Jack told David to tell Macmillan he wouldn't meet in Bermuda again because there was no—in the governor general's house there was no hot water for the bath. *[Both laugh]* So they met at Nassau. Then I don't think Jack saw Randolph Churchill—not until later. But I remember the next day, sitting out, when Godfrey McHugh came running in with a dispatch that whatever company it is that shot Skybolt and saying, "Look what wonderful news, Mr. President!" And I said—I told you before about him saying, "Goddamn it, Godfrey!" It was just too awful to be true. And then he got on the phone and tracked everyone down and Gilpatric said he didn't know, and McNamara was away. I don't know if you've read Dick Neustadt's thing on Skybolt, have you?

I haven't.

Well, Jack gave me that about Novemb—on November 20 and said, this is the—usually he never brought anything home—and he said, "This is the most fascinating reading," and he said, "Read it." And so I took it to Texas with me. It's been in my briefcase ever since. I've never read it. But anyway, it explains all the little hitches back and forth.

Well, you think the President was deeply concerned?

Oh, he was just crushed because Nassau had gone so beautifully and Macmillan had—Macmillan was really in trouble at home, I guess, and whatever they'd worked out was Polaris—hadn't been quite what he wanted but together they'd both done the best they could to get something that would be all right for them. And I remember David's face. He just looked like he'd been kicked in the stomach, and Jack saying, "Ugh, you know, what are we going to do?" And he felt as if he betrayed the prime minister. So David went in another room, carrying his little red dispatch box, and talked on the phone to Macmillan and they made up what their announcement would be. But they were both just sick about it. I think Jack always felt that contributed so to Macmillan's troubles. And as he said, it's always some third person down the line somewhere whose fault it is. It turns out on that thing, which he just explained to me briefly, it's Thorneycroft, who Jack always did think was stupid, doing some little thing and someone not being there when someone called, I don't know.

Do you remember anything about the President's mood, before he went to Nassau?

Well, not exactly. What would it have been? Well, some anticipation.

Yes, and concern, because it did weaken Macmillan's political position. And I think the actual solution was worked out by the President and Mac Bundy and David on the plane down to Nassau.

And I remember Jack being really mad, either talking to me on the phone from Nassau or telling me before. He hated Diefenbaker, and Diefenbaker had made some snotty condition that he had to come down there and have lunch with him one day, or something. He was mad about that. But, you know, they had a good time, always, he and Macmillan—I mean, sort of it was rather wry laughter. You know, they always managed to have their jokes, even though they were tinged with despair a bit. But that was too bad, that whole thing.

Actually, the problem of the testing of Skybolt, although it was a big thing then, didn't have the effect that everyone feared and—it did for about a week, but I think it was so well handled that it—

Well, maybe here, but it really caused trouble for Macmillan at home, didn't it?

Well, to some degree—for a time. But Labour didn't want Skybolt either, so they weren't in a position to exploit it for themselves.

I see. And then I remember Randolph Churchill, when Jack went to Washington, came over. Well, he was so pro-Jack in all of—that was very nice. I don't think he saw Jack that time. Maybe he did.

Yes, he came to Washington thereafter, and was very proud of the fact that he'd written the one pro-Nassau piece to appear in the British press.

That's right.

The next big thing was de Gaulle's veto of British entrance into the Common Market.[2] The President was rather fascinated by de Gaulle, wasn't he? As a historical phenomenon?

Well, of course, he was always interested in him, but really it was more Churchill. And I think probably because I read, or said I did, de Gaulle's memoirs and because he used a sentence from one of them when he announced for the presidency—"I've always had a certain image of America"—that's taken from the opening line of de Gaulle's—"I've always had a certain image of France." Just that. But he saw—he used to talk to me about de Gaulle so realistically. You know, that *that* man was just consumed really with grudges, and he'd explain of how he'd never forgotten the slights of the last world war, or practically, that we didn't come earlier into the first world war. When everybody that he was dealing with then is dead, and everything, and he just— he was nice about it. He never got mad the way he did about the Germans or anything. But he just seemed to have such distaste for someone who was so spiteful. I remember he asked him, in Paris and he was very interested, who he got along with best—Churchill or Roosevelt. And de Gaulle said, "With Churchill I was always in disagreement but we always reached an accord. With Roosevelt I was always in agreement but we never had an accord"— or some lovely little French wordplay—but, you know, so when de Gaulle did that, well, I wouldn't be surprised if Jack almost expected it. And I remember one time later—oh, I was having to answer a letter to Malraux or something—when Malraux came over for the *Mona Lisa*,[3] which was way after that, I think. He came for dinner one night alone, afterwards, and Jack said he purposely wasn't going to talk to him about all this—you know, France

---

2. In January 1963, de Gaulle abruptly vetoed British membership in the European Common Market, saying the organization would otherwise appear to be "under American domination and direction."

3. The *Mona Lisa* came to Washington in January 1963.

and England and everything, the kind of thing that Hervé was always so frantic about. He talked to him only about Red China. Bundy could tell you that conversation. He said, "Why are all of you worrying about this and that and your *force de frappe* and all?[4] You know, you should just think of Red China and what's going to happen when they get loose." And Malraux was rather impressed. But—and later on that spring I had to answer a letter—or else it was about coming back from Morocco, when I'd said I wouldn't land in Paris, or something.[5] I just never wanted to go near the French again. But there was no way to get home without doing it. And Jack said, "No, no, you mustn't be like that. Don't you see you're the one avenue that's open, and they think I'm a so-and-so but they think you're nice because you like France. And you must always leave an avenue open and you mustn't—" Again that thing of conciliation always. You know, he said, "What's the point of you getting mad at them too and writing Malraux an insulting letter?" But he was just so—it was just so un-Christian of de Gaulle, and Jack gave so much and that spiteful man gave so little. And I think he sort of saw that in the long run, de Gaulle would do all of this work for "*la Gloire*" and everything, and he'd really be remembered as—well, the man who, with Castro and Red China, didn't sign the test ban treaty. Like he used to say about Nehru sometimes, "Isn't it sad? This man did so much for independence and everything, but he stayed around too long and now it's all going, bit by bit, and he's botching up things." And, you know, Nehru's image really did change a lot in his last years because Nehru got to be awfully sanctimonious—I mean, the difference between Hungary and Goa and all of that.[6] What was the thing Jack had about that? A very good expression. Something about, "It's like the town preacher being caught in the whorehouse." You asked me about him and Nehru the other day—he had that sort of feeling about him. And also, what I forgot to tell you about Nehru—it was so funny, Nehru wanting to come on this very private visit but

---

4. The *force de frappe* refers to the independent nuclear deterrent that de Gaulle was trying to create.

5. In October 1963, after their Greek cruise on the Onassis yacht, Mrs. Kennedy and her sister Lee stopped in Morocco. Irritated by de Gaulle's rebuffs of her husband's efforts to improve French-American relations, as well as her own, she balked at a stop in Paris on the way home.

6. In December 1961, the sanctimonious Nehru ordered his troops to seize Portugal's colony of Goa, which lay on India's west coast, surrounded by Indian territory. The Indian prime minister labored to explain how this differed from the Soviet invasion of Hungary.

because there weren't any crowds purposely arranged, out of desperation, the man went to Disneyland, which seemed so unlike Nehru, but there'd be a lot of children who'd yell, "Cha-cha Nehru *Zindabad!*" I mean, this funny thing of ego. So he thought that that was de Gaulle's horrible failure, and I don't think he did think much of him.

Were there any Frenchmen whom he liked and trusted, particularly?

Only one I know is Segonzac.[7]

Not Hervé.

No, Hervé amu—I mean, Hervé's whole sort of way of life and his desperation about David Gore—I mean, he always tried to be so nice to Hervé and sometimes he'd say, "We should ask him to dinner because he's about to explode again." But no, you know, basically he didn't like the French, and I loathe the French. There's not one French person I can think of except— maybe two very simple people. Maybe Boudin,[8] who's so un-French. You know, they're really not very nice. They're all for themselves.

How did the President and Malraux—how did that work?

Well, Malraux would talk brilliantly and so would Jack, and Bundy would always be there. So, you know, it was a wonderful exchange, but Malraux sort of off in a marvelous fog or— It was very interesting and they never, you know, really got into policy or all that. Well, he was interested in Malraux, but he saw that de Gaulle treated him like Muggsy O'Leary—not as well.[9] So, you know, no one—that was the thing—no one spoke for de Gaulle. There was no point giving really Malraux any messages, but—

---

7. ADALBERT DE SEGONZAC (1920–2002) was Washington correspondent of *France-Soir*.

8. Stéphane Boudin, who was advising her on the White House restoration.

9. The cigar-chomping John "Muggsy" O'Leary (1913–1987) was JFK's driver during the Senate years, then an agent for the Secret Service.

But he wasn't astonished by de Gaulle then. He rather expected that de Gaulle would have a headstrong—

Well, maybe he was a little astonished in the beginning because he really tried hard and went over backwards. But, well, maybe he was a little astonished, but then he got to see that it was this classic pattern and it just wasn't going to get any better. And he was really irritated, I told you before, at what de Gaulle said after Cuba.[10] And that's another time that I think there was some sincere irritation that that proved we'd never defend Europe. I mean, just a damn troublemaker that man was!

Yet he wanted de Gaulle to come to the United States, and I think de Gaulle had agreed to come in March of this year.[11]

Yes, or it was going to be January, even, and it was going to be at Hyannis. And Hervé always said, if only they could talk and meet the way Macmillan and Jack met—anywhere, you know, halfway, this and that, but do it a lot. And then this time I think Hervé was right. He said, even if nothing's accomplished. But for de Gaulle—he would want it to be some momentous meeting, and I think that meeting would have had terrific results in a way, or some results, and for finally de Gaulle to agree and all that—

The President had some expectations a meeting with de Gaulle might ease things.

Yes. You know, de Gaulle respected Jack and the whole way his opinion changed of him in Paris. I mean, I don't know what his opinion was, but obviously, everyone thought, "Who is this young President?" And, you know, the way he'd speak to me of him during the endless dinners—we sat next to

---

10. De Gaulle said that the missile crisis had shown that when the crunch came, the United States was willing to act on its own, and therefore might not reliably fulfill its commitments to defend Western Europe.

11. When President Johnson's diplomats tried to make good on de Gaulle's promise, the French president refused to schedule a visit to America, insisting that his attendance at Kennedy's funeral had already fulfilled his pledge.

each—you could just see that he was—or, what he told me about him after his funeral, upstairs.[12] And then what—

What did he say?

Well, I mean, that he just was one of these—you know, so impressive. And then Segonzac sent me a letter which I can show you that Burin des Roziers, who I think is de Gaulle's chief of cabinet,[13] told Segonzac what de Gaulle really thought of Kennedy and, you know, he thought—I mean, as long as Kennedy was alive, he was the leader of the West. And maybe de Gaulle didn't like it sometimes, but he really looked up to him. And then, apparently— Bobby told me this later—Bohlen[14] or someone—tried to say that Johnson would be all right, he was the one Kennedy had chosen as vice president—you know, reassure him in the first days. And about a month or so later, he said, "Kennedy may have made a mistake," or "You all may have made a mistake about that man." In other words, his opinion of Johnson fell very low. So he wouldn't have dared to—he never would have recognized Red China, I'm sure, if Jack had been alive. There are so many little things like that, because he respected him.

Did the President have any particular—did he ever talk about Europe, in the sense of European unity and unification—Jean Monnet, for example? Did he mention him that much?

---

12. After the funeral, Jacqueline received de Gaulle in the Yellow Oval Room and told him that every-one had become so bitter about "this France, England, America thing," but "Jack was never bitter." De Gaulle allowed that President Kennedy had had great influence around the world. With her insistence that every nuance be right, at six that morning, before walking to the service in St. Matthew's, Mrs. Kennedy had called the White House curator and asked him to replace the Cézannes from the Yellow Oval Room with American nineteenth-century aquatints: she wanted the atmosphere for her meetings with de Gaulle and several other foreign leaders to be not French but American. De Gaulle's relation-ship with JFK had not been wholly negative. During the missile crisis, when Dean Acheson offered to show the French president photographic evidence proving that Soviet missiles were in Cuba, de Gaulle replied that Kennedy's word was good enough for him.

13. ÉTIENNE BURIN DES ROZIERS (1913–) had served under de Gaulle since World War II.

14. CHARLES "CHIP" BOHLEN (1904–1974) was an old Soviet hand who became JFK's second ambas-sador to France.

THE BURIAL OF PRESIDENT JOHN F. KENNEDY

Well, he always, in the very beginning, thought of Jean Monnet one of the first for the Medal of Freedom, and you know, so he thought he was a most wonderful man and that all that he worked and believed in, and everything.[15] So I think he did think that was a marvelous idea. But he never—you know, he never really sat and talked to me an hour about European unity, but I know he thought—he was for it, wasn't he?

Yes. I think it was quite characteristic. He was very much for it but he was much less interested than a lot of the people in the State Department about the questions of structure and all this kind of thing. And I think quite rightly so, because he knew if it came, it would come in its own way and you could get obsessed with the sort of tactical questions about it.

Yeah, he never seemed to be pressing it, or anything, but—

I think he saw it as a historic inevitability.

Oh, and then he told me something very interesting. Oh, if he'd only written these things down because I've forgotten them. But what made de Gaulle veto the Common Market and what Macmillan had told him and how Macmillan had been out at Rambouillet about two weeks before.[16]

That's right.

And everything seemed to be fine and then there was some little thing here or there, some typically French thing of—like Hervé always being mad when he's not given precedence. Well, something that some country or person did that irritated him and bang-o, he turned around and did the other.

---

15. JEAN MONNET (1888–1979) was considered the architect of an integrated post–World War II Europe. Upset that there was no proper award for civilian achievement, only military, President Kennedy had established the Presidential Medal of Freedom in 1963, but did not live to present it to its first recipients, including Monnet, in December 1963.

16. De Gaulle hosted Macmillan at the French diplomatic retreat Château Rambouillet in December 1962.

I think he may have have felt—was it possibly this, that—

Oh, well, maybe Nassau made him change it?

Yeah, that he—that—

That Macmillan told him at Nassau about Rambouillet.

Yes, but Macmillan at Rambouillet had not said anything to de Gaulle about the Nassau agreement, and de Gaulle believed—did not understand that the Nassau agreement was drawn up—that the Nassau plan was drawn up on the plane down to Nassau—and supposed that Macmillan had already known about it then, was holding out on him.

I see.

Might that have been it?

That's it. I guess so, yeah.

Because I heard somewhat that sort of thing from the French here—that Macmillan came to Rambouillet and held out on de Gaulle and, therefore, de Gaulle regarded that as a personal betrayal.

And that's why he suddenly did the Common Market, though at Rambouillet it had all looked wonderful. And I think—yeah.

Though, or certainly why he did the Common Market so brutally. I think that, in any case, he might have done it but not in that kind of contemptuous way that he— that he did it. On other European leaders—Fanfani came here a couple of times. In fact, when I saw Fanfani, he reminded me that he first met the President at the Chicago convention in 1956.[17]

---

17. AMINTORE FANFANI (1908–1999) was Italian prime minister for most of the Kennedy years, the third of his five tours of duty in that job. As leader of his Christian Democratic party, he had attended the Democratic convention of 1956 as an observer.

Well, he liked Fanfani. You know, that was sort of the opening to the left and everything, I suppose—they got on well and—but I mean, he wasn't just, you know, inspired beyond belief by him.

No, no.

I can't think of any other leaders. I wasn't—Tito had a violent temperature when he saw him, so that was difficult.[18]

Well, how was the Tito thing?

I wasn't there. And I guess the poor man had a fever of 102 and couldn't eat anything. So it was mostly, you know, polite and all of that, but nothing much. I don't know really much about that.

How did the Indian trip, which you and Lee took, happen to come up?

Well, Nehru brought it up when he was here at dinner, or something. And then Ken Galbraith jumped on the idea. Then it was—it was delayed so many times. I was still so terribly tired after John and I didn't really want to go on that trip. But yet I sort of wanted to go to India. So, once it was delayed, you just weren't up to it, or something was happening—I forget what. Could it have had something to do with Cuba? I don't know. It was put off—anyway, just to show you one thing how sweet Jack was. The schedule came back for two weeks. All over India! My God, it would have killed him, campaigning! And you wrote back and forth, and you tried to change it and he—and Ken would keep saying that the children at Mysore were weaving garlands, and this and that. So finally, we cut it, with a map, to very small—you know, just mostly Rajasthan and around India. And it was—we were in Florida, either Washington's Birthday, or Easter or something, I forget when we went—and Jack got through to Ken Galbraith, and Ken was really protesting on the phone, and he spent the whole last day of his little holiday there, shouting to

---

18. **JOSIP BROZ TITO** (1892–1980), the unifying founder and strongman president of Yugoslavia, was given a luncheon by JFK at the White House in October 1963. Mrs. Kennedy was still in Greece.

JACQUELINE KENNEDY ENCOUNTERS INDIA

MRS. KENNEDY BEING PRESENTED WITH A HORSE BY PRESIDENT AYUB KHAN OF PAKISTAN

Ken on a bad connection—you know, saying, "It's too much for her," and, "Ken, I don't care. Everyone complains. It's just what they say in campaigns when you tell them you can't. I'm not going to let her. She's tired." You know, he really fought to have that chopped off. Well, then—so he did that. You know, I guess he—it was wonderful to go to India, and he didn't really care if I went or not, but I guess he thought it would be nice.

I think he was very pleased with it and very proud of the success and I think he thought that—well, as you mentioned yourself in connection with France, that quite apart from it's nice for you to get a holiday and get out of Washington, I think he helped—think it helped the country and it helped him in important respects.

You know, it was so funny, the difference between India and Pakistan, because India was really just getting to know Nehru, who did like Lee and I—Lee and me. And never mentioned Pakistan or anything. And then there was Ken Galbraith and B. K. Nehru and Madame Pandit and her sister.[19] It was much more like a family group. The meals were pleasant. And when we got to Pakistan—of course, I basically like the Paks more than the Indians. They're sort of more manly, and Ayub never stopped talking politics or how he hated Nehru or couldn't stand him.[20] And I did get a message from the State Department from Ken to make sure that it looked like McConaughy was an old friend of Jack's.[21] So the first thing I did when McConaughy and Ayub—McConaughy got there the day I did—the day before, as the ambassador. So, I tried to sort of say—set it up that they'd known each other from when and everything. And McConaughy said, "Oh, no"—that's right in front of Ayub—"That's not true at all, Mrs. Kennedy. The first time I ever met the President was two weeks ago when I gave—" And the only time I ever wrote Jack a letter, which I wrote coming down from the Khyber Pass and gave him when I got home, was what a hopeless ambassador McConaughy was for Pakistan, and all the reasons and all the things I thought the ambassador there should be, which was a gentleman, a soldier, and a friend of the President's. And I suggested some other people—Bill Blair and Bill Battle.[22] And Jack was so impressed by that letter, he showed it to Dean Rusk, whose big choice McConaughy had been, and said, "This is the kind of letter I should be getting from the inspectors of embassies." I mean, he'd never been for McConaughy, who was a sweet man, but just such a— When we went to Rawalpindi, that *Paris Match* reporter was yelling, as we got off the plane, "*Bonjour*, Jacqueline!" And that night McConaughy said to Ayub Khan, "Mr. President, I was so interested to hear all that French at the airport today. I never realized

19. VIJAYA LAKSHMI PANDIT (1900–1990) was sent by her brother, Prime Minister Nehru, to London, Moscow, and Washington as his ambassador.

20. MOHAMMAD AYUB KHAN (1907–1974), president of Pakistan from 1958 to 1969, was the leader for whom the Kennedys had arranged their glittering dinner at Mount Vernon in 1961.

21. WALTER MCCONAUGHY (1908–2000) was a career Foreign Service officer who had previously served in Burma and South Korea, and was the American ambassador to Pakistan from 1962 to 1966. The State Department wished to suggest that, as with New Delhi, the President had sent an old friend to Islamabad.

22. WILLIAM MCCORMICK BLAIR (1916–) was an investment banking heir and close Stevenson aide who became Kennedy's ambassador to Denmark. William Battle (1920–2008), who had helped to rescue JFK in the South Pacific during World War II, was his ambassador to Australia.

there was so much French influence in Pakistan." Well, Ayub just looked at him and said, "I think if—you will find out that the influence here has been mainly British." But you know—Dean Rusk! Anyway, that was my trip. And our trip was so exhausting that all through Pakistan, Lee and I were having nosebleeds every day and night. So we were really tired when we got home.

Did the President talk much about Africa? The Congo?

Yes. Once he said about Ed Gullion and Bill Attwood—and Bill Attwood had gotten sick there and everything and, you know, you were so sorry for him—he said, "Those are so much more the important places to be now as a diplomat." And he said, "London and Paris and everything don't matter anymore. There's the telephone and, you know, it's really done that way. But," he says, "it's those far-out places in Africa that are, you know, the exciting places for a diplomat to be, and where you can do the most." Well, Ed Gullion, he'd always had a special feeling for, because when he was doing his Indochina speech, which was the year before we were married, because I'd had to type it all up from that summer—I mean, translate all these French books and everything—Ed Gullion was the only person in the State Department who would sort of talk to Jack, and who would really say how awful Indochina was and the way it was going.[23] And I guess he got fired because of that, or—or else he got—no, he got put in some—

He got shifted out of that area and given other things.

Yeah. And put in some pathetic little post. We always used to see him all the time and, well then, I think Jack named him to the Congo, just showed what he thought of him. He really thought he was exceptional.

In 1963, one of the big things on the President's mind was, of course, Vietnam and Diem and Madame Nhu, and all that.[24]

---

23. The postcolonial Republic of the Congo suffered domestic upheavals during the Kennedy years. Edmund Gullion (1913–1998) and William Attwood (1919–1989) were JFK's ambassadors to the Congo and Guinea, respectively. In 1963, Kennedy considered Gullion for ambassador to South Vietnam before choosing Henry Cabot Lodge, Jr., whom he had defeated to enter the U.S. Senate in 1952.

24. In the summer of 1963, President Diem was cracking down on critics, especially Buddhists. When

Yes, well, you know, obviously it was trouble for so long and you didn't ask Jack about it when he came home, and everything. But I know once—I forget how long Lodge was out there before things really got bad. About how many months?

He was out about, I guess, about three months before Diem was thrown out.

Well, I know that he started acting rather strangely, and he said he wouldn't answer their cables and you couldn't get through or—anyway, as if he was kind of taking it into his own hands, or something. And what I can remember is when the coup came, Jack was just sick. I know he'd done something to try and stop—Lodge had started something and they'd stopped. All of this you can learn from other people because a lot of it I learned later. But he'd done something to stop it. But anyway, when Diem was murdered, Jack was—oh, he just had that awful look that he had at the time of the Bay of Pigs. I mean, he was just so—just wounded, and he was shaking his head and it was home in our—you know, in our room at the White House— and he was saying, "Oh!"—you know—"No! Why?" And he said Diem fought Communism for twenty years and everything, and it shouldn't have ended like this. He was just sick about it. Madame Nhu tearing all around, saying things about him—I suppose she was more of an irritant. But once I asked him, "Why are these women like her and Clare Luce, who both obviously are attractive to men, why are they—why do they have this queer thing for power?" She was everything that Jack found unattractive—that I found unattractive in a woman. And he said, "It's strange," he said, "but

---

a Buddhist priest burned himself on a Saigon street, Diem's cold-blooded sister-in-law, Tran Le Xuan (1924–2011), known as Madame Nhu, dismissed the event as a "barbecue." That summer and fall, the President was forced to think seriously about how much he wished to use American military force to support a South Vietnamese leadership that, although anti-Communist, was growing more erratic, autocratic, and corrupt. He approved a coup d'état by South Vietnamese military officers against the Diem brothers, which went out of control and culminated in their assassination. Madame Nhu blamed Kennedy for the deaths of her husband and brother-in-law. When JFK died, American policy toward Vietnam was at a pivot point. In ironic retrospect, this historical moment was like the one Kennedy had asked Professor Donald about. For Lincoln, it was what decisions he would have made about Reconstruction, had he lived, and whether they would have changed history. For Kennedy, the question was about Vietnam.

it's because they resent getting their power through men." And so, they become really—just hating men, whatever you call that. She was rather like Clare Luce. *[whispers]* I wouldn't be surprised if they were lesbians.

Clare Luce wrote very favorable pieces about you, remember?

Yeah, but Clare Luce had come to lunch with Jack once in the White House when Tish was still there.[25] And I remember—oh, she so badly wanted to come to see him as a man would. She wanted to see him in his office, or something. Anyway, a sort of a male lunch was arranged, and Tish told me she was so nervous before, she'd had about three martinis.[26] And I was so mad at her that I stood—I managed to be just outside our dining room, standing there, pretending to shuffle through my desk, and I just really cut her dead, so that when Jack introduced us and I just stood with my hands at my side and finally walked over. He said to me later, "You know," he said, "if you're going to cut someone dead, dear"—you know, he was sort of touched at my loyalty because it could only make Mrs. Luce hurt me more,[27] but he really wasn't very pleased at my doing that. He said, "Do it naturally, but don't just set it up and lay the trap for them." And apparently, all through that lunch, Mrs. Luce, who I guess was a bit loaded, just went on and lit into him and told him all these things. And finally—he was always, you know, so courteous to women—he said, "Well, I'm sorry, Mrs. Luce, but unfortunately you're not in a position to do anything about these things, and I am." And that's how it ended. And the sad thing about that is they'd been friends and she'd been a friend of Mr. Kennedy's and he'd helped her so. You know, the time when Morse and all that, when she didn't go to Brazil?[28] Well, both Harry

---

25. During their lunch in 1962, Mrs. Luce grandly told him that every president could be described "in one sentence," and that she had been wondering what his sentence would be.

26. Tish Baldrige had worked for Mrs. Luce in Rome. She had not looked forward to watching her former boss do battle with her current boss over this luncheon.

27. Not to mention, antagonizing Mrs. Luce's powerful husband.

28. WAYNE MORSE (1900–1974) was a Democratic senator from Oregon and JFK colleague on the Senate Foreign Relations Committee. After Mrs. Luce's stint in Italy, Eisenhower had nominated her for ambassador to Brazil, but then she publicly said that Morse's bad judgment in opposing her appointment must be explained by the fact that in 1951 he had been "kicked in the head by a horse."

Luce and Mr. Kennedy told her she shouldn't go and Jack called her up especially and said, "You know, now, they're wrong. You know, you'll be much happier there. You need to be doing something." And he said, "All this will blow over and, you know, I really advise you to take it." And, "My father's older and he sees things his way." Well, she didn't take it and I think Jack was completely right. What did she do? Then she went back to Arizona and made little mosaic tables, and got bitterer and bitterer and more and more venomous.[29]

And swam underwater.

Yeah. And he tried to help her. So for her to turn on him like that—well again, this resentment of men.

And Harry Luce remained friendly.

Yeah, I think. Well, I know Jack saw him a couple of times and, you know, it was all right—I mean, he might blow up at him for certain things, but they would— it never got bitter that way.

How did Luce happen to write the introduction to Why England Slept?

Oh, that was Mr. Kennedy, because Jack had gotten Arthur Krock to do it. And then Mr. Kennedy thought that it might look as if Arthur Krock had written the book or something, because he'd been an old friend of the family—and that it would be better if Henry Luce did it. So it was sort of changed midstream, and that's one thing Arthur Krock never forgave Jack for. I mean, the last time we saw him, he even brought it up.

Oh, really?

(Morse was severely injured in the accident.) In the face of outrage from other senators, she refused to retract her insult and asked Ike to withdraw her nomination.

29. The Luces had built a house in Phoenix. She also took up scuba diving.

Or forgave Mr. Kennedy for it. It was a real slight. And you know, so that's where this queer enmity that Krock had for him, who, after all, he'd known as a young boy and known me and he'd sort of been his mentor—not exactly mentor, but you know, seen him and everything. This sort of bitterness started. And that's when. Mr. Kennedy changing it.

I can remember in the first winter, the dinner at the White House, when the Krocks were there, so there was still a slight relationship then, but then Krock became absolutely hopeless.

You try over and over. You see, he'd been a friend of me growing up, gotten me my job in the *Times-Herald*, always a friend of my grandfather's—we used to write poems to each other, for both of us. And you try, over and over, to do something about the relationship, and each time you just get slapped in the face with a wet fish, and finally you gave up. He was too bitter, and he couldn't bear to see someone young coming on. And we went out of our way to be nice, and we even went to their house for dinner—as President.[30]

You did? When was this? In the beginning or—

Yes, sometime that year. I think it was in the spring.

On Vietnam, it was rather interesting that the President should send Cabot Lodge, whom he had defeated in the Senate in 1952 and who ran on the opposite ticket in 1960. Had he and Lodge maintained particular personal relations in this period?

No, the only time I can remember, we asked Lodge to the dinner for Abboud of the Sudan. And Lodge was really nice that evening. I mean, I think Jack had always thought of him as rather arrogant and everything. Well, he seemed so touched to be there and so sort of, well, polite. And I remember Jack walked him to the door. Once he was President, he did these extraordinary sort of thoughtful things, to go out of his way. Lodge was just very nice then, and

---

30. In April 1961.

when we went upstairs I said, you know, he just seemed so nice that evening, and Jack said, "Yeah." I think he probably did it—don't you think?—rather thinking it might be such a brilliant thing to do because Vietnam was rather hopeless anyway—and put a Republican there. I don't know. That's what I read in the papers. I never really asked him why he sent Lodge there.

I'm sure that entered in. I think Rusk suggested it, and I think the President was attracted to it partly for that reason, and partly because Lodge had served as liaison officer with the French army in the Second World War and spoke excellent French.

Oh, that's right.

And partly because he wanted to figure out that we had enough prestige to recapture control of our policies from General Harkins[31] and the military. I think all those things may have entered in. I think Latin America was something the President cared about a great deal, obviously. And you mentioned earlier about his admiration for Betancourt and for Lleras Camargo. Did he ever—do you remember Frondizi of Argentina?

No. That was a men's lunch.

That was a men's lunch. Um-hmm. The Brazilian trip was always about to take place.

Oh, we always had our bags packed for that trip. And I remember one so interesting thing that he said about Quadros[32] when Quadros resigned. He did resign, didn't he?

Yes, he did.

And Jack shook his head. He was rather disgusted and he said, "You don't

---

31. PAUL HARKINS (1904–1984) was the American commander in Vietnam.

32. JANIO QUADROS (1917–1992) was Brazilian president from January 1961 until he quit in August of that year.

have the right to do that." One doesn't have the right to do that. "I mean, you don't have to run again, or something, but you don't have the right, once you're in there and the heat gets too strong, to just get out of the kitchen." So I think everyone had thought quite a lot of Quadros before, hadn't they?—and pinned a lot of hopes on him. And Jack was—well, not horrified, because that's—too strong a word—but that just wasn't in his way of doing things. I mean, when he took on something—just the way he was always prepared to lose this election—I don't think he would have, but he would be talking about it—on civil rights. Sometimes when things were bad, and he'd say, "Well, maybe"—but you know it was something that had to be done. You could never really be a great president unless you were prepared to be hated or to lose on something that counted. Again the whole thing of *Profiles in Courage*. And that's just what Quadros was the opposite of.

Do you remember any particular reaction to Goulart?[33]

No, that was—that lunch, again, I was sick. And I think he thought Goulart was sort of a shifty character and—you know, I mean, well, I mean, you know—Goulart was really messing everything up, wasn't he?—in the economy and the Communists. I thought—I think he thought he was a faker and a robber and a—but I don't know what he exactly thought.

Did he have any particular—do you remember anything particular about Peru?

Yes, you know, Prado of Peru had been here on a state visit. He was really rather a comic character. But anyway, when he was overthrown, it reminds me so now of everyone saying that the United States recognized the junta in Brazil too quickly, because we held off recognition or something. We cut—

We suspended relations and stopped aid.

---

33. JOAO GOULART (1918–1976) was president of Brazil from 1961 to 1964. JFK was not delighted by Goulart's inclusion of Communist sympathizers in his government, his opposition to American sanctions against Castro, and his efforts to improve relations with Soviet-bloc countries.

That's right. And later on Pat's—Rosita Prado, who Pat[34] went to school with, wrote Jack a letter saying, "You saved my father's life"—because they were going to execute Prado and, I guess, his wife. And because of what we did and everything, they let him get out and get to Paris and all that. But, you know, just making it rough for them for a while there. Finally, it made it better in the long run, instead of just saying, "Hooray, hooray, they've overthrown"—and I guess—no—

No, you're absolutely right.

That's right, no—yeah.

What we did was we suspended and said, we will resume if you agree to do certain things like give parties political freedom, restore freedom of the press, agree to hold elections. They finally agreed to do these things, and then we resumed relations, and it made a great difference.

And in Brazil, the minute the junta took over this time, everyone just had cheers. And that was the most disillusioning thing. Betancourt was here talking to me about it, two months ago. He said all—half of Congress, or Parliament, whatever it is, all the great writers, everyone has their civil liberties taken away from them. And that was one of the most despairing things in Latin America—the difference between Kennedy and Johnson. It affected all the countries. Jack never would have done it that way.

Charlie Bartlett played a role in working out the conditions with the new government in Peru. Do you remember anything about that?

No, I didn't know that.

He helped—I think Charlie and Berckemeyer[35] were kind of playing on that. Did

---

34. JFK's sister Patricia Kennedy Lawford (1924–2006) was married to the British actor Peter Lawford (1923–1984).

35. Fernando Berckemeyer was the Peruvian ambassador.

the Dominican Republic—was there anything particular there? John Bartlow Martin or Bosch?[36] Not much.

Well, he just said how insurmountable Bosch's problems were going to be. You know, he hoped so it would work, and then it didn't.

What was his general feeling about the Foreign Service?

Oh, and the State Department.

The State Department.

Well, it was just despair, and he used to talk all the time. You know, he had such high hopes for Rusk in the beginning, when you read his dossier of what the man was. And he liked him, sort of, personally. I mean, you could never say Dean Rusk is mean, or anything, but he saw him get to sort of be the tool, really, and he saw that that man was so—well, could never dare to make a decision or any—he never would make a decision. And Jack used to come home some nights and say, "Goddamn it, Bundy and I get more done in one day in the White House than they do in six months in the State Department." I remember once they'd—they'd asked for some message to be drafted to Russia, a very unimportant one—something like wishing Khrushchev happy birthday—maybe a little more important—and either six or eleven weeks went by and nothing had come. And then—this is another very late example—when I came back from Morocco, I told him of this brilliant, young, very low man in our embassy there, who'd been attached to the Secret Service, who learned all the Berber languages and everything—had been there two years and he was going to be transferred to the Caribbean or something, and he wanted so to go to that part of the world—Algeria or something. Well, when I told Jack that, he was really mad because he said, "I wrote Rusk a memo about that six months ago, that you shouldn't have this policy of moving everyone every two years. That it's so much better to let them build up some knowledge,"

---

36. JOHN BARTLOW MARTIN (1915–1987) was a journalist and onetime Stevenson aide who was JFK's ambassador to the Dominican Republic, which was led for seven months in 1963 by Juan Bosch Gaviño (1909–2001), the country's first legitimately elected president, who was deposed by a military coup.

or something. And he used to say that sending an order to Rusk at the State Department was "like dropping it in the dead letter box." And the one thing he was thinking of—you asked me once what he was planning to do after the election? It was to get rid of Dean Rusk.[37] But yet he so hated to hurt anyone. And I said, "Well, can't he go back to the Rockefeller Foundation?" And he said, "No, no"—so sadly. "You know he's given all that up. He really burned his bridges." And I think he was sort of toying with the idea of putting McNamara in there, but it really wasn't firmed up because I don't know if he thought exactly McNamara would be right for foreign policy. And he didn't want to let Bundy go because he needed Bundy with him. But he wanted someone in there, you know, almost like McNamara or Bobby, who could just flush out all those— And it was so funny, one day three ambassadors came in to say goodbye to him, and he said they all had on striped shirts with the white collar and cuffs—you know, very English, with umbrellas on their arms—and two of them had on what he called slave bracelets. I don't know if he meant identification bracelets or elephant hair.

These are our U.S. ambassadors, about to go overseas.

Yes. And one was going to Africa, and one was going to the Near East—I don't know, Lebanon or Turkey or somewhere. And these sort of precious flits came in his office and he was just so—you know, it was the wrong idea of the kind of people he wanted to be sent out there anyway. He wanted a more rugged America sent. And he called up Rusk the minute the last one had left his office—I guess there weren't three in a day, but say, three over a week—and said, "I want you to send out a memo to everyone in the Foreign Service that not one of them can wear a slave bracelet anymore."[38] But, you know, those were the kind of people who took Rusk over in the end. And he cared so about the little—like where was Rusk? He wasn't in on either part

---

37. In his 1991 memoirs, Rusk insisted that he and JFK had had a private understanding from the start that he could only afford to serve one term at State. But if this was true, it was obviously unknown to Jacqueline, and Rusk clearly changed his mind, since he continued for five more years in the job under President Johnson.

38. Nigerian slave brokers once used Portuguese coins to create ornamental "slave bracelets"—not the most helpful image for a U.S. diplomat at a time of tumult in his country over civil rights.

of the missile crisis or something terribly important because he'd have to go to a—

Nassau—

Oh, Nassau—

He did not go to Nassau because he had to go to a dinner for the foreign ambassadors—the annual diplomatic dinner for the foreign ambassadors in Washington.

Yeah, well, little things like that, I mean, he turned into—I mean, Jack said one terrific thing about Angie Duke, who he was so proud of in a way, because Angie does have the most beautiful manners in the world and did so much helping all that way. But Angie wanted to get out of being chief of protocol, and Jack was so surprised where Angie wanted to go. It was Tanganyika. And Jack thought he would have wanted—

Denmark.

Yeah, that he was—sort of wanted to be a Bill Blair, going to eternal parties. He was rather disillusioned at Bill Blair for that, by the way. But you know, he said, "I'm not sure Angie's quite up to Tanganyika." But he was very impressed that he wanted to go where life could be rugged, and as I said, "What about Africans?" And another thing about Dean Rusk. You know, Jack was very formal. He never called anyone by their first names until he really knew them well. And Dean Rusk was the one member of his cabinet—probably because he was older and he hadn't known him before—who he called "Mr. Rusk," right up until the last year. And suddenly one day, they broke down and he called him "Dean." But people don't know that he was that. It was part of his English—admiration for things English. He never liked it if anyone called you "Jack," or me "Jackie," or—except in the campaign, when they yell it. But then it's a sign of liking you. And he never would call anyone— He always called my mother and stepfather "Mr. and Mrs. Auchincloss."

Oh, really?

314

He called my mother "Mummy," because he thought it was such a funny name—as sort of a joke. But he always called my father "Mr. Bouvier."

He never called your mother "Janet"?

Never. And yet, you know, he knew them so well. But he just—he didn't think it was right.

What about some of the other people in the State Department? George Ball?[39]

Well, I can't exactly remember what, but I can remember he wasn't always entirely pleased with George Ball.

And of course, poor old Chester.

Oh, yeah, Chester. Chester Bowles would give some endless talk in a meeting about we should enslave—take the mud huts out of enslavement and raise the standard of the, blah—you know, go on with these rolling phrases for hours, and then Jack would say, "Yes, Chester, but I'm not asking you that. I'm asking you what we should do about this problem—X-Y-Z." Something rather simple, and Chester would never have an answer. And so he couldn't wait to get him out of there.

Averell he liked.

Yes, Averell he did like. Walt Rostow[40]—it was funny, one night I was at a seminar at the Dillons. Jack was out of town, and making a speech somewhere, and he called me up, and I was called out of the room, and he said, "What's the seminar?" And I said, "It's Walt Rostow, talking about underdeveloped countries." And a lot of people like you, and Bundy, and everyone were there. And he said—so loudly, I had to put my hand over the receiver—

---

39. The orotund Chester Bowles was Kennedy's first undersecretary of state, George Ball the second.

40. WALT ROSTOW (1916–2003) was a development economist at MIT, then Bundy's deputy before going to State as director of policy planning.

"Jesus Christ! You mean all those people are—Walt Rostow's got all those people trapped in there, listening to him?" Because he really thought Walt Rostow went on and on, and was hard to listen to. He said, "I'm glad I'm not at that seminar." But he liked him. He never said anything mean about him. He said Jerome Wiesner always used to peek through his door.[41] He'd come around through Mrs. Lincoln's office and peek—he said it used to drive him crazy. Every time the door would be open, Wiesner's head would peek in and out, and it would finally drive him so crazy he'd say, "All right, come in or else go away," and it was usually something unimportant.

He liked Wiesner, though, I think.

Oh, yes.

On this—when it came to appointing ambassadors, there was always the—the State Department always wanted to appoint a Foreign Service officer, and the White House people always wanted to send some non–Foreign Service officer— someone like Bill Attwood, or someone like that. Did he ever comment on that general problem?

Well, just as I said, that the Foreign Service ambassadors were usually so awful. And, you know, sometimes you obviously had to send one. You couldn't demoralize the State Department so completely. Then he went over there to give a talk to them once and to tell them—and he really prepared that talk. He said, it's so awful in the State Department. They get so demoralized. They get sort of trained not to take a position one way or the other, but by the time they get way up—and he said younger people should get up quicker—they just can't give you any answer but the answer that's no answer—safe on both sides. And so the whole point of the speech that he gave to them was that you must, you know, be prepared to take an answer one way or the other, and you must be prepared to go to Congress, or—I don't know. Just that their training was wrong, and they were brainwashed

---

41. JEROME WIESNER (1915–1994) had been MIT's president when JFK appointed him as his science adviser.

by the time they got there, and, mostly too effete to do any good, which was sort of the standard the people at the State Department admired. And just to say something rather interesting and unfair about someone who was a friend, which Jack never said to me but I saw this later, this winter when he came to see me—it's Chip Bohlen. He loved Chip Bohlen, and when Chip Bohlen was around. And sometimes I used to tease Chip Bohlen, and say that he was too stuffy or State Department–ish. I used to just see this side in little things. But he was appointed ambassador to Paris just about the time of the missile crisis—

That's right.

And Bobby asked him to stay, and I think Jack asked him, but sort of vaguely, but Chip Bohlen couldn't wait to get on that boat.[42] And I said to him this winter—he came to see me in this house—something about it or "Why weren't you there?" And Bobby told me the reason he wanted Chip Bohlen to stay so much was that he'd been their Russian adviser for so long and Llewellyn Thompson had just sort of come in and they didn't really know Thompson that well. So here they were, entering this crisis with a new Russian expert. But Bohlen had to take the boat—he wasn't even going to take a plane. And so I said to Bohlen, "Aren't you sad?" or "You missed it," or "Why did you go?" And he said, "Oh, well, I didn't think it was very important. It didn't seem so bad." And then he said, "I thought I could perhaps do more good over there, from that side." Which was so much baloney because he just barely got there. And he said, "Was it really all that serious? It didn't seem that to me." And I thought, "My Lord, the greatest, most awful thing that's happened in your lifetime—and all you can say was that it was not that serious?" And the thing is that even Chip Bohlen was so imbued—who is

---

42. LLEWELLYN "TOMMY" THOMPSON (1904–1972), son of Colorado sheep ranchers, joined the U.S. Foreign Service in 1929 and came to specialize in the Soviet Union, serving as ambassador to Moscow from 1957 to 1962. At the start of the missile crisis, JFK had wanted Bohlen to delay his departure. He knew Bohlen well and that, as ambassador to Moscow from 1953 to 1957, Bohlen had developed a sophisticated understanding of Khrushchev and his circle. Instead it was Thompson who advised JFK during the missile crisis. Although the President had been little acquainted with him, as it turned out, the self-effacing Thompson was in a position to provide insights on the Soviet leadership that were of more recent vintage than Bohlen's.

a brilliant man—by that State Department thinking, that the one thing that mattered to him most—he'd finally been made ambassador to Paris, where, he said, he hoped and assumed he would stay, he told me—this is under Johnson. But once that happened, he didn't care what was happening, he was going to get there. I just think that's sad. Though I love Bohlen, it makes me think so much less of him.

I know. It's very puzzling. I did an oral history thing with him, and he went through all this, and I asked him and got the same unconvincing—and he said, "Well, everything was set up, and if I went to Paris, I could explain what our policy was." And it was not convincing. But then he loved the President and said one marvelous thing about him. He said—I mean, this is on the tape—that he said if—"When the President was killed and Johnson came in, I felt this was the future giving way to the present or the past."

Oh, then another thing that disappointed me about him—he named— he was there at the ceremonies where they named a street after Jack in Paris and he sent me his speech. Well, one line of it was, though there was "a certain sadness about this day," the naming of this street shows that Franco-American relations—is a great step forward for Franco-American relations, or something. Well, I just thought, this day *"une certaine tristesse"* was the words. I wanted to write him back—but the poor man sent me the speech, so, of course, he was trying to do his best—and say, "Is that all you think of this day? A certain sadness? You sound like Hervé with your 'Franco-American relations'!" So, Bohlen had so much but he didn't—I don't know, a little extra thing.

He's the best of the Foreign Service officers, but even he has been deformed in some way by that—

And, for instance, if he, who's brilliant, could have been made secretary of state, it wouldn't have done any good because he would protect his own, and that was just what Jack wanted to get out of there—the people who would protect their own.

On the domestic side, economic policy and so on, Walter Heller.[43]

I don't really know what he thought about what Walter Heller did or everything. He didn't have the same personality as Walter Heller, so whereas Galbraith and everyone you would have home or for dinner, we never saw Walter Heller. I think he thought he leaked a lot of things—didn't he?

Yeah, I think he did.

Or that he was talking to the press, or something. I mean, I never heard him say anything against Walter Heller. I always thought Walter Heller was sort of a—well, a jerk when you meet him. I never could believe he was such a brilliant economist.

He did a good job, I think—

But—

And has been very unhappy—since.

So, I never heard him—but I mean, we didn't—Jack and I didn't really talk economics, so—I guess he thought he was fine.

On the Supreme Court, the President—

Oh, he loved Douglas Dillon.

Yeah.

But—and he thought a lot of Dave Bell.

---

43. WALTER HELLER (1915–1987), chairman of Kennedy's Council of Economic Advisors, was the Buffalo-born son of German immigrants and a University of Minnesota economist.

Yes, he relied heavily on—did he?—on Dave Bell. When Kermit Gordon became director of the budget, did—was there any particular reaction?[44]

Well, that's because he wanted what? Dave Bell—

Dave went over to AID.

AID, yeah.

Yeah, but Gordon didn't—

I don't know anything about that. Wasn't he sad that Dave Bell had to leave being director of the budget? Yeah, he was really sad about that.

He felt Dave was the only man who could straighten out the AID situation.[45] You remember Fowler Hamilton[46] had—

Oh, that's right. And he was very sad, the way it came out about Fowler Hamilton. I can't remember exactly but it looked as if he—oh, no, no. Labouisse.[47]

Labouisse.

Labouisse. It looked as if he'd been fired for incompetency or something, and he—Jack so badly wanted to have it come that he was being promoted by being ambassador to Greece. However, that story came out, he was sorry for Labouisse—he was sad. It shows a certain charity again.

---

44. DAVID BELL (1919–2000) and Kermit Gordon (1916–1976) were Kennedy's successive chiefs of what was then called the Bureau of the Budget.

45. In November 1961, JFK had created the Agency for International Development, which dispensed foreign aid and was suffering growing pains.

46. FOWLER HAMILTON (1911–1984) was Kennedy's first AID administrator.

47. HENRY LABOUISSE (1904–1987), known as "Harry," a social friend of the Kennedys, had been chief of AID's forerunner agency and became JFK's ambassador to Greece in 1962.

The President made two appointments to the Supreme Court, you remember. Byron White[48] and Arthur Goldberg. Did he talk much about the Court or about—

Well, I remember he was really happy that he'd have two appointments to make and I think he thought both his appointments were good.

Yes.

And I know that Justice Frankfurter, he knew wanted him to appoint whoever it was—Paul someone?

Paul Freund.[49]

Yeah. And he knew of that wish. He was—he went to call on Frankfurter a couple of times and again once—brought him to his office. But he wanted to put Goldberg in there.

He used to be—he and Bill Douglas used to be—at least, Bill Douglas—was a great friend of Mr. Kennedy.[50]

Of his father's, and then really of Bobby's. They were always going off all through Russia and everything together. We never really saw Bill Douglas much, but I think he liked him.

He wasn't around the White House much.

---

48. BYRON WHITE (1917–2002) was an All-American football halfback from Colorado, where he gained the nickname "Whizzer," and a Rhodes Scholar whom JFK had met in London before World War II. By coincidence, he was one of the naval intelligence officers who wrote reports on Kennedy's heroism commanding the PT-109. White joined the Supreme Court in April 1962 and proved more conservative than Kennedy and his people had expected.

49. PAUL FREUND (1908–1992), a Harvard Law School professor and giant of constitutional law, turned down President Kennedy's invitation to be solicitor general. JFK also considered him for the high court before choosing Arthur Goldberg.

50. WILLIAM O. DOUGLAS (1898–1980), liberal, civil libertarian, and environmentalist, had been a close Kennedy family friend since his work with Joseph Kennedy on the Securities Exchange Commission in the 1930s.

No, never.

Never.

But none of those people were. Arthur Goldberg used to be around our house in Georgetown a lot for the time of the labor bill, but that was always for breakfast. And Arthur Goldberg—I said to Jack once—some dinner where I sat next to him—"He is the biggest egomaniac of any man I've ever seen in my life." And it's true. I've never seen a man who never stops talking about himself.

Yeah, he does it with sort of an innocent, joyous way, but it is hard.

Well, I find that horrifying. I'm not sure Jack didn't make a mistake putting him on the Supreme Court because that just seems to make people think they're more and more special.

And as they're out of the newspapers, they feel they have to make up for that by talking more about—

And the decision that I thought this winter—you know, that was made after Jack's death, this case where it's all right to print anything, even libel, about someone in the press. It's a little more complicated than that, but you remember.

The New York Times case.

Yes. But that seemed such an awful thing to do—and Goldberg was the one who held out and said that it could even be malicious and completely untrue. And I thought, that's right after that ad of the day in Dallas, of the picture of Jack—"Wanted for Treason." And there you, his appointee, go and say that everything, even this, is all right? But it's because the Supreme Court is so isolated. They're never affected by newspapers, anything. So Arthur Goldberg's head's going to be even more swelled in a few more years. So, I guess, Jack always said he was the most brilliant labor lawyer that ever was.

What about the President and the press—apart from Charlie Bartlett and Ben Bradlee, who were—

I suppose so many of our friends before the White House were in the press. I mean, there's Rowlie Evans, Hugh Sidey—Bill Lawrence he played golf with.[51] You know, he basically liked them. I always thought in Washington, politics and the press—you're both sort of involved in doing something. So many of his friends were there. Bill Kent in Florida would be around, sometimes. He liked the kind of badinage and everything you could have with them. Much more than his colleagues in Congress, though we had some there. And then—people always used to say that he was so thin-skinned by the press, but that really wasn't true. And it was so funny, because one night Ben Bradlee was taunting him—or, no, he was saying to Ben Bradlee something that was written was untrue. And Ben Bradlee came one night for dinner in an absolute rage because some tiny little Republican newsletter that his John Birch mother-in-law subscribed to had had a paragraph written by—not Tony Lewis but Tony someone who wrote for Nixon—

Ralph de Toledano.[52]

Ralph de Toledano had written something bad about Ben Bradlee. You would have thought it had been over the front page of the *New York Times*. Just one or two sentences, and Ben was in a rage. And Jack just sort of lean—I mean he didn't really rub it in, he just leaned back and looked amused and said, "Well, see how you fellows feel when something unfair is written." I guess the one thing he admitted was a mistake was canceling the *Herald Tribune*.[53] He was a little bit more that way in the beginning, but at the end he'd

---

51. Rowland Evans of the *New York Herald Tribune*, Hugh Sidey (1927–2005) of *Time,* and William Lawrence (1916–1972) of the *New York Times* and later ABC News.

52. RALPH DE TOLEDANO (1916–2007) was a founder of the conservative William F. Buckley's *National Review* who was close to Nixon.

53. Sick of criticism by the New York paper, the goal of which—he suspected—was to boom Nelson Rockefeller for 1964, Kennedy cancelled his subscription, causing a momentary Washington cause célèbre.

never mention unfavorable things, or if I'd say, "Oh, I think so-and-so is so awful"—when I'd come home to him and he'd say, "Don't think about it. Don't read those things." You know, he just accepted it as part of the—you know, when there was something good, I mean, he wouldn't mention it. I'd say, "Wasn't it wonderful what"—I don't know—"someone said today?" If I could find it.

What about the great statesmen of the press, like Lippmann and Scotty and all the rest of them—and Joe Alsop?

Well, Joe was his friend. And, I think, Lippmann and Reston—Reston was awfully sanctimonious and sort of—so they were never close. I mean, I'm sure Jack saw them in his office and things. And, of course, they had this kind of jealousy or resentment of Jack because for the first time there was a president who probably was brighter than they were, who was younger, who was—Lippmann had two things against Jack, partly his father and partly being Catholic, strangely enough. And you hear this in conversations with other people but he could never sort of purge from this—

Yeah. And I think Lippmann's wife was an ex-Catholic. She was brought up and went to a convent and broke with it and I think that had some—

Well, I remember when—

Though, remember in 1960 that Lippmann wrote marvelous columns.

Yeah. I can't really remember what they wrote and what they didn't, sometimes. But—I mean, he wouldn't sort of be a sycophant to them. I mean, he wouldn't suck around. In the press, he really saw the people who—he liked. Someone funny like Bill Lawrence, just—you know.

But you don't feel that he was unduly sensitive—

Unh-unh *[meaning no]*.

—to the press. One thing a lot of people have written about the administration

is that no administration was more interested in its own image, to use that odious word, and so on.[54]

Well, that to me, it's like reading about someone—you know, it's so untrue. And then they'd all talk about the public relations setup that we had going before the—during—before the campaign, and the this and the that, and our image. Which I'd never thought of as image. And there was never anyone in public relations, except—Charlie Bartlett always used to say, "You're doing too many articles." But he used to say to Charlie, "You know, I have so many— much against me. The only one—and in a certain position that mightn't be the best way to get what I'm aiming for—the nomination. But this way, it is. You know, to just get more and more known and bombard them." So many public relations things were that when they asked for interviews, and he would do them. But he never had anyone advising him and he never thought about our image. In fact, our image—when you think of something so incredible about me, I was always a liability to him until we got to the White House. And he never asked me to change or said anything about it. Everyone thought I was a snob from Newport, who had bouffant hair and had French clothes and hated politics. And then because I was off and having these babies, I wasn't able to campaign, you know, and be around with him as much as I could have. And he'd get so upset for me when something like that came out. And sometimes I'd say, "Oh, Jack, I wish—you know, I'm sorry for you that I'm just such a dud." And, he knew it wasn't true and he didn't want me to change, I mean, he knew I loved him and I did everything I could, and when I did campaign with him, I did it very hard and I spoke French all through Massachusetts to counteract Henry Cabot Lodge—until people came up and used to be surprised that I could speak English! He was, you know, proud. So, he never asked me—there I was the worst liability and there were Lee—Princess Radziwill and every-thing. And—and I was so happy, I remember thinking, once you got in the White House—it's really true of any president's wife. Everything that was bad is suddenly new, and so it's interesting. So whereas, then that you have decent French food is a plus instead of a minus—that you don't like, stay in a kitchen all

---

54. In the early 1960s, such a practice, routine for modern presidents, seemed so new that at a press conference, JFK was once asked about his efforts to "manage the news."

PRESIDENT AND MRS. KENNEDY GREETING GUESTS
AT A WHITE HOUSE RECEPTION ON LINCOLN'S BIRTHDAY, 1963

day making Irish stew. And when I did the tour of the White House, he was so proud of that. He used to show that and ask people about it. And then I did the guidebook over everybody's objections. They all said in the West Wing that it would be awful to have money change hands in the White House.[55] But then he was proud of me, and I was so happy that at last I'd been able to be something that he could be proud of. But, I mean, that shows you he wasn't thinking of his image or he would have made me get a little frizzy permanent and be like Pat Nixon. You know, "Pat and Dick," and he never—he never would hold hands in public or put his arm around me, or—because that was naturally just distasteful to him, as I think it is for any married— So he didn't do

---

55. As a girl touring the White House in 1940, Jackie was disappointed that there was no guidebook available.

anything for his image. And he used to tell me—sometimes he'd tell me I should wear hats instead of sc[arves][56]—oh, and all these letters about my skirts too short. And I said, "But they're not too short," and he said, "Oh, I guess you're right." But, you know, he never said, "Lengthen them" or—

He never tried to ask you to do—not to stop behaving—stop being yourself for any political or public relations purpose?

No. And I think he liked that I was—I mean, he knew I was being myself and that I did like to stay in the background. I think he appreciated that in a wife. And he married me, really, for the things I was, but then when they

56. JFK preferred hats to scarves.

PRESIDENT KENNEDY AND MRS. KENNEDY SPEAK TO ISAAC STERN
AT A DINNER IN HONOR OF ANDRÉ MALRAUX, 1962

didn't work out politically, he was never going to ask me to change, which I just think was so nice about him. Because he wouldn't be fake in any way, and he wouldn't be fake about his children and he wouldn't kiss babies, and so all that was really written by people who just didn't understand him. The one thing he was, which people can't understand and which was—where I felt so sorry for poor Nixon, who had such a disadvantage—Jack was the most unself-conscious person I've ever seen. He just naturally could be attractive in a crowd or a room. He was unself-conscious about walking around with a towel on. If it fell off or something, you know, he'd put it on again, but— So many people are worried or nervous in public, or public appearances. Nixon was and, you know, he would sweat and everything. So the people who weren't sort of sure of themselves, or had that wonderful

PRESIDENT KENNEDY SPEAKS WITH PEARL BUCK AND JACQUELINE WITH
ROBERT FROST AT A DINNER HONORING NOBEL LAUREATES, 1962

ease of Jack, were in a way jealous and you know, attributed all these funny things to him, which weren't true. He was just always so natural.

How did he feel about the White House staff?

Who do you mean by that?

Well, the—we're talking about the public thing. Pierre, and—

I think he—you know, loved them all. I used to get so mad at Pierre because he did have a certain hamming-up thing that really didn't help protect my children much. I mean, he'd give a long interview about some drunken rabbit.[57] And I'd blow up at Pierre, but then I'd say to Jack, there's the nicest thing about Pierre. You can really say the most terrible things to him, which I did sometimes, and he never bore a grudge. It would be over, like that. So Jack was grateful to Pierre for that. And when I look at it now, without Jack, you see that his White House staff is the most extraordinary collection of people, who are so different—who now, a lot of them, dislike each other. I mean, maybe they did then, but you never knew it then. But I mean, there were the Irish Mafia. There was Pierre. There was Mrs. Lincoln, who was jealous of anyone who came near Jack. There were the professors—you know, there was you, there was Bundy, Ralph Dungan, Mike Feldman.[58] And all adoring Jack and knowing—and then, there was me and our private life and friends. All kept together because they knew he thought highly of each of them, and that their contribution was to their utmost. And he loved all of them, and they all loved him. And Jack held together this motley band, who now—from some of them, at least from the Irish—are just so bitter about everyone else in there.[59] But you never saw that.

I thought it was the most exceptionally harmonious experience. And you know, everyone warned me, before joining it, that there would be feuds and knives out, and so on. I had no—I just thought it was the best possible experience of dealing with—of the people around the President because of the way he, you know, managed everybody.

Yeah. And I often thought it was—well, not exactly, but you know, you hear it said that mother love is infinite and it isn't that you can love two children— and then, if you have nine, that means you love them just that much less. Well, there weren't really any jealousies or favorites. No one ever thought Jack had a favorite—

---

57. Eager to preserve her children's privacy, Jacqueline was horrified when Salinger once told a reporter about one of their pets, a beer-loving rabbit called Zsa Zsa.

58. RALPH DUNGAN (1923–) and Myer Feldman (1914–2007) were both White House staff members.

59. She refers here especially to the turf-conscious Ken O'Donnell, who disliked Sorensen and Schlesinger. One sign of JFK's ability to keep all of these disparate factions working together is the fact that he never had a chief of staff. Always wary of finding himself on the "leading strings" of an aide, he had all top members of his staff report directly to him.

That's right.

—unless it was Dave Powers, who was a favorite for what everyone hoped he would have a favorite for—someone to relax him, you know. But he didn't have any favorites. And so that way, they could all work together. There was no intrigue of "who's in" and "who's out." And as Kenny said—he didn't put Kenny in the position of being the only man you could get to see the President through. They could also sneak around through Mrs. Lincoln's door, or Tish would manage to—you know, there were so many ways.

Yeah.

Well, he was so accessible, and yet he got so much more done—than now. He was accessible, but when he worked he really worked. He didn't, you know, break things up.

When would the President see the children?

He'd see the children—I didn't tell you all our day once, did I? Of how in the morning George Thomas would rap on our bedroom door about quarter of eight, and he would go into his room, and the children would come in. And they'd either turn on the television, going absolutely full blast, and he'd have his breakfast, sitting in a chair, on a tray, doing all his—reading the morning papers, going through all his briefing books or, you know, those sheets of typewritten—his agenda for the day.

He'd do that before he got dressed?

Yeah. He'd—yes, he'd sort of have—

A dressing gown on or something.

No, he'd take a bath first and they'd come in while he had a bath. I told you all of John's toys were by the side of his tub. And then he'd sort of have breakfast in his shirt and underpants. And on the television—gosh, sometimes it was loud because I'd often come in because it—sometimes I'd like to just, sort of, stay in bed until about nine. But I'd come in there and sit with him, sometimes. But there'd be cartoons, and there was this awful exercise man, Jack La—

LaLanne, yes.

So Jack would lower—and there'd be Jack LaLanne, and he'd be telling Caroline and John to do what they were doing, so they'd be lying on the floor. Sometimes he'd touch his toes with John a bit. But he'd have them tumbling around. He loved those children tumbling around him in this sort of— sensual is the only way I can think of it. And then he'd always come out in the garden during their recess in the morning and clap his hands, and all the little things from school would come running.[60] The teachers—he used to call out his two favorites, Caroline and Mary Warner. And then the teacher said it wasn't fair for him to give them candy. She told Caroline she could only get candy if there would be some for the entire class. So Mrs. Lincoln had an entire box of Barracini candy that—but he'd go out or, if I was around there with John, he'd call us in and a little bit in his office, and then he'd send them out and then John would play on Mrs. Lincoln's typewriter. Then they'd come over in the evening, just as he was finishing up for the day, and just play around his office. One of the last days I remember—well, you know, there's that wonderful picture of them all talking about Berlin and Jack—which was an awful, sort of a crisis—and John tumbling out from under his desk. But, oh, and then one of the last days, Charlie the dog came in and bit John on the nose, and Bundy had to get Dr. Burkley.[61] You know the children were never bratty but he liked to have them underfoot, and then he'd take them swimming and—or else, if it didn't work out quite that way when he'd come upstairs before dinner, no matter who we had for dinner, they'd come in. You know, they'd have their time with him in their pajamas. He really would play with them first, even if it was a state dinner. He'd always say—or even when it was a state lunch or just a man's lunch. Usually, he'd have me in the room and

---

60. While living in the White House, Caroline attended a school established by her mother in the White House solarium. Most of her fellow students were children of administration officials.

61. GEORGE BURKLEY (1902–1991) was a navy admiral and served as the President's primary physician after Dr. Travell was removed from his case (in keeping with JFK's compact with Dr. Kraus), although Travell publicly retained her official title.

THE WHITE HOUSE SCHOOL

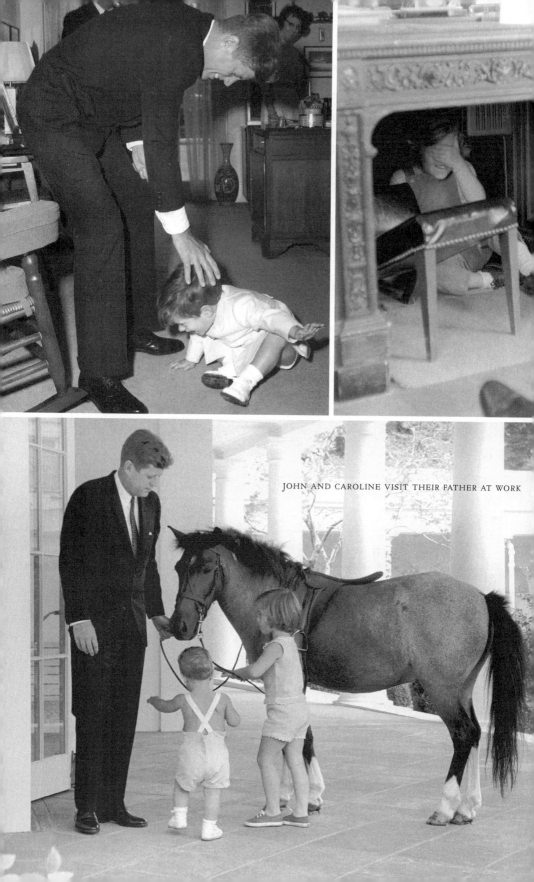

JOHN AND CAROLINE VISIT THEIR FATHER AT WORK

he'd say, "Go get the children!" And, of course, they'd always be in their naps in their underwear or something, and I'd have to bring them out in their underwear because he'd never give you warning before. But he just loved to have them around. And then he'd—he really taught Caroline to swim. He made her dive off the high diving board. He made her swim the length of the pool in Florida, the last Christmas she was there. Well, she got a quarter of the way and did the rest under water. He was saying, "Come on, you can make it!" You know, he did so much with them. And he told her all these stories. He'd make up "The White Shark and the Black Shark," and "Bobo the Lobo," and "Maybelle"—some little girl who hid in the woods. And then one day, he was desperate and I said, "What?" He said, "Gosh, you've got to get me some books, or something. I'm running out of children's stories." He said, "I just told Caroline how she and I shot down three Jap fighter planes." But—

Were there any books that he liked reading or the children demanded that he read?

No, he didn't read—he didn't like to read books to them much. He'd rather tell them stories. But he'd make up these fantastic ones. Sort of that they were just riveted by. Oh, and then he'd have ponies for Caroline—White Star and Black Star. Caroline said to me, "Daddy would always let me choose which pony I wanted to ride and which pony my friend would ride." And then he would make some race and he would always let Caroline win the race. And then he had a—oh, Miss Shaw was in a lot of them, rather ludicrously—and Mrs. Throttlebottom was in the race. And how Caroline went hunting—the Orange County hounds and then White Star and Black Star—she went in the Grand National and beat every—you know, little things that had to do with their world, where they did absolutely extraordinarily. John got his PT boat and shot a Jap destroyer, or something like that. But, he never got impatient. They'd come in his bed, you know.

What—when you went to Hyannis Port or Newport or Palm Beach, where he'd have more time with the children. Of course, he couldn't lift them or play with them himself, could he, with the back?

He'd get on the floor, then he could really roll around with them. And he used to—he could lift Caroline up and—at least, a little—he used to throw her around an awful lot before we got to the White House.[62] But, well, they'd be in our room in the morning, and then he'd swim with them for about an hour, and then he always wanted them to come out on the boat with us. A lot of times, you know, they really were quite young. They'd get awfully cranky if they missed their nap. But he always wanted them to come, so you'd put them to bed inside for half an hour or something, and maybe they would get whiny, but he always wanted them there. Or, at Camp David and things, you'd sort of sit out and have supper with them or you'd run on the lawn, and everything.

What place relaxed him most, do you think, of the various places you went?

It was really the boat that relaxed him the most. Before he was President, it was to go out on his father's boat, the *Marlin*—and then the *Honey Fitz*. And the reason for that was, there was no telephone. He was awful about the phone. It could—never—ring but he wouldn't answer it. You know, calls would come, or else he'd be getting ten people on the phone. So, there, I mean, rain or shine—I can remember him taking Adlai Stevenson out on the *Honey Fitz* one day in late October in Newport—hurricane season. I got two polo coats for Adlai and a pith helmet of my stepfather's. And Jack was sitting in the back in a black sweater, the hair—the wind blowing his hair, blissfully happy with fish chowder. And I was inside, with two blankets on, and drinking hot soup. That's how cold it was. He just thought everyone would love that boat because that was his away from care. It was for him what getting out on a horse was for me—in the air, no phone. I'm not that mad for riding horses or hunting. But the release from tension in the air. He loved the sun and the water and no phone. And you know, friends there—you always had friends there that—he never used the boat for working—but whoever you want to relax with.

What did he think of all these skits about himself, like The First Family, *and so on? Did he ever listen to them?*

---

62. After damaging his back in the Ottawa tree planting, JFK once privately forecast that John would be able to lift him before he could ever expect to lift his son.

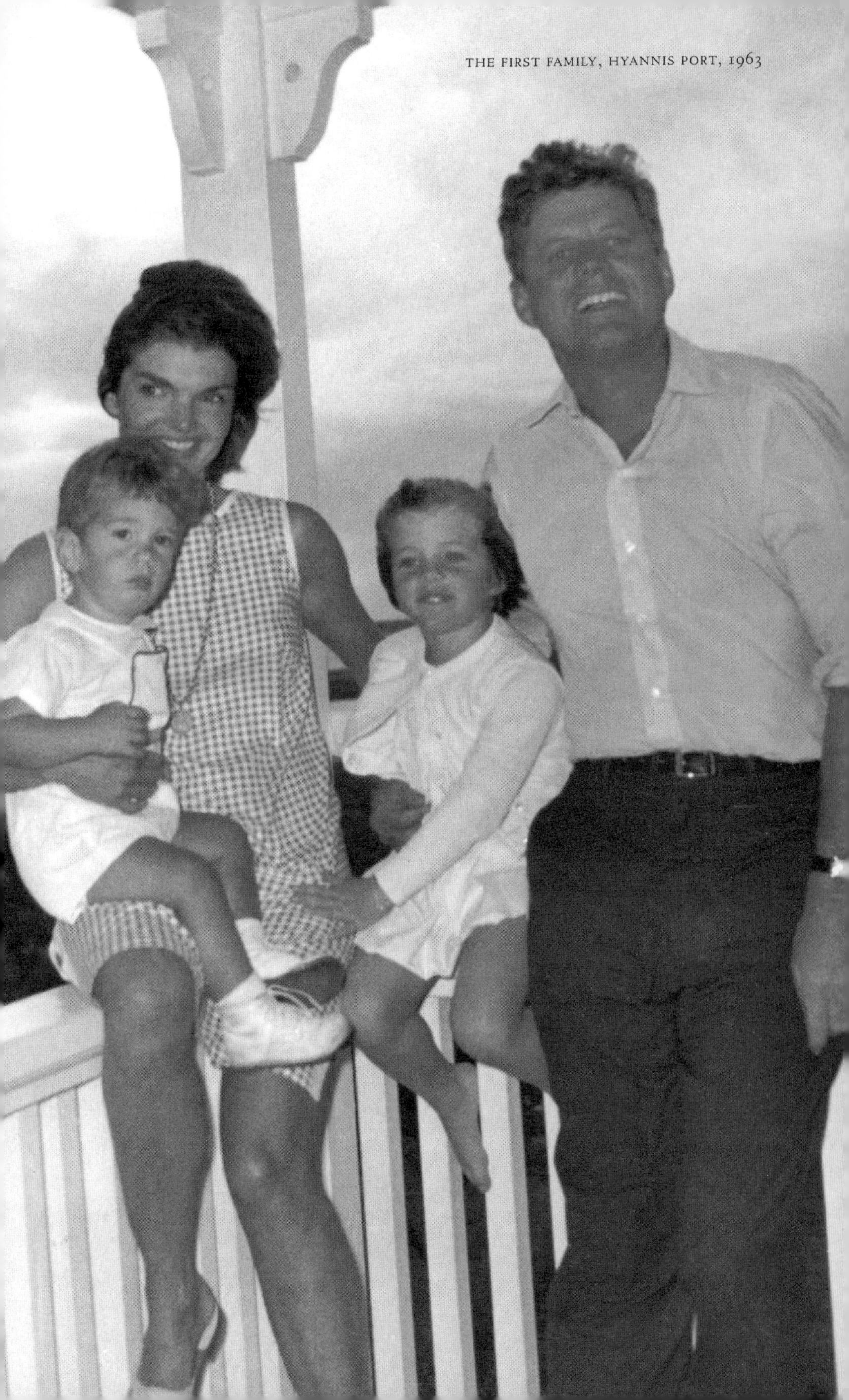

THE FIRST FAMILY, HYANNIS PORT, 1963

THE *HONEY FITZ*

I think he listened. I'm not sure he listened to all of that record.[63] I listened to one side, and then I threw it away because I didn't want my children to see it. And I guess, he sort of took it. You know, I thought it was so unfair that he didn't—I guess he just accepted it. I mean, he obviously didn't like it, but I was the one who got much more worked up about those things. I thought it was so mean. I didn't care if they made fun of me or anything, but

---

63. *The First Family* by the nightclub comedian Vaughn Meader was the fastest-selling record in history, selling an astonishing 7.5 million copies. As Kennedy told a press conference, he thought Meader's impersonation of him sounded "more like Teddy than it did me."

PRESIDENT AND MRS. KENNEDY SAIL WITH HER
MOTHER AND STEPFATHER OFF NEWPORT, 1962

when they made fun of little children— And the first year he was President, I went to the Women's Press Club dinner. He had a fever that night, and so Lyndon took me. It's a tradition for the President and his wife to go— and a woman named Bonnie Angelo came out on a tricycle as Caroline and sang some awful song.[64] And the next year, I wouldn't go and that Bonnie Angelo was president. Pierre really got upset by that. And I said, "I'm not going to go, and you can either tell them why, Pierre—for what they did last year—or you can make up any excuse you think is best." And then I explained that to Jack. I just felt so strongly about those children. It was hard enough protecting them in the Kennedy family, where some of the cousins, especially, Eunice's children, are—were so conscious of the position, and would always wear Kennedy buttons and would play that record, "My

---

64. **BONNIE ANGELO** (1924–) covered Mrs. Kennedy as First Lady for *Time* magazine.

THE PRESIDENT AND CAROLINE ON THE *HONEY FITZ*

Daddy Is President, What Does Your Daddy Do?,"[65] or *The First Family*. And I hid all those things from my children and always taught them that the White House was sort of temporary. I'm so glad I did, for the way it ended. But that it was while Daddy was President, and presidents had lived in it before. I'd tell them when Franklin Roosevelt would come to dinner—and Mrs. Longworth or President Truman. I'd tell them little stories about other presidents, and then there would be a president after Daddy, and then we would be living in Hyannis. And, you know, so they never got to think that all this was going to be forever in this power, which the others were awful about. So I'd get upset about those skits, but he didn't like to see me get upset. But, I guess, he knew it was part of being President. And because it was such a different and young family, there was so much more to make skits about with us, which he said, sort of wryly, to me once.

Did the President often talk much about the things he would like to do? You mentioned a new secretary of state.

I know he was going to get rid of J. Edgar Hoover, the minute—and he always said that those were the two things he did first—you know, Hoover and Allen Dulles, which I guess he had to do at the time. He couldn't have not.

Did he have any—ever talk about who—what he would do with the FBI?

No, he didn't say who he'd make, and then Bobby was going to leave the Justice Department. I think he might have made Nick Katzenbach[66] the head, I'm not sure. And, well, I know there was going to be a domestic peace corps, but I guess that was sort of started, wasn't it? And I know he was going to do this poverty thing.[67] And I know he really cared about—Kentucky was the

---

65. In 1962, *My Daddy Is President*, by the seven-year-old "Little Jo Ann" Morse, sung in baby talk with a bossa nova beat, was a 45-rpm jukebox favorite. Among the lyrics: "No matter what I do, it makes a news event. / 'Cause my Daddy is the President."

66. NICHOLAS KATZENBACH (1922–), who was imprisoned by the Italians and Germans as a prisoner of war for two years during World War II, served as RFK's deputy, and under President Johnson, as his successor.

67. It was ultimately LBJ who established "Volunteers in Service to America" (VISTA) in 1964 as part

place he spoke to me about and we were going to go to Kentucky sometime, and I mean I know it was mentioned.[68]

Yeah, Appalachia.

That's it, Appalachia. And he was going to Russia.

Yes. That's—I wanted to ask you about that.

Sometime in the second term we were going to go to Russia and that would have just been so incredible. And we were going to go to the Far East. I guess, I always thought he was going to go in December, but then as he wasn't talking about it, I guess, with Indonesia and everything, it was sort of—

Yeah, but I think it was—I think he was planning to go in April—in the spring, to the Far East.

And it would have been so incredible for him to go to Japan, when you think Eisenhower couldn't go there,[69] and the crowds and everything you would have gotten. If all this had to happen, I just wish he could have seen some more good things come in, that he worked so hard for. The tax bill, the civil rights bill, the economy up so high. You know, think of all those businessmen who still say awful things about him, and suddenly the gold flow is absolutely stopped, the gross national product has never been so high. To go to Japan and to go to Russia. If he could have just seen all those and—and won. If he could have just won, and he was so praying it would be Goldwater that he'd have to run

---

of his "War on Poverty"—another program that adapted some of the ideas JFK was considering at the time of his death. Worried that his proposed tax cuts would do little to help the jobless and poor, Kennedy had wanted to help poor families like those who had so affected him while campaigning in West Virginia in 1960. Told about this, the new President Johnson seized the notion with both hands. In January 1964, during his first State of the Union message, a speech written largely by Sorensen, Johnson declared "unconditional war on poverty in America."

68. And in 1964, President Johnson was the one who posed for pictures with poor families in Appalachia.

69. A planned trip to Japan by Eisenhower in June 1960 was cancelled just before his planned arrival because of anti-American riots.

against. He used to say, "Let Barry alone. He's doing just fine." You know if he could have just seen some of the good things.

He would have liked to run against Goldwater.[70] Did he think Goldwater was going to get it, or was that—

Oh, it was just too much to hope for. I mean, it was just too good to be true. I don't think he did. In the beginning, quite a while ago, he thought Romney would, and he was nervous about Romney because he said he'd be sort of hard.[71] But then I think later on, he didn't think Romney would so much. I don't know who he thought would.

Did he ever talk about Rockefeller?

Yeah. He said Rockefeller, in a way, was sort of a coward, because he should have done what Jack did and run in those primaries.[72] But either he was— had cold feet or was nervous about not going into New Hampshire and all that. And he said if he had, he would have been president.

---

70. BARRY GOLDWATER (1909–1998) was Republican senator from Arizona and the most prominent conservative of the day. JFK had met Goldwater before World War II when he went to an outdoor work camp near Phoenix, and they remained warm and jocular friends for the rest of their lives. Kennedy presumed that voters would find the Arizonan so extreme that, if nominated, he would lose to Kennedy in a landslide in 1964 (as Goldwater ultimately did to LBJ). Goldwater later insisted that JFK had agreed, if they should be the two presidential candidates in 1964, to fly around the country and debate together, almost like Lincoln and Stephen Douglas in 1858. There is no doubt that when Goldwater raised the idea, the President responded pleasantly, but it does not seem likely that in 1964, the competitive JFK, eager for the biggest victory possible, would have so gingerly offered so weak a challenger as Goldwater the benefit of being seen all over the country arguing with the President as an equal. Kennedy had, however, committed himself to face his 1964 opponent in televised debates like those of 1960 with Nixon.

71. GEORGE ROMNEY (1907–1995) was president of American Motors before his election as Republican governor of Michigan in 1962. RFK later recalled in a 1964 oral history conversation that for a time, Romney was the opponent his brother "feared the most. . . . He thought he had this appeal to . . . God and country. . . . He spoke well, looked well. He perhaps would cause some trouble in the South, where we were in trouble anyway [over civil rights]. . . . That's why . . . we never talked about Romney."

72. NELSON ROCKEFELLER (1908–1979) was elected governor of New York in 1958. Two years later, he seriously considered challenging Nixon, whom he loathed, in the 1960 Republican primaries but decided to stay out. JFK had worried that Rockefeller might be a strong opponent when he ran for reelection; however, he divorced his wife and in May 1963 remarried a younger woman, which at the time was a mortal sin in presidential politics.

Yeah. Oh, the President did feel that if Rockefeller had gotten the nomination in 1960, he would have been elected. I think that's right.

And he said, you know, he just didn't have the—I don't know whether it was gumption or judgment or just timid soul, or something. And of course, now the poor man's doing it all with completely the wrong sense of timing. And, I don't think he thought very much of Rockefeller, but he didn't really say anything mean against him. He didn't like Nixon and he really thought he was dangerous. You know, and that he was a little bit—

I thought he was sick.

Sick, yeah.[73]

Scranton?

Well, I don't remember talking with him about Scranton.[74] You know, he was sort of coming up, and I suppose he thought he might have had it. But I never can remember talking to him—

Did he look forward to the '64 campaign?

Oh, yes. And I looked forward to it so much. It was one you could do to-gether. Campaigning's so different when you're President. It wouldn't be those awful things of plodding through Wisconsin, forcing somebody to shake hands with you. I mean, he really looked forward to it, and then to winning and then to just sort of solidifying. You know, he really did so much.

---

73. After the 1960 campaign, JFK told Bradlee that Nixon was "mentally unsound" and "sick, sick, sick." When Nixon was defeated in 1962 for governor of California, Kennedy called the victor, Edmund "Pat" Brown (1905–1996)—the President's hidden tape machine was on—and marveled at how the loser had told reporters in Los Angeles that they wouldn't have Nixon "to kick around anymore" because it was his "last press conference." JFK explained to Brown, "You reduced him to the nuthouse." Brown agreed: "I really think he's psychotic. He's an able man, but he's nuts."

74. WILLIAM SCRANTON (1917–) was a moderate Republican congressman when elected Pennsylvania governor in 1962.

There wasn't that much more to do, except it would have jelled. And it would have been relations with other countries. I mean, it would have been Latin America and with Russia and de Gaulle never would have recognized Red China, and all of that—if he'd stayed alive.

Did he ever talk with regard to the Russian trip about anything particularly he wanted to see or do?

Just that there would be the most fantastic crowds.

Did he—was it just Moscow or would it—

I think it was just a Russian trip. You know, he never really went into it. And, oh, what did he say? When things got nicer about Khrushchev, you know, after the détente[75] and everything, he always used to say—well, remember what he said after Vienna, that he really is a gangster, and so everybody mustn't get deluded. But if you deal with him out of firmness—it's different. But he never wanted people to think that now Khrushchev is the sweet, benign, undangerous person.

Did he ever talk about his letters, his correspondence with Khrushchev?[76]

Well, just that there was one. But he never told me what. I didn't ask him what was in them. If I'd asked, I could have seen them, because every time I'd ask about something like that he'd say, "Get Bundy to show you." Bundy did, and for a couple of months there, Bundy was sending me all the intelligence—top briefings and everything. And then finally, I got so bored—no, not bored, discouraged—reading them. I said, "Please, never send me another." And when I'd read those things which Jack had to flip through every day, I didn't see how he could be so cheerful at night, or have a drink or go

---

75. Referring to the relaxation between Washington and Moscow that began after the missile crisis and ripened with the test ban treaty of the summer of 1963.

76. JFK pursued a frequent private correspondence with the Soviet leader, which Bundy puckishly called "the pen-pal letters."

out on the *Honey Fitz*. He'd just read twenty pages of problems. And then I thought, "Well, I'd better not read them anymore, because I can just read the good things and be in a good mood for him." And I remember we gave a little dinner—farewell, for Ros Gilpatric, and Mrs. Gilpatric was saying to Jack all through it—it was the TFX time—"I say to Ros when he comes home every night, 'How can they say those things about you? Aren't they all awful?'"[77] And he said to her, "My God, you don't say that to your husband when he comes home at night, do you? That's not what you should do. Find one good thing they say, say, 'Isn't that great?' or bring up something else that will make him happy." And so, that's how I sensed what he wanted me to be, and that's really when I stopped reading all those briefings and things, because I didn't want to have to worry about anything. I wanted to, sort of, take your cue from him and—

One of the greatest gifts was his capacity to switch from one thing to another and not be nagged at by problems, to put them aside knowing that he can't do anything more at that moment about them and not let them worry him.

And that's—did I ever tell you about him making me move my desk?

No.

Well, I used to have my desk in the West Sitting Hall, where we always sat, and it would be piled high—and especially when Tish was always sending in those damn folders. Just when you'd be sitting happily with Jack, some other messenger would come running in, I think—and he said, "Move your desk out." I knew I did tell you this.

You told this. Yes.

---

77. In 1963, the Senate Permanent Investigations Committee examined the award to General Dynamics of a $6.5 billion contract, the most lucrative such mandate in American history, to build a new TFX fighter plane. Before his appointment as McNamara's deputy, Gilpatric had been counsel to General Dynamics and was criticized for participating in the TFX decision. Although in March 1963 Gilpatric had announced his return to the law, he remained at the Pentagon until January 1964 in an effort to clear his name.

Down to the Treaty Room. Well, and I couldn't get problems off. But he could always go to sleep, too, which I thought was so important. He didn't have this in—you know, he could just turn it off. And I always thought one thing, and I think it's true of Lyndon Johnson, and I think it might have been true of Adlai Stevenson. That these things get on you and on you and there's indecision or something—and you can't sleep. You really become—I always thought any president would become an insomniac. But Jack had this built-in thing that Ted Reardon[78] told me about before—like soldiers in a foxhole. When it was time to go to sleep, he just could. And that was one of his greatest—it was fortunate he had that. That's about all.

[John enters the room and plays with tape recorder]

---

78. TIMOTHY REARDON (1915–1993) was JFK's administrative assistant in the House and Senate and a special assistant in the White House.

THE PRESIDENT AND FIRST LADY, WASHINGTON, D.C., MAY 3, 1961

ACKNOWLEDGMENTS

There are many people whose support and encouragement have helped immensely during the preparation of this project. First, foremost, and always to my husband and children for their love, integrity, and interest. I would like to thank the family of Arthur M. Schlesinger, Jr., especially Alexandra Schlesinger, for her gracious enthusiasm; and Bill van den Heuvel for the same wise counsel and joyful outlook that made him such a beloved friend to my mother. I couldn't have completed this project without the help of Lauren Lipani, who read, listened to, and checked every detail along the way.

I am grateful to Tom Putnam, the director of the John F. Kennedy Presidential Library and Museum, as well as to the Library's dedicated archivists, Karen Adler Abramson, Jaimie Quaglino, Maura Porter, and Jenny Beaton. The unusual and unfamiliar photos that add so much to this book result from the efforts and expertise of Laurie Austin and Maryrose Grossman. Thanks also to Sharon Kelly, Jane Silva, and Stephen Plotkin for additional research assistance. I am also grateful to Tom McNaught, the director of the John F. Kennedy Library Foundation; Rachel Day, for coordinating requests and new technology in connection with this book; and to all the Foundation staff for their commitment to excellence in all they do to strengthen the legacy of my parents.

For their legal and publishing advice and expertise, I would like to thank Bob Barnett, Deneen Howell, Jim Fuller, Tom Hentoff, and Esther Newberg.

People always did their best for my mother, and this project was no exception. She would have been especially pleased that the talented team at Hyperion are all women, including Sharon Kitter, Linda Prather, Kristin Kiser, Jill Sansone, Marie Coolman, SallyAnne McCartin, and Ellen Archer. For their work on the audio restoration and production, I am grateful to Marcos Sueiro Bal, as well as Paul Fowlie and Karen Dziekonski.

I wish my mother could have had the good fortune to work with Gretchen Young, who is exactly the kind of editor she was herself; with Shubhani Sarkar, who has brought creativity and insight to this design; and with Navorn Johnson, who managed this project from beginning to end. For their ongoing wisdom and wise counsel, I would like to thank Ranny Cooper and Stephanie Cutter, and for bringing their expertise and skill to this project, Debra Reed and Amy Weiss.

Finally, I am indebted to Michael Beschloss for his illuminating Introduction and comprehensive annotations, which benefit this book tremendously.

—CAROLINE KENNEDY

SOURCE NOTES

xx   "tall thin young congressman": Carl Sferrazza Anthony, *As We Remember Her* (HarperCollins, 1997), p. 37.

xx   "across this great crowd": Charles Bartlett oral history, John F. Kennedy Library.

xx   "a spasmodic courtship": Robert Dallek, *An Unfinished Life* (Little, Brown, 2003), p. 193.

xx   "start to cry again": JBK to Lyndon Johnson, January 9, 1964, transcription of recording of telephone call, in Michael Beschloss, *Reaching for Glory* (Simon and Schuster, 2001), p. 22.

xxi   "his acid wit": *New York Times,* March 1, 2007.

xxi   "I return your letters": JBK to Arthur M. Schlesinger, Jr., December 3, 1963. JBK letters cited here and below appear in her still-closed papers at the Kennedy Library and, in most cases, in the archives of the recipients.

xxi   "much on my mind": *American Archivist,* Fall 1980.

xxii "a matter of urgency": Ibid.

xxii "thousands" of people: *New York Times,* April 6, 1964.

xxiv "an historian of the twenty-first": *American Archivist,* Fall 1980.

xxiv "From time to time": Ibid.

xxv   "flighty on politics": Journal of Arthur M. Schlesinger, Jr., July 19, 1959, Schlesinger Papers, New York Public Library.

xxvi "nobody wonders": John F. Kennedy at Fort Worth Chamber of Commerce breakfast, November 22, 1963.

xxvii "pass a law": David Finley, memorandum of conversation, February 19, 1962, Finley Papers, National Gallery of Art Archives.

xxvii "ripped down": JBK to Bernard Boutin, March 6, 1962.

xxvii "practically nothing": *White House History,* #13, 2004.

xxvii "Hold your breath": JBK to David Finley, April 18, 1962.

xxvii "may be the only monument": *Time,* November 20, 1964.

xxviii "would walk halfway": JBK to Edward Kennedy, September 17, 1970.

xxviii "early Statler": Mary Van Rensselaer Thayer, *Jacqueline Kennedy: The White House Years* (Little, Brown, 1971), p. 93.

xxviii "my predatory instincts": JBK to Adlai Stevenson, July 24, 1961.

xxviii "ran a curio shop": JBK to Lady Bird Johnson, December 1, 1963.

xxviii "the setting in which": *A Tour of the White House,* CBS-TV, February 14, 1962.

xxviii "a New England sitting room": *New York Times,* January 29, 1961.

xxix "She was a worker": Lady Bird Johnson oral history, Kennedy Library.

xxix "What has been sad": *Ms.* magazine, March 1979.

xxix "It is the major temple": JBK to John F. Kennedy, handwritten, undated, 1962.

xxix "Egyptian rocks": Richard Goodwin, Kennedy Library Forum, November 4, 2007.

xxx   "remind people that feelings": JBK to JFK, memorandum entitled "Abu Simbel," handwritten, undated.

xxx   "excruciating": *Look,* November 17, 1964.

xxx   "a new life": JBK to David Finley, August 22, 1964.

xxxi "So now he is a legend": *Look,* November 17, 1964.

xxxi "things I think are too personal": JBK to Arthur M. Schlesinger, Jr., handwritten, undated, 1965.

xxxi "if I could steel myself": JBK to Lyndon Johnson, March 28, 1965.

xxxi   "Close your eyes": *U.S. News & World Report,* July 26, 1999.

9   "I had publicly endorsed": Ted Sorensen, *Kennedy* (Harper and Row, 1965), p. 80.

10   "a stormy meeting": Ibid.

15   "My sweet little house": Gordon Langley Hall and Ann Pinchot, *Jacqueline Kennedy* (Frederick Fell, 1964), p. 141.

18   "I'm going to get in": William Manchester, *The Death of a President* (Harper and Row, 1967), p. 186.

25   "as if Jack were President of FRANCE": Oleg Cassini, *A Thousand Days of Magic* (Rizzoli, 1995), p. 29.

27   "a Stevenson with balls": Dallek, p. 259.

32   "You remember in my oral history": JBK to Schlesinger, May 28, 1965. Her first draft was sold at auction in 2009.

42   "treasured friends": Ted Sorensen, *Counselor* (Harper, 2008), p. 399.

46   "a lot of money": *New York Times,* December 12, 1996.

47   "I am no Whig!": James MacGregor Burns, *John Kennedy: A Political Profile* (Harcourt Brace, 1960), p. 268.

48   "He was the only President": JBK to Edward Kennedy, September 17, 1970.

52   "I think you underestimate": JBK to James MacGregor Burns, handwritten, undated, 1959.

55   "forgot Goschen": Winston Churchill, *Lord Randolph Churchill* (Macmillan, 1908), p. 647.

61   "that I had privately boasted": Sorensen, *Counselor,* p. 150.

63   "Can I be godfather": Edward Kennedy, *True Compass* (Twelve, 2009), p. 24.

64   "could see around corners": Anthony, *As We Remember Her,* p. 60.

69   "Go to Germany": Michael Beschloss, *The Crisis Years* (HarperCollins, 1991), p. 608.

81   "a good Democrat": Schlesinger, *Robert Kennedy and His Times,* p. 201.

85   "resting up": Schlesinger, *A Thousand Days,* p. 103.

85   "renege on an offer": Clark Clifford, *Counsel to the President* (Random House, 1992), p. 318.

85   "such fun if it had been": James Olson, *Stuart Symington* (University of Missouri, 2003), p. 362.

86   "How's my little girl": Lyndon Johnson to JBK, December 23, 1963, transcription of recording of telephone call, in Beschloss, *Reaching for Glory,* p. 18.

87   "Johnson had 'grabbed'": Robert Kennedy oral history, Kennedy Library.

89   "That doesn't surprise": John Connally, *In History's Shadow* (Hyperion, 1994), p. 10.

90   "For Christ's sake": Manchester, *The Death of a President,* p. 116.

113   "the brightest boy": David Halberstam, *The Best and the Brightest* (Random House, 1973), p. 44.

124   "nut country": Manchester, *The Death of a President,* p. 121.

127   "My life here which I dreaded": JBK to William Walton, June 8, 1962.

131   "if Jack makes it": Letitia Baldrige oral history, Kennedy Library.

138   "The President told me": JBK to David Finley, March 22, 1963.

138   "I must be quite honest": David Finley to JBK, March 27, 1963.

138   "I never dreamed": JBK to David Finley, March 22, 1963.

142   "but there were about a hundred": Sorensen, *Kennedy,* p. 383.

143   "I've learned more": James Abbott and Elaine Rice, *Designing Camelot* (Wiley, 1997), p. 86.

143   "Boudin's masterpiece": Ibid., p. 101.

167   "the most private place": JBK to Eve Fout, July 1962, in Sally Bedell Smith, *Grace and Power* (Random House, 2004), p. 113.

170   "twenty times a day": The Estate of Jacqueline Kennedy Onassis, April 23-26, 1996 (Sotheby's, 1996).

170   "minimum information": Mary van Rensselaer Thayer, *Jacqueline Kennedy,* p. 31.

173   "as excited as a hunting": Ibid., p. 318.

173   "Why are some people": JBK to Henry du Pont, September 28, 1962.

184   "Hell, Mr. President": Beschloss, *The Crisis Years,* p. 122.

189   JFK to Raskin: Interview with Raskin, and Raskin unpublished memoir, both cited in Beschloss, *The Crisis Years.*

201 "A wall is a hell": Ibid., p. 278.

203 "It is all going to be involved": JBK to William Walton, June 8, 1962.

210 "Obviously she was quick": Sergei Khrushchev, editor, *Memoirs of Nikita Khrushchev: Statesman, 1953-1964* (Pennsylvania State University, 2007), p. 304.

211 "You're offering to trade": Beschloss, *The Crisis Years*, p. 325.

226 "Nous pensons a vous": Manchester, *The Death of a President*, p. 446.

237 "the worst head-of-state": Arthur M. Schlesinger, Jr., *A Thousand Days* (Houghton Mifflin, 1965), p. 526.

239 "every weekend since": J. B. West, *Upstairs at the White House* (Coward, McCann, 1973), p. 235.

242 "Can't you control": Schlesinger, *A Thousand Days*, p. 28.

247 JBK-Macmillan correspondence: Harold Macmillan Papers, Bodleian Library, University of Oxford.

256 "interview them all": Arthur M. Schlesinger, Jr., *Robert Kennedy and His Times* (Houghton Mifflin, 1978), p. 404.

266 "There's always some": Richard Reeves, *President Kennedy* (Simon and Schuster, 1993), p. 416.

273 "several glowing references": Sorensen, *Counselor* (Harper, 2008), pp. 408-409.

277 "the steam really went": Benjamin Bradlee, *Conversations with Kennedy* (Norton, 1975), p. 226.

291 "under American domination": Schlesinger, *A Thousand Days*, p. 842.

295 "this France, England, America": Manchester, *The Death of a President*, p. 710.

306 "one sentence": Ralph Martin, *A Hero for Our Time* (Macmillan, 1983), p. 431.

307 "kicked in the head": *Life*, May 11, 1959.

332 "leading strings": Schlesinger, *A Thousand Days*, p. 50.

346 "mentally unsound": Bradlee, *Conversations with Kennedy*, p. 32.

346 "You reduced him": Recording of John F. Kennedy telephone conversation with Governor Edmund Brown, November 7, 1962, Kennedy Library.

PHOTOGRAPH CREDITS

⁀

INDEX

NOTE: Page numbers in italics refer to illustrations. The letter "n" indicates footnotes.